"How drunk were you when you thought of this idea?"
Jeffrey Leestma, president of the Automotive Hall of Fame

"Did you come out of the same gene pool as Ken Kesey?"
Elliott Eki, AAA

"Alyce, you are amazing!"
Anne Fletcher, author *Thin for Life*

"You touched my life. I'm sure I'm not the only one.
I think that's why you're on this trip. You didn't just stop by.
You were sent."
Ken Blinn, Director of Programs, The Barnum Museum

"You will be my inspiration from now on."
Jackie Kindestin

"So impressed with your individual style and love of life."
Terry Dickman

"You are a great adventure. The greatest adventure."
Kristi Unger

"You are one brave lady."
Faye Carr

"You lifted my spirits 100% and improved my attitude 100%.
My friends and co-workers noticed."
Janet Swan

"Impossible not to have been inspired! Just reading and
learning about you sparked that 'Go after it, babe!'
Thanks for the inspiration!"
Susan Rogers

"Loving every word."
Kevin Cook

"What I enjoyed most...one on one encounters in
out of the way places."
Ken Barratt

"You are so cool. What do you do to top this?"
Steve Striharsky

"Other people are saying 'I may do it, I may go, I might go next year, maybe when the kids are grown, maybe once they're married and we have time,' and maybe, maybe, maybe, and you are actually doing it. YOU GO GIRL - YOUR LIFE IS AN OPEN ROAD!"
Liz Kitzul

"I'm very excited for you. What you are doing is super. You are awesome."
Alissa Ann Douglas

"You are extraordinary."
Stephen Booth

"Your insights are fun to read; descriptions make for an enjoyable vicarious experience for the reader."
David Balding

"The great thing about your very own trip is that you get to make the rules. You have already mastered your fear by making this trip. That will never change. Americans are kind, helpful, generous and empowered far more than we ever expected. Everything changes when you travel alone. The impact is life-changing."
Carolyn Fox

"You are the only one I know with the determination to do this. If anyone can do it, you can. You've already accomplished more than anyone else could have."
Jan Browder

"I was quite impressed with your approach to life and its hazards."
Leigh Hendry

"You have blessed me and my family."
Chris Grebenc

"I love fearless women."
Ingred Taylor

Marianne
Aug 7, 2008

HIT THE ROAD,
Across America in A Topless Car

The True Story of the 8,458 Mile Epic Journey
Coast to Coast to Coast
Across the United States of America

Alyce Cornyn-Selby

by Alyce Cornyn-Selby

Beynch Press Publishing Company

Also by Alyce Cornyn-Selby

What's Your Sabotage?
Procrastinator's Success Kit
Did She Leave Me Any Money?
Why Winners Win
Teamwork & Team Sabotage

www.justalyce.com

www.GoingTopless.info
(Across America in a Topless Car)

ISBN 0-941383-27-X

Published by BEYNCH PRESS PUBLISHING COMPANY
1928 S. E. Ladd Avenue
Portland OR 97214
(For catalog, write to above address)
503-232-0433

Order books: 1-800-937-7771

NOTE:

The 1927 Bugatti roadster replicar had
no radio,
no heat,
no doors,
and absolutely NO TOP.

"I thought I was taking this trip alone.
It took a small army of very surprised people
to help me with this trip.
You know who you are."
--*Alyce*

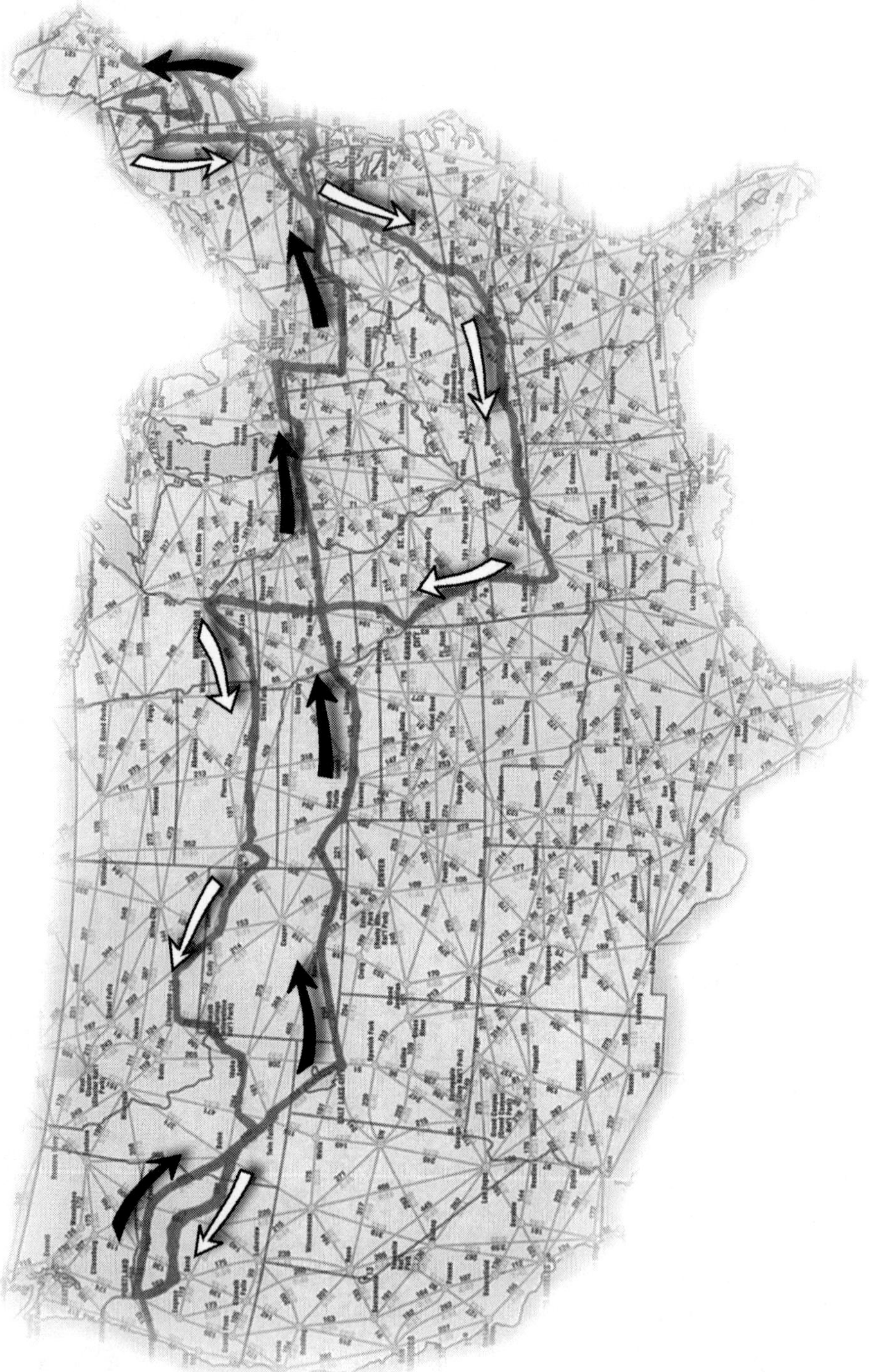

PREFACE

Some day you're going to write a book. Some day you're going to lose the weight. Some day you're going to go to Vienna. You may come to the chilling conclusion that your "Some Day" may have been yesterday. This was my "Some Day" Drive.

Will you wake up some day and say, "Oh, my, I forgot to live my life"?

Come take the trip but don't say, "Oh, goodness, she missed the Shelburne Museum in Vermont," or "How about the Smithsonian?" or "She drove right by Mt. Rushmore!"

That's because I've seen these places. Some of them several times. If I missed your favorite spot, I may have already seen it. "I notice you didn't mention Disneyland or the Grand Canyon," said one reporter, who wrote about my story: TRAVELER FINDS BIZARRE STUFF. Before the trip, I had already been to all 50 states and 23 foreign countries. I had seen Niagara Falls, Monticello, the Field Museum, the Statue of Liberty and all the "majors."

And don't say, "She was so close to Ruby Falls, why didn't she go there?" or "What about Lake Winnipesaukee?" Those places are scheduled for the next trip.

If you lived to be 200 years old you couldn't see all there is to see of America.

I could get in my roadster tomorrow and follow the very same route and have a completely different experience. Because the weather changes a place and so do the people you meet along the way.

And do not say, "I couldn't travel like that." You'd be surprised by what you can handle when you're out there in it. You have your own lessons to learn and Mother Road is an excellent teacher. She is relentless, generous and always there for you.

I learned a lot; some of it I didn't want to know. I identified 23 Roadster Lessons--there were probably 100 more. The most important:

"Life should not be measured by the number of breaths we take but by the number of moments that take our breath away."

Alyce Cornyn-Selby

1

In the Great Overall Scheme of Things, why does anybody do anything? Have the motivational experts ever considered the profound effect of DISGUST on motivation?

I was disgusted the morning of September 13, 2000. My office looked like a paper recycling plant. There were whiny requests to "fill out our forms," there were quarterly taxes, there were computer registration forms and membership update forms. Who was responsible for this chaos? If I could get my hands on 'em, I would fire their incompetent carcasses! It was every entrepreneur's nightmare; the cause of this chaos was me. I work alone.

Did you know that paper could scream? (If pie can call from the kitchen, then you understand that paper can also vocalize.) Every paper demand was a screaming brat in my business playpen. I wanted out of this adult day care center that had cast me as Nurse Ratchet. I desperately did not want the part. It was clearly time for Rand McNally's School of Problem Solving: Hit the road.

Living in Oregon I was supposed to have a relationship with the Pacific Ocean. You are morally obligated to look at an ocean if you live within 100 miles of one.

My only beach time, for nearly two years, had been short strolls along the Atlantic when I had East Coast speaking engagements. I was in danger of being ticketed by the Stop & Smell the Roses police. This suddenly seemed a situation in immediate need of correction, probably brought on by an overexposure to paper. So midmorning, in complete disgust on this clear, sunny Wednesday I chose the roadster and headed west; I needed to see my own neighborhood ocean. That was the goal that day.

It took hours to make it from Portland to the Pacific, ordinarily a drive of an hour and a half. The wimpy engine could barely push me and the car body over the low Cascade range. It was a delicious distraction from my papier mache'd office, but it was quite an all-comsuming task to go putt-putt-putt along Highway 26. At some inclines we could have been passed by a riding lawn mower. Inching along, I imagined that soon we'd actually start rolling backward down the hills.

I bought the obligatory salt water taffy in Seaside and as I walked out of the candy store, white bag in hand, I contemplated the drive home. "I like your car," a grinning 9-year-old said who was being dragged down the beach by a large yellow dog. "I do too," I replied and waved. I looked at the roadster. If he had been a dog he would have been some sort of terrier, a leash-straining ankle-biter in need of a bath.

In fact, the car had been more of a pet than a mode of transportation for the three years that I had owned it. With no doors, no top, no heat, no radio and no windshield wipers it couldn't be seriously considered a vehicle...not in a state where truck sales consistently outpace car sales and the Portland concept of "roughing it" is not using cruise control. No, I'd used the car as a "grocery-getter" and until I'd split for the beach that September day, I hadn't driven it outside the city limits of Portland.

Now I looked at the car and had this thought: "This car is just too much fun."

On that 180-mile round trip to the beach I lost one of my vintage 1927 license plates. No, I didn't hit anything, it just fell off. The right front fender also broke a weld and hung like a split fingernail. The next day going up MLK Boulevard to the welding shop, the left rear fender broke loose and I drove the rest of the way steering with one hand and holding onto the fender with the other. The cost estimate to weld the two fenders back on was daunting. Fenderless cars are legal in Oregon (as long as it isn't raining, what a joke!) so I gave the amputation order: cut them all off.

What remained resembled a blue cigar on four tires. I drove the car this way for several months.

"Howard," I asked my car buff friend, "what would it take to make this car go like a normal car?"

"A new engine."

"Matthews," I asked the guy I bought the roadster from, "where can I go to get a new engine put in this thing?"

Those two little conversations and $2500 later, a 1200 cc engine was in the junk pile at Ron's Auto Repair and I was on my way with a beefier rebuilt mill (that's an engine to you civilians) down 82nd Avenue. Dr. Ron's orders: return after 300 miles for a valve adjustment. I made it five blocks. Not an impressive start for what I hoped would be an engine that would make my life wonderful. Life wasn't wonderful. I was pushing the car; it wasn't carrying me anywhere.

The good news: the car is so little that even I can push it.

I'm no Einstein on the subject of cars. I'm more Gertrude Stein on the subject of cars. I know just slightly more than I knew 20 years ago when I bought my first car, a 1940 Ford coupe. That's a whole story in itself. Yes, I still have it. And no, it's not for sale.

Unbeknownst to me, having an old car was an instant fat-fendered ticket into a strange universe complete with its own language. I learned that a deuce wasn't just a card in a deck and running board wasn't jogging when you didn't feel like it. I used to think that the reference to a "mill" meant a large factory where paper is made. I was so oblivious to the language of automobiles that I had to have the lyrics to "Little Deuce Coupe" *translated.* I mean, what exactly are "lake pipes"? A drainage system for pond scum?

Gone are the days when I thought:
woody was a famous woodpecker,
V-8 was a vegetable juice,
competition clutch meant stage fright at a sporting event,
drive train was what the engineer did for Amtrak,
409 was stuff you sprayed on your kitchen counters,
raked was something I need to do to my lawn,
headliner was a lead newspaper story,
chopped was something done to liver,
flames were in my wood stove,
pinstripes were in my lawyer's business suit,
small block was a short neighborhood street,
pink slip was something I wore under a pink dress,
and stroked and bored meant you were being touched by an uninteresting person.

When I bought my first car I didn't know a carburetor from a washing machine part. And even my best friends will say, I still don't know. So what's a nice girl like me doing in a story like this?

I have no explanation. I engage in inappropriate age and gender behavior. It's been like this for as long as I can remember.

2

Leafing through the foreign language dictionaries at Powell's Book Store, I found the appropriate nickname for my roadster. The little car was a reproduction of the Italian Bugatti family's Model 35, one of the winningest cars of the 1920s. I found: "A Seno Scoperto" means "topless" in Italian. At least I think it does. So I named the car "Seno."

The little roadster was a tad odd looking and people frequently asked, "What is it?"
Sometimes I answered, "It's a 1927 Seno."

They usually nodded and said "oh" or "yeah, I thought that's what it was."

3

People are walking mysteries. For instance, we have no idea why we say we want to lose 20 pounds *while we're eating a hot fudge sundae.* It is as if the brain's desires, although escaping through the vocal chords, does not extend all the way down to the hand that holds the spoon.

At one time I thought that maybe hands were the problem. All the potato chips I had ever consumed was through my fingers that money slipped when I purported to want to save it. These same hands rearranged the paper clips on my desk when I had something really important to do, like taxes. And my hands could not seem to be coerced into cleaning the garage. Clearly something must be done to these misbehaving hands. It's tax time, let's go get a manicure.

When something is our favorite, we say it's the "hands down" favorite. When it comes to foreign policy we don't extend our butts across the sea, it's always our hands.

"I can't keep my hands off the donuts."
"I can't keep my hands off the intern."

If you've ever sabotaged yourself, chances are your hands were involved.

Your mama said to "keep your hands to yourself." But did you listen? I didn't either.

So imagine my surprise when I watched my hand writing checks for car stuff for this impractical little roadster! I had other things to do with the money--little things, like new gutters for the house, tattoo removal or accordion lessons. Many purchases would have made more sense. But when Seno needed axle boots (I'm hoping there are purses to match) and his wheel bearings packed (in ice? in Gucci bags? what?), there seemed to be no hesitation in my hand as the checks were written. Whatever Seno wanted, Seno got.

In the Pacific Northwest, winter is one giant postnasal drip. It seemed incomprehensible that someone deep inside me had become smitten with this seasonal little car and had assigned some sort of priority to it.

I watched my hands buy gloves. It was actually much worse than that. I became the purchasing agent for gloves as if I were stocking a sporting goods store. I collected leather and Gortex and Velcro'd gloves, some that heated themselves electrically with batteries. I bought soft leather gauntlets at a Renaissance fair. I bought nylon glove liners at the Harley Davidson shop. Hands, of course, are the first things to get cold when you drive a topless car.

Seno's amputated fenders were reshaped and welded back on. I could have treated myself to minor liposuction and reshaped myself for less. I noted other signs in my behavior. My AAA card was upgraded to Plus, good for extra towing.

And I had to ask, "Am I going somewhere....in this car?"

Internally I seemed to have selected some sort of adventure for myself but I wasn't letting me in on it.

Perhaps only a compulsive overeater would understand this. It's the old "there-was-a-box-of-cookies-here-this-morning" syndrome (and you live alone). Or you look around your house and you say, "Where did all this stuff come from?" Or you wake up and say, "Who is this guy in my bed? I don't recall the captain turning on the 'I'm crazy' sign. Where is the *nearest* divorce attorney!"

I never made a conscious decision to put myself in a topless car and fling myself out there into the American highway system. The idea was conceived somewhere deep in my inner landscape, that place where creativity and madness and husband-selection is done. You know the place. That place where you convince yourself that blue nail polish won't really make you look like a corpse or that you can find a parking space downtown.

If my granddaughter said she was going to do this, I'd nail her foot to the floor.

Meanwhile, Seno's master cylinder was replaced and I dealt with tire shop owners who said, "They haven't made that tire in 25 years." I learned what powder coating is and it has nothing to do with finishing your makeup. When I picked up the dingy wire wheels at Portland Powder Coating, I was stunned to see what $250 can do to metal. I pulled the soft white packing from around the wheels as if I were opening a bridal gift.

"They're jewelry!" I exclaimed (to the delight of the guys in the shop). The wheels looked as if they'd been dipped in red fingernail polish and were still wet.

Part of me was saying, "Who is this person who is breathing heavy over wheels, for gawd's sake! In 20 years of being around vintage cars and owning a few, you've never gotten excited over wheels! Who are you anyway?"

It was unnerving to hear a very soft voice reply, "You'll find out."

4

Journal Entry: September 11, 2001

Every time I watch it, I hope that the plane doesn't hit the building. And every time it does and every time the horror grows. I am as stunned as the rest of the country. I want to reach out and hold the plane back.

I feel like I have a hole in my chest. My lungs feel bruised, like I've been center punched.

College classes are canceled. Flights are canceled. Surgeries are canceled. Regularly scheduled television is canceled. The meeting planner for this weekend's conference in Coeur d'Alene called me and said the committee would be gathering to decide if they should cancel their conference. I am their star speaker with three of my programs scheduled, including Saturday's evening banquet speech.

The mystery did not unfold that day, of course. Things got murkier. I was 95 percent sure that my speaking assignment in Coeur d'Alene, Idaho would be canceled. People were canceling press runs and church spaghetti dinners. In 16 years as a professional speaker, I had only one gig canceled. Cause? A hurricane.

I think all Americans hugged each other a little tighter that night as we settled down to try to sleep.

The next morning in typical "Now what?" mode, I checked on my options. The airline ticket that the conference chair had sent me was now, of course, worthless.

Journal Entry: September 12, 2001

Everyone is moving in slow motion. The entire nation is screaming that they don't understand. I don't understand either.

Amtrak, sticking to their never-convenient schedules in the West, is not an option. I picture myself in the Spokane train station at midnight and it is not a pretty sight. I've checked the bus schedule and when I did finally get through, they were sold out. I have never in my life missed an engagement; if it's still on I will find some way to get there. I hope they don't cancel this conference. But people are canceling dental appointments, mud wrestling and bird watching! (The dental appointments make perfect sense to me.) We are all in the most amazing pain, not knowing how to help each other.

Wednesday afternoon a resolute meeting planner called from Coeur d'Alene and said they were going ahead with their conference. I told her it was going to be great and I would be there in 48 hours. I stood for a moment in my office and then turned, turned again, and turned again. I must have looked like a dog trying to lie down.

Something had gone "ping!" in my head, like a silver spoon gently striking a crystal glass.

I picked up the phone in my office and I called Spike's Auto Upholstery. "I'm the one who came in with the Bugatti roadster," I said. "You gave me an estimate for a tonneau cover. Can you slamdunk that cover for me in 24 hours?"

"Maybe...if you get it over here right away."

I don't remember hanging up the phone. I was out the door and delivering Seno to the shop on 6th Avenue.

The only way for me to get to Idaho was to drive. I would have to leave within 32 hours to make it. I could do that. All the props and books and my suit, everything was already packed.

Journal entry: September 13, 2001

The only thing left to make Seno ready for a Road Trip is the tonneau cover. I've wanted to take an overnight trip as a test drive to see if I can stand driving long distances in this car that is barely a car. Is this the opportunity? I hate the idea of risking a speaking engagement on an unknown quantity like this open car. There is too much at stake. I cannot let these people down. At the same time I feel this panic, as if Life as we know it in this country will never be the same. Transportation has come to a standstill all over America--all over the world! Joyce is stuck in Chicago; Alexis is in Canada. What's next? Rationing coupons for tires? Roadblocks at state borders? Permission slips to travel? I may have lost my chance to do my dream! (OK, so it might be a nightmare--but I don't know that!) I've always said "Some day I want to drive across country." Well, I'm getting the chilling feeling that my "Some Day" may have been yesterday.

I don't know if the car is mechanically sound enough to make it--everything is so new, so untried. And I don't know if I can physically drive the silly thing that far! It's more than 800 miles roundtrip and I don't think I've driven it 800 miles in all the time I've had it. Can I hold it to the road in the wind? Can it keep up with the trucks on the interstate? Will I be an accident just waiting to happen? Mouse potato that I am, am I physically fit enough for such a journey?

I've decided to leave it up to the Universe to decide. If Spike's Auto Upholstery can get the cover done in time, I'll take Seno. If not, I'll take Milk Toast.

Milk Toast was my white, normal car, the safe car with the car seat for grandkid Gracie. A four-door nondescript, American-made reliable form of transportation. A car that always starts, has electric windows and air-conditioning. An accountant's car. A *real* car.

Journal Entry: September 14, 2001

4 AM. The tonneau cover is tan with a zipper in the middle. I am scared to death and I am leaving anyway.

I used a flashlight to find my roadster in the dark. More than an hour away from first light, I couldn't get the key to slip in the ignition without the aid of the light. (There was only one simple dial on the dashboard and it didn't light up.) The single dashboard gauge was like Joe Friday: it gave just the simplest of facts, m'am. Typically the fuel indicator in an old car should be regarded with suspicion. The speedometer liked to speak in ball park figures too. The honest answer to "how fast will it go?" was truthfully, "I have no idea." At least the headlights worked. And I needed them. The morning was so black that I couldn't see my house just 20 feet away. I pulled the shift down and to the left and backed out of the drive-way. One very nice thing about a roadster with no top: no blind spots.

I-84 was 30 blocks from my house. It was already so cold that I zipped my down parka up to my chin. Just before the on-ramp next to Benson High School I pulled my red motorcycle helmet over my hair. It didn't feel half as ridiculous as I thought it would--driving a car while wearing a crash helmet. But then, I was a woman on a mission. Traffic, startled to see a person in what appeared to be an Indy racer shot out of a Time Machine, made room. I concentrated on exhaling and became acquainted with that familiar trucker's advice to put the pedal to the metal (or in my case, fiberglass).

Soon I was beyond Portland's suburbs and it was just me and Seno and the trucks. We were all taking the gentle curves through the Columbia Gorge, my favorite part of the Pacific Northwest. Inter-state 84 laid down between the Cascades and the wide, cold Columbia River, past a garden of waterfalls--Horsetail, Multnomah, Bridal Veil. But I might just as well have been in Nebraska because in the dark all I could see were mud flaps and How's My Driving messages and plenty of truck lights. Over, around, left and right and through a tunnel.

To the trucks I must have seemed like something insignificant, like gnats at a picnic. But to me, the trucks moved like giant icebergs with jet engines attached, afterburners at full bore. The sound pressed me against the car seat. When they passed it was an all-consuming experience and I gripped the wooden steering wheel as if I were going to be sucked out of the car. I was terrified.

It was Hood River before I could see the horizon lighten. I was hoping that maybe I'd lighten up too. Seno and I were so small and things can happen so fast at 65 miles per hour. Eventually a few pick-up trucks joined the parade eastbound and then finally some passenger cars. Occasionally some driver would honk a friendly greeting and the people inside their cars would wave at me. What they didn't realize was that I'd have a bonafide heart attack every time they'd blow their horns and I couldn't get my grip off the steering wheel to wave back. They had, obviously, never in their lives ridden in an open car. Sound was magnified. A simple car horn sounded like the *Queen Mary* was docking on the end of my bumper.

An open car was a sensory experience. I felt all the air, the pockets of warmth from a roadside pond, the chill of a cold breath down a canyon. I could see everything above me, hawks and sheer cliffs and spectacular skies. I could smell the soy sauce as I drove up Hawthorne Boulevard. I could smell the lawns dampened by sprinklers. I felt *everything* when I was in my open car. The richness of the experience was sensory overload. Comparing driving a roadster to driving a regular passenger car was like comparing lightning to a lightning bug.

When I pulled into the first rest stop I wanted to cry with relief. My forearms were beginning to ache and I learned Roadster Lesson #1: Gripping the steering wheel does not improve the performance of the automobile.

5

It was now 9-11 + 3 and I was grateful that:
  a) I had an all-consuming task requiring complete concentration.
  b) I had no radio.
At this precise moment in history the only thing I could do for the rest of the world was grieve and keep moving.

The Cascade mountains began to drop away from the Columbia River around the dam at The Dalles, Oregon. The towering cliffs and white lacy waterfalls started melting into round, rolling hills. Seno and I passed through the Rain Curtain where the green and the damp just disappear. The air was suddenly lighter, warmer, drier. The dawning sun looked at us as if to say, "What's the matter? You don't recognize me? I'm over here in Central Oregon all the time. You should come visit more often."

Biggs Junction was basically a truck stop. I've never noticed any churches there or schools or even a post office. The price of diesel was spelled out in yellow and black letters about the size of the Hollywood sign in L.A. I had completed 84 miles east on I-84 and could now live to tell about it. It seemed a momentous occasion--even though I had 328 more miles to go before I was within walking distance of the final destination, the conference center in Coeur d'Alene, Idaho. Then there was the little matter of 412 miles return trip but that problem felt as close to me as Mars.

Most of Oregon was high desert, not rain forest. The people clumped together like moss in the Willamette Valley but the cowboys and the crops were all over here east of the Cascade Range. Biggs Junction really was a significant junction because US 97 presented two amazing possibilities. Go south to Shaniko from here and Shaniko was a ghost town and the ghost resided in the reconditioned hotel. Or go north to...well, if you've never seen it or heard about it, you wouldn't believe it.

Up to this point the prevailing westerly wind had helped push me eastward. The Gorge was a large natural wind tunnel and home base for world class wind surfing. The little surfboards with their delicate single sails gyrated like butterflies by the dozens in the wide river and the tugboats, hauling commercial freight, were supposed to dodge these bugs. What the wind freaks didn't realize was that it takes an entire *mile* to stop a tugboat. And that was on a calm Columbia River day when the wind was only hitting gusts of 40 miles per hour. This same wind blew me and my little car all the way to Biggs Junction. I probably could have turned off the engine and made it in the same amount of time.

The forces pulling on the Biggs Junction bridge were probably comparable to the moon pulling the tides. The Mighty Columbia, moving thousands of acres of melted mountain snow, careens *westbound* and the wind, strong enough to pull the dandruff right off your head, blows *eastbound*--the Great White Knuckle Crosswind of the Pacific Northwest. Caught in the middle of this chaos was a long, thin two-lane bridge, a narrow strip of asphalt that connected Oregon to Washington. That skinny bridge stretched straight out in front of my fiberglass roadster. Coming at me was the chrome face of a Freightliner with stadium lighting all over it. Seno handled like a box kite on the bridge. The wooden steering wheel shuddered back and forth. There were no shoulders and there was no turning back. The bridge had a slight hump in it, so now I was also pulling against gravity. It was almost seven o'clock in the morning and I was sure that the trucker in that oncoming Freightliner had been driving all night and was now looking forward to getting to Biggs and a good strong mug of coffee. My headlights, all of three candle watts, were headed toward his two spotlights and our combined speed was 120 miles per hour. I realized that if I should live long enough to reach a cross point with this semi his big body would momentarily block the wind. Any overcompensation on my part with the steering wheel and I would be shmushed like Silly Putty on the side of his trailer. He would be wearing me and probably not even know it.

I couldn't close my eyes at a moment like this. I wanted to, I really, really wanted to but it was not recommended. It was the Zen experience. Yes, I was in the Now Moment. I was *not* worried about the scrambled files in my office or the five e-mails I didn't send or the crumbs on the kitchen counter. I was *not* thinking about how things could be better between me and my relatives. I was *not* aware of the unemployment rate, the crippled stock market, the voting debacle in Florida or even global warming. I was only aware that this Freightliner was so big it created its own weather and on the off chance that I would survive its going by, there was a passenger car right behind it, following closely in its vortex.

The only trick left to me was speed. If I slowed slightly, I would have a nanosecond more to deal with the sudden block of wind. I wondered how slowing down was going to go over with anyone behind me. Yes, of course, I *would have* the twin brother Freightliner in my rearview mirror! His headlights cleared the top of my head. Tiny whitecaps, thrown up by the wind, lapped at either side of the narrow passage across the river. It occurred to me that a human being could survive in the cold of the Columbia River for only 60 seconds before hypothermia would set in. I could hear Butch Cassidy laugh and say, "Hah! The fall will kill you!"

The Cummins diesel behind me growled and all of us went rushing toward each other. The wall of the oncoming truck went by my left side. Seno and I hit that dead space of air and my helmeted head flopped as if on a spring. The momentum of my forward motion got us safely into the wind again and although I think the wheels left the ground and we were officially airborne, I was still in the game, now going by the passenger car. Up ahead I could see land where the bridge connected with Washington State. My fingerprints were etched permanently into the wooden steering wheel.

Roadster Lesson #2: You can't be like the kamikaze pilot who flew 188 missions; when you commit, you commit.

(Three months later a truck and trailer blew off the Biggs Junction bridge. The driver was found still in his seat belt in 30 feet of water.)

6

Almost 90 years ago, a guy who looked like Dom Deluise with hair saw this collection of rolling brown fat-fendered mountains in Washington State and said, "Hmmmmm, Stonehenge." With money and land to spare and a fondness for concrete, Sam Hill had his own Stonehenge built. I suspect that the phrase "what in the Sam Hill?" first came from the lips of people who saw what Sam Hill was up to and wondered if there was some pharmaceutical explanation for his behavior. This was before LSD, remember.

Sam was up to quite a lot if you read between the lines of his life, depicted at Maryhill Museum across the river from Biggs Junction. Road baron and visionary (seems there were a bunch of those guys in the 1920s), Sam was responsible for helping to rebuild Europe after WWI and he brought much joy to that part of the world, especially to the women. And the women (artist, dancer, queen...the usual) got together and said, "Let's make an art museum out of Sam's place." And now you can stop by and see Rodin and Thomas Hart Benton and Charlie Russell. The Queen of Romania took one look at the desolate, uninhabited thousands of acres and said, "A perfect spot to leave my coronation gown." And she did. It was all there in a spacious, elegant museum now, inconveniently located on Highway 14 across from Biggs Junction, Oregon. I am not making this up. There's nothing else out there but wind, wind and more wind...and snakes. (www.Maryhillmuseum.org)

Although I was hell bent for Idaho, there was no way I was going to pass up a stop at Stonehenge. It was like a "Bakery Open" sign; I had to stop. The neolithic impostor was four miles east of the museum, sat atop a 600-foot bluff and it overlooked 100 miles (50 to the east and 50 to the west) if I could buck the wind long enough to stand up and see it all.

Washington State's Stonehenge, practically in my backyard compared to the British version, was a war memorial to 13 men of Klickitat County who died in WWI. At the turn of the century it was believed that Stonehenge on Salisbury Plain in England had been used for human sacrifice. It was this thought that gave Sam Hill the idea. The human sacrifices to the god of war should cease everywhere. His version, and Sam was also buried here, was not just a replica, it was a recreation of what the original was *before* it started falling down and being used to provide stone for houses around the English countryside. My recommendation: see *both* Stonehenges.

This neighborhood Stonehenge in Washington State took two million pounds of cement and 11 years to build. It was actual size. Sam's crew with their concrete mixer didn't know at the time that the original was a calendar and that the alignments were critical, so the Maryhill version was about five degrees off from the original. But a booklet by astronomer Ernest Piini, available in the store next to the monument, explained how to correct for the difference. (1980 Sarsen Press ISBN 0-937324-06-X)

When I visited, I liked Stonehenge all to myself. It pulled me like the English original pulled dowsing rods. The strong wind never died down here and gave me the impression that the gods were trying to airhose visitors off their cliff. In the early morning hours of September 13, 2001 when I drove Seno into the monument's area and felt the popping gravel under the tires, the magic of the place was already starting. I had survived my drive across the Biggs Junction bridge and the familiarity of Stonehenge felt like being greeted by a congratulatory and eccentric friend.

If I listened with an ear reserved for cathedrals, past the wind and the distant roar of I-84 trucks, I could hear something like a hum. I walked clockwise around the 16-foot high outer circle of 30 pillars (never counterclockwise), then stepped into the inner circle of 30 sarsen stones. I turned slowly as if tuning stations on an old-style radio dial and hit the mild vibration of this place.

I've analyzed what specifically resonated so profoundly in me about Stonehenge. I think it had something to do with the structure of the trilithons, the two tallest pillars capped with a slab forming something that looks like the symbol for "pi." Why would I, for instance, take a fired clay class just to create my own model of Stonehenge? Picture a class with everyone making cups and plates and Alyce molding lumps of clay into little sarsens and trilithons. Something about this design strikes a memory in me, like hearing an old familiar song when you're strolling in a foreign city.

Although this area of Washington State was rough, dry country and the wind was relentless, I got a feeling of blessing and "safe travels" from my old friend Stonehenge. I was encouraged and the fright of the bridge was breathed out of me. After recording the visit with Kodak film--Seno dwarfed by the pillars--I jumped back in the driver's seat and left wild, crazy Stonehenge in my rearview mirror.

7

Brushstrokes of high thin white clouds covered horizon to horizon. The white sun took up much of the sky and so perfect that it seemed more like a hot summer postcard. The 75-mile stretch between Pasco and Ritzville, Washington may be described by most people as "there's nothing there on US 395." What they mean is, no McDonalds, Wal-Marts, bowling alleys, gas stations, the opera or shoe stores.

I saw a great deal.

The land looked like a great lumpy blanket and this visual was enhanced by the patchwork of green striping, semi-green, dirt brown, black, dusty tan, wheat blond and in the distance, the illusion of purple. Over this quilt came a tiny toy car and I was in that car. I imagined what we might look like from a helicopter.

There were just enough people traveling that day to keep me from becoming paranoid about getting stranded. That would be scary on this 75-mile stretch.

My breathing began to feel under my control again. I was no longer puffing off the top part of my lungs but I wasn't relaxed either. With more than 8,000 things that could potentially go wrong with an automobile, I felt sensitive to all 8,000 and this was getting on my nerves. I wasn't "there" yet--within walking distance of the place where I was expected to do my work and until I was, a certain amount of stress would have a grip on me. That's how I was. I knew I was in the zone called "Get There" and I groaned to remember some of my more heroic efforts to make it. When a certain celebrity (who shall remain nameless but had a Cuban father and a comedienne mother) wisely opted out because of a brutal Michigan snowstorm, Alyce still showed up for the conference. I remember being wide awake after 40 hours of bucking the Travel Obstacle Gods, and stepping on the stage and delivering. The last three of those 40 hours I was certain I was going to die in that blizzard. I told the conference organizers *not* to tell the audience about the ordeal. I didn't want a "sympathy applause"; I only wanted a reaction to my performance as given, not because of the fiasco of actually getting there. I got a standing ovation.

My military upbringing did not permit me to wimp out on any speaking engagement. That was why the risk of relying on my roadster, when a perfectly good modern car was in my garage caused me to shake my helmeted head. Now in eastern Washington, as far as the eye could see, there were no Tri-Met buses, no shuttles and no taxis. I had no Plan B.

For miles and miles rows of wheat laid in circles on the hills of eastern Washington like necklaces. Large wagon wheel-like structures suspended lines of aluminum hoses and this irrigation made the whole region agriculturally possible. These spraying contraptions stretched across the landscape. On one wheel nearest the highway a farmer or a field hand had taken the time to strap the Stars and Stripes where all travelers could see it. This week would begin the shortage of American flags.

There was, thankfully, a rest stop. Coming out of the cement block ladies room, I saw that the roadster had gathered an audience of his own. This was my first experience of playing Second Banana to this weird little car. He was obviously the star and had top billing here.

I answered questions for Seno's new fan club while I fumbled for my point-and-shoot camera. A butterfly, the color of a kid's rain slicker, was stuck in his grille--we had picked up a little passenger, already dead from exhaustion. The contrast of the brilliant yellow wings on the neon purple paint was a photo too good to pass up. A silver van pulled up next to Seno and several people leaped out, a common reaction to finding a bathroom 60 miles from anywhere. The driver immediately blurted out, "Trade ya pink slips for the van!"

Sometimes people are joking when they say that; I knew he wasn't. I asked myself, "Alyce, what *would* you take for this car?" My Internal Financial Director reminded me of the purchase price (cheap) and all the remodeling (not cheap) and the bills for paint and wheels. But my Internal Time Keeper stepped up and reminded me of all the time and inconvenience it took to get Seno to his appointments and all the research and phone calls it took to find just the right shade tree mechanics and body shops to do the variety of work. In a way, the car was priceless because I couldn't be paid enough to go through all of that again. I also wouldn't trade this exquisitely beautiful September day and being on the road, driving through the fields of this fertile country. I looked over the entire rest stop parking lot. There were passenger cars, SUVs, several trucks and this guy's van.

"I wouldn't trade this roadster for all the vehicles in this parking lot." I sort of exhaled when I said it so that the weariness of getting me and the car to that spot came through the communication, not that the roadster was so valuable (it wasn't, in terms of dollars). The message was clear: "Not negotiable."

By the time I buckled up and yanked the stick into reverse, Seno had collected a little band of friends in the parking lot and there was lots of waving as we went back to US395. I was the roadie and Seno clearly was the headliner. How strangely comfortable it felt to be next to the spotlight rather than in it! Probably nobody in that rest stop would be able to pick me out in a line up, but they'd remember the car for a long time.

Roadster Lesson #3: Value's got nothing to do with the price.

8

A lot would have to happen before I'd forget that September conference in Coeur d'Alene, Idaho. I have had larger audiences and have been at more memorable venues and with stage partners like Henry Kissinger. But this conference won one of my "most memorable" awards.

The topic of my banquet speech, selected nearly a year previously, was "Everything I Know About Life I Probably Learned from My Car." I had no idea when I agreed to do this that I'd have the most appropriate visual aid available right in the parking lot.

I scoped out the conference center and was disappointed but not at all surprised to find the large banquet room completely windowless. In a way, that was good for a speaker because then there was no competition with a sunny day or a great view. But it also shot down any scheme for unveiling the roadster to make a dramatic point. I walked around the swimming pool and backtracked through hallways. Conference exhibitors were setting up displays and draping tables. They may have thought I was casing the place; they seemed relieved when I was introduced as the speaker. I was darting in and out of backstage doors when I discovered that the large banquet room was actually just half an even larger hall. A collapsible wall separated the two. Somewhere in a dark passageway I startled a hotel worker. I made an effort to explain my creepy behavior...

"I've got this car and..."

He showed me that the solid wall in the dark was actually another movable screen and there was a set of double doors that opened to the outside for deliveries. With his help I woke Seno out of his blanketed nap and very quietly drove him around to the double doors. The hubcaps cleared the opening with only a half inch to spare. The hotel helpers, now gathering backstage to watch the unusual sight of a purple roadster being pushed into the carpeted hall, found pots of live mums and created a display worthy of a car show. Seno sat there hidden all day while I pretended to act like this was going to be a typical banquet speech, memorable, of course, but with a surprise ending.

The rest of the day I welcomed any diversion to take my mind off of my upcoming evening performance. I autographed books at the author table. My policy was to sign anybody's book, whether I'd written it or not. The conference planners were as calm as camp counselors on a field trip to a glass factory--a marginal sense of hysteria barely under control. It was always like this. And I was always relieved that I did just my part of a conference and not the whole Titanic thing. Meeting planning appeared to be a thankless job where there was frequently competition among attendees to complain about smaller and smaller things.

Journal Entry: September 16, 2001

I don't care WHAT that car cost me, it was worth every cent to have it in that banquet hall last night.

For one brief, intense moment, the disturbing images of 9-11 were overtaken by a jolly little purple roadster.

When the hotel staff pulled the wall open, the audience acted like they had just seen a flying saucer land and watched Robin Williams get out of it. Sure, the car was cool but their reactions were overwhelming. And because I got to be the opening act for Seno's appearance, the group poured over me like warm butter. They were amazed and delighted and noticed all kinds of things about Seno, like the wooden steering wheel, the lips smiling on the front, the emergency brake located outside the body ("What's this thing?"). Cameras came out of everywhere. They wanted a group shot and individual shots, they wanted in the car, leaning over the car, standing behind the car. At some point I wanted to say, "Look, folks, it's just a CAR!" Spouses nudged each other and said, "Honey, remember when we had that old Studebaker..." At that moment the car was worth its weight in what? silver? bronze? Well, at least more than fiberglass. And it took a little bit to convince them that I had indeed driven it all the way from Portland, Oregon to Idaho.

"And I get to drive it all the way back," I reminded them.

And that presented its own challenge. With only 24 hours of terra firma, I was back in the driver's seat. The Idaho Tourism Bureau claimed that it was always beautiful in Idaho. Believe them. The air was clean and warm as I found the entrance to Interstate 90 westbound Sunday morning.

I had always couched my dream of crossing the country in Seno with "if I decide to" or "it may be nuts but" or "perhaps some day I will." Somewhere between Portland, Oregon and Coeur d'Alene, Idaho, however, I had broken a fear barrier. There's nothing quite like *doing* something to give you the idea that you can *do* it. "Thinking will not overcome fear," wrote W. Clement Stone, "but action will."

I discovered a connection between my fear and sound. If you've ever been totally numbed in a dentist's chair, *knew you absolutely could not feel any sensation whatsoever* and still freaked when you heard the dentist's drill, then you can comprehend what I will tell you next. The key item that made it possible for me to drive this tiny car hundreds of miles: ear plugs. So when I left Idaho without inserting them, my stress shot up to Megawatt Level. It was not healthy to be that frightened and it was probably not safe to be driving around in high anxiety. Before I made it to Post Falls, just eight miles from the Washington State border, I pulled over, got the helmet off and literally corkscrewed the industrial-strength ear plugs into either side of my head.

The unfettered sun was rapidly turning the ribbon of interstate into an open furnace. I had prepared myself for cold weather but I hadn't given a thought to the affect of hours in searing heat. I bought a long-sleeved silk shirt in Spokane and dabbed sunscreen on the tops of my hands. The lower half of my face took the brunt of the 65 mile per hour wind. I was being sandblasted. "This can't be good for a person's skin," I thought. The sun got higher, the air got drier and I reached for my water bottle, drinking it for awhile and then shaking it on myself, wetting the silk for relief.

As long as I could keep the car in motion, I could stay this side of fainting. But Highway 395 zigzags through Pasco and Kennewick, six lanes and long stoplights, strip malls with no greenery and no trees to hold back the monotonous sunlight. A 27-year resident of Oregon (where skin cancer was the lowest in the nation) and I felt like an earthworm on hot concrete.

Thunderstorms had been predicted but there was going to be none of that. I started taking on the mentality of a pilot, however, noticing clouds to the west and wondering how far away they were and how soon I'd be under them. I couldn't judge such distances because as a passenger-car owner, I had never needed this information. I mentally took photos of the cloud bank and noted my position on the map. I would find out how far away they were and remember it for future reference. Suddenly clouds were becoming very important to me.

The silk shirt was a good idea except for one thing. My motorcycle riding friends had never warned me about shirt collars. There's a reason bikers don't have shirt collars. When a collar, even a soft silk one, is flapping at your chin and you're doing 70 miles per hour, it stings like an electric prod. I tucked it in but it would gradually work its way out again. If I'd had a scissors I would have cut it off.

Foremost in my mind was, "How can I get comfortable in this car?"

A few adjustments were going to be in order, the shirt being just one of them. The water shaken on the silk was a very workable solution for the heat. But there was no vent (at all!), no air circulating around my legs. My feet might just as well have been in Phoenix on a windless day. By noon I was ready to take an ice pick to the fire wall to get some air.

The roadster's benchlike seat was surprisingly comfortable and felt more like sitting in my aunt's living room. The pedals and the steering were not adjustable (tilt steering wheel? what's that? new fangled invention?) and it was just a blessing that everything fit my size perfectly.

The only music I had was what I could imagine in my mind. Seno had no radio and I heard no news reports. Somehow I was massaged by the car's vibration and the slowly moving hills. They only appeared to be moving slowly because they were so rolling and so large. Despite my alert stance at the wheel, I was soothed. I lapsed into a state of "witnessing" where it seemed that I was watching all this on a domed movie screen. It was the magic of the Mother Road. This was what I came for. This was the answer to: why go? and why this car? Because to move through this land and through this air, feel it all and see it all, unobstructed by anything--this was as close to the Divine as a person was allowed to come and still be breathing.

My "Greatest Generation" fighter pilot dad was fond of a poem. It was etched in metal, mounted on walnut and always hung next to his bedside at every base he was stationed. As I drove home from Idaho I remembered some of "High Flight":

"Oh, I've slipped the surly bonds of earth
and danced the skies on laughtered-silver wings;
...
I've chased the shouting wind along, and flung
My eager craft through footless halls of air.
...
I've topped the wind-swept heights with easy grace
...
And, while with silent lifting mind I've trod
The high untrespassed sanctity of space,
Put out my hand and touched the face of God."

(*High Flight* by Pilot Officer John Gillespie Magee, Jr, an American RAF pilot.)

I used to think, "Oh, geez, Pop, it's just flying." Not any more.

Roadster Lesson #4: There's always more to it than you think.

9

Journal Entry: September 17, 2001

I have learned that I am slightly more physically fit than I thought I was. After driving that distance, delivering three programs and then immediately driving home, I feel like I've only been hit by a Toyota.

And I have learned that a Roadster Mile is one and a half times longer than a regular car mile...two miles if you're bucking that headwind in the Gorge. Trying to drive Seno westbound into the wind was like trying to push a turkey platter through water.

I am not the same person who left Portland three days ago. Something has changed. I don't know who it is, but there's a person inside of me who is saying, "See, I told you we could do it." Who IS that person? And how did they get inside of a grandmother who still doesn't know an air filter from a coffee filter?

Seno seems unfazed by the adventure. He almost appears perky, like he can't wait to go again.

10

A month later part of me was still reluctant to acknowledge that I really wanted to take myself across country. When it was evident that this part was losing, it tried a different tact--it suggested that I take a different car, even rent a car. I listened to the Voice of Reason for several weeks. It just didn't work.

The best I could do was say to myself, "We're not really going to do this, but if we *were* going to, what would we have to do to make it happen?" Then my brain would relax and begin to play.

"Luck is when preparation meets opportunity."

OK, if this is true then I needed to: a) create the opportunity because it wasn't likely to create itself and b) prepare.

Prepare what? Seemed like I needed three things if I was going to get serious about this as a real project: information, skill and endurance (physical and fiscal).

What I needed to prepare:
1. Talk to women who have mileage.
2. Tweak the car with special interest on comfort.
3. Increase physical stamina.
4. Research the route.
5. Increase driving skill.
6. Examine all "what if's."
7. Get current with Life.

If all this could be done, I challenged myself, then maybe...

1. Women who have mileage.

Most of my women friends didn't ask why I wanted to drive a topless vehicle across America. A few of them probably wondered why I hadn't done it already. I needed advice and I went to the experts. Joy had logged over 175,000 miles on two wheels; she didn't even own a car anymore. Carolyn celebrated her 50th year by closing her law firm and riding a Harley through all 50 states. Beth hit the road once for more than a year and now can curl up and camp anywhere. Sheila stepped out of a very active business life and traveled worldwide for two years. You meet people like this and pretty soon you begin to feel like slug bait. And my idea of camping was when room service was late.

I listened to advice on...places to stay, places to avoid, hostels, KOA, awnings and overpasses are your friend, packing a gun or not (split vote on this one), self-defense in general and what to do until the tow truck arrives. I was a seasoned air traveler but long distance car trekking alone was a new challenge and I just wanted to lessen my weiny factor. I got an earful from "women with mileage."

2. Tweak the car with an emphasis on comfort.

"What do you do when it rains?" was the most often asked question. Well, my plan wasn't too elaborate: pull over and meet interesting people. This was not going to be a race across the U.S. so if I had to sit out a rainy day in a motel room watching cable, OK. But if for some strange reason I really, really felt that I needed to drive in the rain, I also wanted that option.

It was Joy, former fashion design student, who helped me design something kayakers call a "splash apron." The tonneau cover was a tan canvas oval that snapped into buttons that go all the way around the cockpit area of the car. It kept the rain and vermin out of the car when I wasn't in it. There was a zipper in the middle that allowed me to drive the car without removing the entire cover. So I would unsnap the driver's half of the cover, unzip the middle, get in and sit on half the cover to drive the car.

Howard donated his military issue rain poncho to the cause. I was stumped, however, on the details of how to attach it to the car. Joy, with a working knowledge of sewing, played with the idea until we had something that I could describe to the upholsterer. I drove Seno back to Spike's and left them to create a solution to the rain problem.

I few days later I arrived to see the finished result. I got into the driver's seat, put my head into the poncho's hood and snapped the snaps to the body of the car. (Never mind if you don't understand this--you'll probably never see one and if you're of average intelligence, you'll never have to get in one.) While I was checking to see if I could still move enough to be safe in the car, another customer showed up at the shop.

"First time I've ever seen anybody wear their car," he said.

Now the bright purple roadster looked as if it had an olive drab mummy growing out of it. On the short drive home, at only 25 miles per hour, air filled the inside of the car and puffed up the poncho making the car look like it was being driven by a green Michelin man. At 35 miles per hour the poncho fabric swelled so much it blocked my view as if an air bag had deployed. Tying the poncho down with cords didn't help. This whole idea had to be scrubbed.

"What do you do when it rains?" I didn't have a nailed-down answer to that question.

Other purchases for the trip included a car cover that was to prove invaluable, a personal heating/cooling collar, tools, emergency flashers, lightweight face mask, a cooler on wheels, a new motorcycle helmet (this one full-faced), an amazing collection of gloves, wet weather gear and extra ear plugs. To help ventilate the car, I found a plastic copper cleaner container with a twist off cap and my buddy Howard inserted that into the car body right about ankle level. It was a perfect little ventilation system. The next item up was a new horn, a bit of a challenge with this 6-volt system. I also made friends with the aviation and marine supply folks for miscellaneous fasteners and locks.

I had the ignition wired with a "kill switch" that would prevent anyone from driving the car, even if they had a key. A second hidden kill switch shut off the battery.

3. Increase physical stamina.

"Buff" was what I did to furniture; it was not a condition of the Alyce body. *Anything* more in the area of movement would be more exercise than I had been doing. When they said, "You need to get in shape," I usually responded with, "Back off. Round *is* a shape." I'd clean an oven before I would go to a gym.

Without the aid of stairmasters, aerobic instructors, diets centers, surgery or drugs, I had lost 100 pounds.. I was currently as active as I was when I outweighed Arnold Schwartzeneggar, which means, not much. To the best of my knowledge, I had no will power. I hadn't participated in anybody's program or paid one cent to diet gurus, weight loss centers or therapists. This was nothing to be proud of--it just proved that in some areas, I was a bit hardheaded. I've written extensively about the system I used for overcoming the weight sabotage (*What's Your Sabotage?* Beynch Press ISBN 0-941383-28-8). For most of my life I could be passed off as a really effective paperweight. My idea of physical fitness was: do I fit in my jeans? Then, I'm "fit." I knew this was a lousy attitude. I also wrote a book called *Take Your Hands Off My Attitude!* (Beynch Press ISBN 0-941383-02-4).

Well, this clearly needed to change. It seemed a tad ironic that something with wheels got me on my feet. After yoga strengthening exercises for my neck to support that three and half pound motor-cycle helmet, I signed up for a hiking class and was pretty pleased with myself when I met the qualifications--walk a 20 minute mile over rough terrain with normal breathing. Then I showed up for Tai Chi, that graceful, quiet meditative mother of all marital arts. For "balance and coordination" the brochure read.

The instructor was built like Peter Ustinov and hadn't been my age for a least a decade. With the unlikely name of Patrick Murphy, he led our little group in an activity called "sculling" which was like piloting an imaginary gondola. Slowly back and forth for an hour and a half. The next day the elation from my success with hiking was replaced with disappointment at my aching thighs from one Tai Chi class.

While mainlining Aleve tablets, I reminded myself about Lyn St. James. When asked about the physical strength needed to drive a professional race car, she answered, "I don't have to lift it. I just have to drive it."

I was not destined to experience exercise withdrawal. The only endorphin high I would experience was during a Nordstrom sale.

Howard also pointed out that if I lost some weight, I'd get better gas mileage.

4. Research the route.

It was possible that this whole idea was brought on by my addiction to maps. The very smell of Rand McNally ink and my fingers started to itch for an ignition key. The thought of going on such a trip was a great excuse to haul sacks full of tour books out of the downtown AAA office and into my bedroom. With pens and atlas and Post-its I indulged in hours of armchair travel in my quiet attic suite. At times, I caught myself humming.

Amazon.com started delivering books like *The Cockroach Hall of Fame and 101 Off-the-Wall Museums, Bad Girls Guide to the Open Road, Roadside America, The Collections and Curators of America's Most Unusual Museums, Fun Along the Road: American Tourist Attractions* and *Road Trip USA.* I marked pages for the Hair Museum in Independence, Missouri, the two-story outhouse in Montana, the birthplace of Paul Bunyan in Maine and the world's largest collection of Edsels in Pennsylvania.

One must love a country that invented jackalopes, rattlesnake eggs and the Hill Billy Diet Pill. America was crammed full of eccentrics like Alex Jordan of Wisconsin and Edward Leeskallin of Florida who had defied gravity and common sense to bring us the best of the country's most bizarre. I could dig for diamonds in Herkimer, New York or Arkansas. I could visit black squirrels in Marysville, Kansas and white squirrels in Olney, Illinois and Einstein's brain in Weston, Missouri. If I were overloaded with testosterone I could bungee jump in most states, go up in the Wright B flyer in Dayton, Ohio or shoot an Uzi in Hot Springs, Arkansas. Find the only volcano within a city limit in Portland, Oregon or see a desert that actually devoured a barn in Maine. Hard to be bored in a state offering a ventriloquism museum, world's smallest church, a wigwam village and a museum dedicated to whiskey--all in Kentucky. How could I want to stay home when there was all that out there?

I could find brewery tours in most states, tour Ben & Jerry's in Vermont and get a lesson (and get a certificate) for pretzel twisting in Pennsylvania. For history buffs, there was Bedrock City in Custer, South Dakota and for pagans there was plenty to do in Salem, Massachusetts. Don't even get me started on world's largest this and that. America was coated with kitsch like thick chocolate frosting on an Iowa 4th of July cake.

Time to Get Serious: I taped a map of the United States to a large sheet of foam core and pushpinned the locations of Chicago and Reno.

These two points were the two non-negotiable sites and they bookended the dates of the trip. I had a speaking engagement in Chicago (April 20) and a speaking engagement in Reno (June 14). These were do-or-die, get-there-at-all-costs anchor points. The pushpins on these two cities were made of silver metal.

Then I selected colorful pins from the box. Jan in Billings, Lynette in St. Paul, Marilu in Arkansas, Irving in New York...nine pins of friends. This became the *sketch* of a route. I wrote to all of them about the possibility I'd actually make it to their doorsteps...and asked for a response if they really wanted a visit. People say they'd love to see me, but how could I be sure? Might have to go find out. When a fellow traveler in Europe said, "Come see me in New Jersey," did they really mean it? What if they didn't? But what if they *did*?

Then I began to fill in with America's bizarre or delightful roadside attractions--Pioneer Museum in Nebraska, Graceland in Memphis, the Barnum Museum in Connecticut.

The truth: I didn't want a carved-in-stone route. I looked forward with glee to a clock-free, scheduleless journey. This proved to be a complete fantasy.

My criteria for route selection went something like this:
a) will there be bathrooms?
b) is it anywhere near a friend's house?
c) will it keep me out of big city traffic?
d) is it free?
e) is there snow and ice?
f) will it get me Pacific to Atlantic and back again?
g) does it get me near something weird to see?
h) is that free?

5. Increase driving skill.

I, like everyone, was a great driver. Ever notice how everybody thinks they're great drivers? Interview anybody, even if they are walking out of traffic court, and they will say, "Hell, yes, I know how to drive! I'm a *good* driver!"

However, I was the kind of driver who disappeared inside my house at the first sign of a snowflake and I didn't come out until it and all of its friends were melted. I'd eat canned stewed tomatoes before I'd risk sliding up Hawthorne Boulevard to Safeway for groceries in a snowstorm. I didn't have a car that I disliked enough to send its tires spinning to do an errand. My way of handling the problem was Typical Alyce, just don't participate.

Besides, that first snowflake caused most Oregonians to put on their stupid shirts and go for a drive! Even if I could handle snow and ice, they couldn't. Most Oregonians didn't even know what a snowplow looked like because we didn't need one that often. So we've never really learned how to handle anything but wet streets. In fact, four straight days of sunshine and an Oregonian gets dumb in traffic. Too much sun and they start careening off guardrails and running red lights.

Face it, *everyone* could use an advanced driving course.

SkidCars were specially equipped cars that simulated icy road conditions. Here in Oregon they were located at Portland International Raceway and the school was operated by an outfit called Pro Drive. The infinitely patient instructors with nerves of titanium would take drivers out to a fairly level asphalt lot where they've seen macho dads, arrogant teenagers, full-of-themselves "experienced" drivers and thrill junkies attempt to learn something. Anything. There's nothing quite as humbling as doing donuts into orange cones when you're trying to avoid a skid...with fellow students watching! What could be done to get out of this mess? The natural response--braking--was what *not* to do. Touch that brake, even tap the brake, even *thoughts* about tapping the brake and failure was assured.

If I could get past the humiliating stomping my ego would endure, I could actually learn how to avoid getting into skids in the first place. I sat in the back seat while other students made fools of themselves and sent my stomach somewhere into next week. Then it was my turn. The car was impossibly goosey and the only curve I took that day was my learning curve.

I earned my certificate for maneuvering the Swedish SkidCars without taking out a guardrail or punching a fellow student in the mouth. I realized that yes, I indeed had the new information but my body was likely to go back to its instincts (all wrong in this scenario) so I signed up and passed the Advanced Course too.

Then one January morning I woke up with too much light in my bedroom. There was the usual grey blanket over the city but it had snowed and diffused sunlight was ricocheting off the white rooftops and white lawns! Ah! A chance to get pictures of Seno in the snow!

I used all my new information and skill to get us to the top of Mount Tabor, our friendly neighborhood mini-mountain and I did it without becoming paralyzed with fear. Families were out building snowmen and dragging sleds up the hill and totally stunned to see my topless roadster coming sure-footed up the street. My ride was even colder than it looked; remember there was no heater in the car.

6. Examine all the "what if's."

What if I get lost? What if I get stuck? What if I get a flat tire in the middle of Wyoming? What if I run into Bad Guys? What if my cell phone won't work? What if there's no room at the inn? What if a tuna lands on the car?

Playing around in "What If" Land can turn anyone into a bonafide neurotic. I could spin around in there like a tennis ball in a clothes dryer. It was *such* familiar territory. After awhile I'd almost get used to all that bouncing and then being calm felt unnatural.

I decided I needed to see if I could sleep in the roadster...just in case. "Just in case" what, I have no idea. Not willing to wait until this unlikely scenario would ever present itself, I slept in the car for two nights...in my driveway. I coccooned into my snuggy red sleeping bag and curled up across the bench seat. It did strike me as odd that while I live in a huge old house only 15 feet away and have a king-sized bed, I was out in the carport huddled in a space smaller than my bathtub.

But it worked. I was certainly more comfortable than I had ever been on any airliner. And there was no asinine pilot pointing out scenes over the radio to the passengers on the left side of the plane. I was more comfortable than when I had to sleep on the floor at O'Hare on a layover from Glasgow. It was more comfortable than Amtrak to Montana. It was quieter than many youth hostels and much softer than the plank I slept on at a Buddhist retreat center in the South Pacific. It was luxury accommodations compared to camping and sleeping on the ground.

Security issues. A person can be as responsible as they can reasonably be and at some point they just have to say, "Now it's up to the Universe." My plan was to concentrate on making me and the car as safe as possible and then just not think about it any more. The standard car alarm, for instance, was designed with the idea that passing strangers will notice a squealing vehicle and rescue it from the hands of evil doers. Even I was not this delusional. I purchased an alarm system that was different from the usual annoying car alarm that goes off in your neighbor's driveway at 2 a.m. Alarms should be on the *owner*, not on the car. (What a concept!) The sensor was in Seno but the receiver alarm was with me and let me know if the car was being touched.

7. Get current with "Life."

Taxes. Estate planning. Insurance coverage. What to do about getting bills paid, mail sorted, utilities checked? What would happen when my ivy started growing across the sidewalk while I was gone? How would I get the pharmacy to give me an advance on my meds? Whose birthdays was I going to miss while I was away? Where were the 1-800 numbers for canceling credit cards if they were stolen? What would I do if I had a dental emergency?

It was called Life . Whoever said "God is in the details" could have God come over and tend to some of these details for me.

I filed my taxes in record time, finished the estate planning and completed all the paperwork, signed the health care directive which basically said "leave me the hell alone," paid all my home's bills in advance, gave the ivy a butch hair cut, drained the hot tub and bought a 7-hour battery for the video camera.

"OK," a voice inside my head said. "I got it all done. Can I go now?"

Then there was the spiritual aspects of this endeavor.

John Steinbeck went 12,000 miles in his truck (now enshrined in Salinas, California) and he wrote: "What I am proposing is not a little trip of reporting but a frantic last attempt to save my life and the integrity of my creative pulse. It would be hard work but to me it represented the antidote for the poison of the professional sick man." (*Travels with Charlie, In Search of America* Penquin Books, ISBN 0 14 00.5320 4)

Jack Kerouac said that traveling across America was "our one noble function of the time."

In *Blue Highways* (Ballantine Books ISBN 0-449-20432-4) transcontinental van driver William Least Heat Moon wrote that he wanted "driving once more instead of being driven" and he observed that "a man who couldn't make things go right...could at least go."

I read the angst books written by men who had "hit the road" and I declared that I was not looking for America, I knew right where it was. It was called a map, guys. And I didn't look to Mother Road to "fix me" either. In fact, if something ailed me, my inclination was to stay home. I wasn't trying to "save my creative pulse" or "make things go right." As for Kerouac, traveling in America has all the "nobility" of a rest stop bathroom.

I noticed that all the upset men who wrote about their road trips chose back roads, avoiding cities. As I read these books a picture began to emerge in my mind of a two-lane highway in Iowa with traffic jams of neurotic men all trying to find something. I, too, planned to take state roads and back highways. Would I run into any of these distraught characters?

Perhaps the sensation of driving was different for women than it was for men. Women could take a car trip without trying to beat their best time. And a need to urinate was not superseded by a desire to stay head of the five semi trucks one just passed.

Freya Stark wrote in 1929: "To awaken quite alone in a strange town is one of the pleasant sensations in the world. You are surrounded by adventure. You have no idea of what is in store for you, but you will, if you are wise and know the art of travel, let yourself go on the stream of the unknown and accept whatever comes in the spirit in which the gods may offer it."

Freya, you enchanted little Buddha lady, you may have hit on something. The ultimate challenge:

a c c e p t   w h a t e v e r   c o m e s.

I wanted to "road test my philosophy." As a speaker who was asked to give an audience information and methods to make adjustments to life on Planet Earth, I wanted to know if my "stuff" would hold up under prolonged efforts and an intense strain.

What would happen to my own motivation during weeks of existing in unfamiliar territory? Taken out of my safe and predictable environment, thousands of miles from home and alone, how well would I do using the tools I suggest to others?

We humans lapse backward into things when under stress. For instance, take someone who proports to be an *ex*-Catholic, put them on an airplane that is about to crash...and see how fast they reach for a rosary.

I wanted to know what I would reach for, what would work, what was lip service and what about my Sustaining Philosophy was real. Would the Oracle of Delphi offer any different advice if they had to deal with speed traps, road detours or pumping their own gas? How would a Zen master deal with it if their car stalled in the express lane at a toll booth? How would your favorite religious leader handle a bladder full of coffee and a sign that read: NO STOPPING FOR 23 MILES.

Journal Entry: April 3, 2002

I have no idea what I'm doing. I'm supposed to leave Oregon in a week and I get the feeling it's going to come as a Big Shock to part of me completely unwilling to accept that this trip is real. All the plotting and planning and doing--stuff, money, bills, insurance, cell phone, maps--I've prepared as if I'm preparing for someone else to go.

But in a week I need to actually get in the car and point it toward the interstate. Hmmmmmmm. I can't grasp it.

I am to the point of compulsion that I won't go in for a pap or a mammogram lest I get bad news and have to cancel the trip. I don't want to know; I just want to go.

11

Voice-in-Head #1: "Is this it? Is today the day we leave?"

Voice-in-Head #2: "(Groan.) It's not today, is it?"

#1: "Remember to pack the charger for the cell phone. Write that down."

#2: "This is such a nice house. I love this house. I've probably got enough projects inside this house to last me the rest of my life..."

#1: "Need a siphon hose...how about the tubing left over from that old fish aquarium we used to have. Would that work?"

#2: "Siphoning gas--gag! I haven't even had my coffee yet this morning."

#1: "Need to get on the net and order the KOA directory."

#2: "Excuse me, I don't camp. What do we need a camp directory for?"

#1: "Gotta get a spare set of keys this morning on the way to Tai Chi. Still haven't read through all of the auto club tour books yet for the Must See list..."

#2: "How can you think about leaving? It is so lovely in May in Oregon. Who could resist an Oregon May? And the Rose Festival in June. Grandmothers with little ones in tow at the Fun Center downtown. I should be one of those grandmothers. Gracie got me on the dragon ride four times last year. And her parents wouldn't take her on the ferris wheel. If I'm not here, Gracie won't get to go on the ferris wheel."

#1: "Don't forget distilled water for the battery."

#2: "Maybe I'll be mugged and killed sometime today and I won't have to go on this damned adventure."

#1: "I can't wait to go!"

#2: "I don't want to go..."

#1: "If we don't go, I'll never forgive you."

#2: "We'll get a thousand miles from home and you'll realize what a truly dumb idea this is."

#1: "Then we'll deal with it."

#2: "And this coming from the woman who considers parallel parking a major accomplishment. Remember the word 'error' comes from the Middle English word 'erren' which means to 'travel about'--when *will* you listen to reason?"

#1: "I can't wait. A *vrooom* with a view!"

#2: "This isn't really going to happen..."

#1: "You just keep telling yourself that while I pack. Life is not measured by the number of breaths we take but by the number of moments that take our breath away."

#2: "I can't breathe...I can't breathe..."

#1: "Here, blow into this paper sack."

12

Ray Atkeson was the Michael Jordan of Photography. With the patience of a troll, he would sit on a spot for six weeks if he had to, just to get the right light. More calendar ink had been spread for his images than probably any other photographer. Ray Atkeson, with his popular coffee table books and dazzling posters, was the envy of scenic photographers worldwide...and, it seemed, half of all scenic photographers lived in Oregon.

So when Ray Atkeson said that the most beautiful spot on the Oregon Coast was (drum roll, please) Cape Kiwanda, a person might want to make special note of that.

April 4, 2002 Seno and I inched onto the sand at Cape Kiwanda very carefully. The waves have been known to suck cars into the briny depths of the Pacific. We had come back to the beach and this time, thanks to all the engine improvements, we cleared Wilson Summit with ease and made good time. We were here specifically because of the name of Cape Kiwanda's town: Pacific City. "Coast to coast" sounded so general, so common. But Pacific City to Atlantic City, now that was descriptive. So in order to start my journey eastbound, I had to travel west first from Portland and touch base at the first goal. That first goal was to find a sign that read "Welcome to Pacific City" and take Seno's picture next to that sign.

The only sign I could find was a little green and white one on Highway 1 and it was about the size of a serving tray. It simply read: PACIFIC CITY. It would have to do. To get a shot of Seno next to the Pacific Ocean I dropped down into Cape Kiwanda's parking lot. A passing tourist was kind enough to use my camera and get both me and Seno with the ocean as the backdrop. As I smiled for the picture, my teeth were chattering and my gloves hid fingers turning blue. Couldn't I use a cup of hot clam chowder at a moment like this? My luck was amazing and right there, rising like a shrine on the south edge of the parking lot, was the home of the "Best on the Coast" winner in the clam chowder division, the Pelican Pub and Brewery.

Seno was beginning to attract an audience again so I beat feet into the restaurant before hypothermia could set in. I'd be hard pressed to find a more comfortable and inviting spot to watch whales and waves than right there. Dark wood, a long bar, wide windows and the entire Cape right outside, blowing and chilly while I was snuggled in a booth trying to decide which award-winning brew to have with my bowl of hot creamy chowder. The Pelican was as unpretentious as it was decorated with awards. Oregon was the center of the known Universe for micro breweries and evidently the Pelican scored big with its MacPelican's Scottish Ale and Tsunami Stout. (www.pelicanbrewery.com)

Sufficiently thawed I went back to Seno and found a 10-year old boy circling the car while screeching for his father to "come see!" The dad fumbled with his camera in the wind. The kid stood stiffly next to the roadster's fender while the picture was taken. I walked up crossing my hands in front of me in a "no goal" gesture and I said, "No, no, no..." They both instantly turned sheepish, caught in the act of what? admiring my car?

"No," I said again. "You gotta get *in it* for the picture!" The boy stared at his dad in that classic "can I?" expression that only good children can muster. The parent hadn't recovered his embarrassment yet so I just took over. "Here, let me help you in." The kid didn't wait for parental approval this time.

He became the first of many kids that I would lift into the roadster. Their unbridled lust for gripping the steering wheel and trying on my helmet became miniature highlights every time it happened on the trip across the country. The enthusiasm of children couldn't be duplicated; there was nothing out there quite like it. It was a gift we were born with and then lost.

"You need to get yourself one of these," I told the boy. By now he was tugging at his father's jacket. The dad was lost in some sort of reverie, like a guy who had long ago given up his convertible for a station wagon. His gaze never left the roadster and I'm not sure he even knew I was there.

"Can we get a car like this?" he was asking his dad. "Where do you go to get a car like this?"

"Well, you probably can't get one *exactly* like this...you'd probably get a better one. Just go see Matthews at Southeast 26th and Holgate in Portland and he'll fix you right up." I was to repeat this line many times over the next three months. When I got in Seno and waved good-bye, father and son were starting what would be, I'm sure, their lifetime of car conversations.

Still searching for a "Welcome to Pacific City" sign for Seno's travel journal, I drove into town and approached the only traffic light. What appeared to be an abandoned gas station sported a faded handmade wooden sign reading: "Pacific City, elevation seven feet." I was maneuvering Seno closer to this little sign when a woman came running across the street. "Who *are* you and what is *this*?" she wanted to know. She seemed to be about my age and I was stunned for a moment that a pre-crone would exhibit such extrovert behavior. I liked her instantly.

Before she could say "mermaids on sale" Sherry and I were chatting like two reunited sorority sisters. I moved Seno over to her gallery, betwixt and between (no capital letters intentional), and we caught each other up on what our lives had been like so far.

"I'm driving this car across country," I said. A photo session ensued with her partner/daughter Cydne pressed into service. Then the storekeeper from Dolls 4 You 'n' Me joined in. I also met the co-owner of Swan's, another eclectic shop, had a giant cookie at the Grateful Bread and stopped by the Library Thrift Store where you could find a lid for any size pot or pan and help the library fund by doing so.

By the time I left I had learned who was getting married, who also has a four year old granddaughter, who still loves her first husband and who was also born in Ohio and how to make fake street signs. I didn't see a typical manufactured souvenir in the whole town. There appeared to be nothing typical about tiny, eccentric Pacific City.

Now that I had touched my western most point, I was officially eastbound. On the way back to Portland, I stopped in Tillamook (best cheese this side of Wisconsin) with its lush pastures and acres of black and white cows that have learned to swim in response to the area's annual flooding.

While I was parked outside Tillamook's St. Vincent de Paul Store (I can pass anything on the road but a thrift store) a Canadian professional traveler--one of those people who doesn't own a house anymore, just a million dollar bank account and an RV--suggested emphatically that I should buy a motorcycle trailer and attach it to Seno's butt. He was a wealth of information about where to buy such a device and how to hook it up and how much better my life would be if I followed his advice that I knew telling him anything about what I actually wanted was pointless, eh? One of my self-imposed lessons of this trip was to live within the space I had and not to drag home every delightful and impractical thing I saw. I had 25 years of that behavior (have a house full of the weirdest stuff imaginable to prove it) and it was a habit I wanted changed about myself.

Roadster Lesson #5: When you drive an odd car, you have a responsibility to be nice to people. You must answer the 800th question about the car as patiently and enthusiastically as the first question asked. If you can't do this, then drive a Honda.

13

After Pacific City I spent a couple of days in Portland before the Big Leaving. It was sort of like when a sprinter digs the tips of his shoes into the track gravel and poises his knuckles to prepare for the starting gun to be fired.

As final preparations were being made (should I take my laptop? where can I buy disposable underwear? where's the address for that hostel in New Jersey?), I made my farewell stop by Darcelle XV, Portland cabaret and the museum for the feminine symbols of chiffon/lace/big hair/spikes/red nail polish. I joined the celebration of the Feast of Fools (*how* appropriate!), a medieval costume party, with the tiara'd crowd of characters I had grown to know and love but never to try to compete with: Lotta Liquor, Empress Poison Waters, Roxy, Monica Boulevard, Meesha Peru, the Lovely Suzanne, Emperor ShelleY, Mr. Mitchell, Maria and Darcelle her/himself. This was the last I'd see of the Royal Rose Court for months. I would be trading in my rhinestones for milestones and my personal perfume would be unleaded regular instead of my usual favorite, Passion by Elizabeth Taylor. I wouldn't be wearing mascara for the next 9,000 miles.

Then on Monday morning Seno and I arrived at Channel 2's TV station and the "AM Northwest" talk show. They did a nice little segment making it appear that the ever-popular and ever-humorous host Paul Linnman was late for the show and was being delivered via roadster. With the experienced help of the staff I brought the car into the narrow studio passage and onto the set of the show.

Once he grasped that I really intended to drive all the way across America, Paul asked, "Are you scared?"

I answered, "Of course. What reasonable person wouldn't be?"

Paul Linnman was all of Portland's buddy, neighbor and good guy. Unlike many of television's talking, hair-sprayed heads that ask a question and never listen for the answer, Paul interviewed as if there were a brain behind that smile. He had been on the air as long as I could remember and Portland watched him age just like Opie.

Our television appearance finished, I could now pack the car. Seno required his own toys: tools, jack, gas can, duct tape, tow strap, flares, can of tire inflator, Rainex, and his stick for checking the amount of gas in his 10-gallon gas tank. What space was left over I could have for boots, more gloves, two helmets (leather and hard shell), first aid kit, power bars, cameras, journal paper, my favorite felt-tipped pens, maps and tour books, water bottle, cell phone, postage and addresses of many friends, chargers for phone and video camera, sleeping bag, small pillow, bull horn, vitamins and film. What was left after that, about the size of a football, was for clothes, sun screen, lipstick, and my travel pookie (the little stuffed lobster that I've carried since my first trip to Maine). I had to select clothes that I definitely loved because I'd be living in them for a long, long time. What I chose would have to do quadruple duty for evening wear, pajamas, hiking, driving, picnicking, restaurants and any crazy events my friends would want me to attend: street fairs, teas, dinners, museums, bar mitzvahs, federal court, ice cream socials. It was an impossible challenge. I packed and repacked the car four times. Discarding, fretting, scheming, stuffing, eliminating.

I had two spaces for gear in the car. One was the space a passenger would normally have occupied and this included the floor space. The other space was in front under the hood. In a front engine car, the mill was under the hood, referred to as the *bonnet*. The storage area in an old car was called the *boot*. With Seno, the cavity under the hinged "hood" on the front of the car did *not* house the engine, that was the storage space. The engine was in the rear. So was the luggage area in Seno the *boot* or the *bonnet*? Whatever. I was too busy cramming things in it.

Travel, as an activity for any reasonably sane adult, is insanity. First off, we become nearly homicidal when preparing to leave town. This seems to be the appropriate time to have the screendoor fixed, have the cat declawed, try out bifocals and all sorts of things we should have tended to a long time ago. "I'm going out of town" becomes the battle cry preceding hysteria. We work harder in the two weeks before a "vacation" than the other 50 weeks combined.

"Is there anything more horrible than starting a trip?" wrote Anne Morrow Lindbergh, wife of you-know-who, one of the few Americans who didn't lose his luggage on a transatlantic flight. She continued, "The last moments are earthquake and convulsion and the feeling that you are a snail being pulled off your rock." Where you are going, no one knows you and, you're convinced, no one will like you. Anything that is supposed to be hot will be cold, anything normally cold will be tepid. At some point during your trip you will be invisible, usually in the presence of waitresses. You are only a few hours away from home and into your trip when you wish you'd never left. We know this. And we do it anyway. When you return there are all the painful repercussions of your absence, stacks of mail, dead house plants, bills on the verge of past due and the cat will never forgive you. You may get the impression you are being punished for having left. You are.

* * * * *

Runes are little Chicklet-shaped stones. Petroglyph-style marks are etched into one side of each stone. They are the Viking form of the I Ching, the Norse Magic 8 Ball. I scrambled the runes in their bag and let the ones that were to speak to me stick to my fingers.

I pulled these runes...

"**Anuz** is the truth heard in the wind. This rune represents wisdom obtained or knowledge delivered." (Yep, I'll be getting enough wind...)

"**Nyd** is frequently seen as a powerfully negative rune, generally represents loss, sorrow and a hard journey with lessons learned. The rune here reversed might be representing a minor loss or a nearly avoided catastrophe. Be careful, things are tricky and require strong attentiveness." (Not exactly what I wanted to hear...)

"**Isa** conveys images of slippery slopes and unsure footing, but also of circumstances that have crystallized and become utterly immutable. Remember that in the cold north, ice is not just the challenge to be overcome, but the very nature of the environment. Be courageous, for you work against this element every day. Will you fight alone or with others?"

That's when I hired Howard, his truck and car trailer, to run along with me (pick up the pieces, so to speak) to Chicago just to make sure I'd make it to that scheduled speaking engagement.

Journal Entry: April 10, 2002

I am desperately afraid that I am going to get in that fiberglass excuse for a car and leave town. Communication has completely broken down with whoever it is inside of me that wants to take this monstrously stupid trip.

14

I had a T-shirt displayed on a wall in my office for months. I bought the shirt at the Mel Fisher Maritime Museum in Key West (www.melfisher.org). Mel was the treasure hunter who located and salvaged the 16th century Spanish ship, the *Atocha* off the coast of Florida. The shirt was a long-sleeved navy blue T-shirt with white script lettering that quoted Mel's telegram to his crew when he finally won ownership of the treasure. It read: *Today's the Day!*

I looked at the shirt and its message every day. It was now time to wear it.

15

"This state called Oregon always has been, and promises always to be, a place of celebrated beginnings."
--Ingrid Wendt, *From Here We Speak*

Backed out of my garage at 5:25 a.m. Thursday, April 11 and headed up the Columbia Gorge in a dark mist. I had wondered how much of the "snail being pulled from a rock" sensation I would feel leaving my comfortable home. I mean, I was so attached to this place that I could almost marry it.

Thanks to Channel 6 News, I shot out of my driveway as if I were off to an appointment because I *was*. Ray Summers, TV news feature guy ala Charles Kuralt and a cameraman were to meet me at the

Columbia Gorge Hotel about 56 miles up the river to cover the story and to film the roadster headed eastbound. So my focus was on getting to that appointment; this lessened the impact that I was actually leaving home. I just had somewhere I needed to go.

Just beyond Corbett on I-84 the sky lightened ever so slightly and made everything iridescent. Felt like driving inside a big, grey pearl. My heart began to fill and feel round and pearl-like too.

Howard, in his orange truck was supposed to be right behind me but I lost his headlights in the wet blur and just continued on, hoping he'd find me if I had trouble. With roadster travel, road noise was so loud that a ringing cell phone didn't have a chance of being heard. So while moving, I was cut off from all outside communiqués. For a solitaire like myself, this was a little slice of heaven.

In 1904 sternwheel steamers paraded up and down the Columbia River and as they approached the hotel at Hood River they would sound a whistle once for each guest on board. This was a signal for the maids to make up the appropriate number of beds. In 1920 Simon Benson had just completed what many of the era claimed to be the world's most beautiful road, the Columbia Gorge Scenic Highway, and he bought the hotel. "Gee, I just finished a highway, I think I'll treat myself to a hotel." I probably would have celebrated with a bottle of champagne and a chocolate dessert, but whatever. Rudolph Valentino and Myrna Loy were said to have enjoyed the pleasures of this opulent hotel--although probably not at the same time. This French chateau-looking place was surrounded by gardens overrun with flowers and little stone bridges and everything that made a brown thumb like myself swoon. The Columbia Gorge Hotel was the place people said, "Oh, yeah, that place with the *breakfasts*!" A totally decadent approach to the morning meal, the hotel served a five-course, you-really-shouldn't extravaganza breakfast. Get a suite on the north side of the building and have a view of the Pacific Northwest's premier waterway, the Columbia River. (www.columbiagorgehotel.com)

About all my I could see at this early morning hour was the white log swing nestled in the trees on the lawn. I pulled myself from the cockpit of the roadster and stood in the drizzle to shake Ray's hand and meet the gorgeous cameraman who looked like a happy Ernest Hemingway, without the edge. And there I was in 40 pounds of wet weather gear. My fashion statement was probably something like "unisex road construction." At least I didn't have to answer the question, "What do you do when it rains?"

Lu Ann Trotebas, buyer and curator of the hotel's gift shop, had never learned how to do anything short of first class. She and I have had dress up events together over the years and engaged in mutually beneficial marketing usually involving fluffy stuff like hats and jewelry. She and her cohort Sally Ruggles convinced several Red Hat Society women to join them at this early morning hour to celebrate my Leaving. More about the RHS later, for now it is enough to know that these intrepid women were dressed in purple and wearing red hats at an hour usually reserved for snooze alarms. The hotel served life-giving hot coffee and these irrepressible, irresistible little cinnamon hummers. If I were Egyptian, I'd want to be buried in a sarcophagus filled with these things.

I was presented with an additional travel pookie (it's a girl thing) in the form of a purple lizard filled with tiny beans. My first hitchhiker. I placed him on the steering wheel and he flopped limply, tail dragging. I thought to myself, "I'll probably look just like that in the coming weeks."

Ray wanted film shot from inside the roadster. I was more than willing to accommodate the cameraman joining me in the tight quarters of the roadster's cockpit but this also necessitated unpacking that portion of the car. That done, we were stuffed like two sausages in one bun and we did a loop of the hotel's acreage waving good-bye to the little group of supporters in the parking lot. Drizzle had upgraded to rain and I took the plastic-wrapped television camera and its operator onto the interstate. We were followed by Ray in a pick-up and Howard with truck-and-trailer. At a prearranged signal, we all pulled over, extricated the cameraman from the roadster and he climbed into the back of the pick-up. Now I was to follow the little truck while heartthrob-with-a-lens filmed my eastbound drive in the rain. So we're doing this little Hollywood film project at 60 miles per hour on a wet interstate at first light.

Then I did one of the most stupid things I've ever done in my life. And, of course, I had to do it on film too. I was overjoyed with finally leaving, really leaving the magnetic pull of my home town and to be totally in the air, wet but still *new* air and new adventure. A grandmother should never do anything to set a bad example for the grandchildren and if she does, a camera should not be near by. I will forever regret doing the gesture from the film "Titanic" with both arms in the air while following the Channel 6 TV truck. It felt totally joyful at the time, I'm sure it made for good TV, but my Internal Grandmother berated me for days about my risky stupidity. My father, the cautious pilot, would have grounded me for good.

The pick-up truck with Ray, the film and my bearded fantasy guy finally signaled and disappeared into the darkness of an off-ramp. Now I really was "eastbound and down, loaded up and truckin'." The clouds were splitting in the distance and white light was shining in rays. The sky was doing the visual equivalent of the *1812 Overture*.

Spots of rain were challenging me. Seno's tiny windshield was the size of an oval serving dish and there was no windshield wiper. It was not like it was broken; it wasn't there and never had been. Blobs of water arranged themselves on this piece of glass. I could see through it until a set of headlights came from *behind* me. Then the shine would strike the roadster's windshield and the resulting light phenomenon made the glass look like a cracked rear window with hundreds of tiny lines.

By the time I reached Biggs Junction, the sky had cleared, the glass had air-dried and my spirit had opened up like the Gorge itself. This time, I didn't have to deal with the Biggs Junction bridge either, I kept it headed eastbound and the sunny miles continued to Pendleton. I was flying, physically and mentally and spiritually. The further I rushed from Portland the less I could actually feel the tires touch the road.

A Christian Youth van passed me and 14 kids waved wildly. A black trucker with a huge smile leaned out of his cab and snapped Seno with a cardboard disposable camera. A construction worker wearing a hard hat over his big, wide cowboy hat shouted "hey!" and gave me thumbs up. I spotted a thirty foot "A" emblazoned on a rounded hillside and I knew it stood for "Arlington" but just for this day, I figured it could mean "Alyce."

When dreaming about the trip, I envisioned Seno and me in the Midwest and New England and cruising through Pennsylvania but I clutched with anxiety when I thought of a certain stretch of road in eastern Oregon. Two words had struck fear in me since I had first imagined the trip: Cabbage Hill. At 4,193 feet the wide curves pulled twice the gravity as the flatlands. Any professional trucker reading this is saying to him/herself, "OK, what are you going to do with *this*, little girl?"

The wild, dry barren landscape east of Pendleton was quiet and sobering. I developed a creepy feeling like something bad had happened here and might again soon. I sailed by big green highway signs: Poverty Flat, Deadman Pass and Old Emigrant Hill. My four cylinders weren't losing a beat, however, and my let's-handle-stress-with-a-joke brain wondered which was old--the emigrant or the hill? Then there were the brown signs: Warning, Dust Storm Area, High Wind and Snow Chains Required. Car parts were thrown beside the road as if a wrecking yard had exploded three miles up in space and showered parts--hubcaps, mufflers, twisted chrome, even car seats. Up and around hills we went like a roller coaster in slow motion. The rain was back when I arrived in La Grande and pulled over for gas. I didn't know I had done Cabbage Hill until I saw a postcard on the gas station counter.

"That was *it*?" I asked. I took this as a sure omen that the trip was going to be easier than I thought. The runes were going to be proven wrong.

The heavy drizzle continued as I traveled between the Umatilla National Forest and the Wallowa mountain range. The Lewis and Clark trail paralleled I-84 for many miles here. Pines appeared. Then more of them and closer to the highway. Then snow, first just carpeting the forest, then more on the trees. The drizzling wet continued even though there was more and more snow and more of it closer to the highway. For almost 45 miles, no towns and no stops, just a very black wet passage of asphalt surrounded by grey pines and greyer snow. The rain turned to splattering snow blobs that hit me and the car at 65 miles per hour.

I kept thinking, "I'm going to get super cold in just a minute."

My glove compulsion had paid off. I had gone into one of Oregon's great outdoor stores and holding my hands up, I had said, "I want what they wear in Antarctica." My hands felt like popsicles even on warm days. There was a dizzying array of choices for protective handgear. What worked for me in the snow at such speeds were Canadian Snowboard Federation Force 10 gloves made out of 65 percent olefin, 35 percent polyester with the outer mitten made of polyurethane.

For the rest of my ensemble I was layered in a fleece vest, a padded satin bomber jacket, a quilted nylon ski jacket and a down parka. I don't mean I had this stuff packed, I mean I was wearing all that.

A very weary Alyce pulled into the Texaco station in Baker City. A grey car pulled into the next bay and a fellow leaped out. He wore a buttoned down shirt with a tie, had dark hair and looked like a soap opera star. He opened his lovely British mouth and asked, "What is it?"

It really doesn't do any good for Seno to be a stud magnet and for me to look like road lint. But with Alyce it was a lot like a dog chasing cars, what am I going to do if I catch one? Absolutely nothing. But I can pant, can't I?

Seno's gas fill spout was inconveniently located under the locked bonnet (or boot, *whatever*) requiring a less-than-graceful bending on my part to open. I unlocked the little padlock and flipped open the fasteners and lifted the hood exposing not only the gas tank but my personal funky luggage as well. I twisted the gas cap off, filled the tank and then noticed the cap in my hand was broken. Not only was I *not* a road bunny, my car was falling apart.

The Englishman headed off saying, "Good travels, lass!"

I had never in my life heard anybody say that. I think I drove all the way from Portland to Baker City that day just to hear those lyrical words. I probably looked at him like a dieter looks at a dessert cart.

The sign read "Bliss, 10 miles." Too late. I was already there. The roadster seemed to glide through southern Idaho as if on a jet stream. I checked the speedometer as I-84 announced Bliss, Idaho and it read 75 miles per hour.

It felt so odd and so terribly wonderful to be in the dream now. It was as if I had seen the scene inside a snowglobe, shaken it, watched the glitter swirl and drift. And now suddenly I was inside the snowglobe watching the magic swirl around me.

Journal Entry: April 11, 2002

Did 580 miles Portland to Twin Falls, Idaho, 5:30 a.m. to 8 p.m. Too much. Had no idea I was going to get this far. Helmet has rubbed off the front half inch of my hair. Idea for Pacific City: Boardman has "welcome to" sign painted on boulders, Baker City has it on a big log arch. Stayed dry and relatively comfortable. My adrenaline took me further than it probably should have. I am finally one day into my great adventure.

16

Howard's truck ran on propane and this required ferreting out the special places that sold it. For Idaho, this meant Twin Falls. While Seno rarely took over six dollars worth of gasoline, Howard's big 1971 GMC rarely gorged on less than $100. My Master Card developed stretch marks in these off-the-trail propane places. But a prescription for Prozac would probably cost me about the same and that was exactly the effect seeing Howard and his truck/trailer had on me. If the roadster and I flew into a thousand pieces I knew Howard would stop and pick up each one. And notify the conference in Chicago that I wouldn't be making it.

Howard hadn't lived in Illinois for 50 years but he considered himself from there and made a pilgrimage to his home state almost every year. Like everyone, Howard had his little quirks, little mysteries. His was: behind the wheel of a vehicle, Howard didn't tire. He could drive for 15 hours with no observable signs of weariness. He could probably get from coast to coast in two days if he didn't drink fluids. Television, however, had a profound effect on Howard. Get him within view of any sized TV set and he'd be comatose in 15 minutes. He would do this regardless of how much sleep he'd already had. There was nothing on film fascinating enough to keep Howard awake for any longer than 15 minutes. It was as if the screen emitted fogs of ether.

I was standing away from Howard's truck while it was being filled because I have a primitive fear of something that smells as awful as propane. A little white pick-up wheeled into the dirt parking lot and stopped abruptly. Two guys, probably in their 20's, stared at my roadster. I wish I could say I'm making up this next part but I'm not. The blond driver, arm on the door of his pick-up, said, "Never seen anything like that." OK, I thought, I haven't either really. Then he asked, "Is it a truck?"

It was a question I'd never been asked before. I looked at the roadster just to make sure it hadn't somehow changed since I'd last looked at it. Perhaps the angle of the view was causing the question. No, I was standing almost right next to the driver. I realized that I was clearly in the presence of someone with vastly different perceptions than my own. I thought I'd better speak slowly.

"This is a truck," I said, resting my two hands gently on the window's edge of his pick-up. "And that is a car," I added, pointing to Seno.

"Oh," he nodded in reply but I wasn't sure he believed me.

I walked over to Howard's truck shaking my head. "What was that about?" asked Howard.

"I don't really know," I replied. "But the guy's a natural blond."

Day Two was a great sunny day to be on the road and I was very happy to cross the gorge bridge in Twin Falls and be back on the interstate. My vision of the trip had been quaint back roads and curving state highways. But this part of the journey was the "Get There" part. This was not touring, this was driving. It would be horizon-to-horizon interstates for five days. The speaking engagement in Chicago was the goal with a date and I had to postpone my dream of goal-less wandering for a week.

Idaho became Utah and Seno chalked up his third state of the trip. The familiar Wasatch mountains, like a dinosaur backbone, crept north-south along northern Utah almost from the border to Salt Lake. They were so familiar because for three years I lived right next to them. My tummy was anticipating a stop here and I'd purposely eaten early and light that morning in Idaho. I was saving up for Perry, Utah and one of my "Mecca" destinations.

Zagat says, "Area's top restaurant and a Utah tradition." Originally called the "restaurant out in the middle of no where", "crazy" Irv and Wilma staked their claim to fame in a tiny Utah town. The restaurant was a small log cabin type of building built on skids so that it could be towed away if things didn't work out. That was over 50 years ago. I wanted to go back to Maddox Ranch House about three miles south of Brigham City on Highway 89. A traveler couldn't miss it because of the retro 50's-pseudospace-looking sign, a spiky neon thing that would either delight or horrify depending on a person's funk acceptance level. (www.brighamcity.net/maddox/index/htm)

"One of the 'best in the west'" claims Aundree Benoit of the Mobil travel guides. None of the reviews did this place justice. I seriously believed that a person could be talked out of suicide by suggesting that their last meal be at Maddox. They'd want to live another day just to be able to eat here again. Here was steak you could almost cut with a spoon. But, honestly, that was not what pulled me there. The rolls are hot, yeasty *air*. There, I've said it. Not very sophisticated, huh? I took most of the gorgeous meal away in a box, preferring instead drizzling famous Utah honey (bees are sort of a role model for Utah people) and feeling my eyes roll back in my head as the buttery bite of roll slid past my lips. I would go into an altered state of consciousness when I ate there.

I was a teenager in Brigham City, Utah in the 60's. This was where I learned how to "tease" hair. I was unnerved the first time I saw it done. Back then you weren't ready to go to class until your head was the size of a waste basket. In my high school yearbook some of the senior girl photos could not include the entire head of hair. The only good thing about this fashion trend was that a space-helmet sized head made the rest of your body look smaller. Cheerleaders looked like lollipops. I haven't seen teased hair since I left Utah in 1964.

We were in luck when we pulled into Maddox's parking lot that April noon and I could see there wasn't a line out the door. I was not the only one who regarded this place with religious fervor usually reserved for temples. I don't know what the square footage of Maddox may be anymore but it was big and the waiting area was ample, full of overstuffed couches and living room decor. The centerpiece of the room was the elevated hostess stand with loud speaker microphone. Several women hustled behind this guard post efficiently moving people with desperate I-have-come-here-to-gorge-myself looks on their faces. I stepped up to the stand and time just seemed to stand stock still. I think the theme of the "Twilight Zone" began to play.

Behind the counter taking names was a bouffanted teenager. As if encased in lucite from Box Elder High School, she had a perfectly rounded beachball of blond hair. I probably stared longer than I should have but I couldn't help it. I glanced at the stack of newspapers on the counter just to check the date. It was unnerving. I had to make sure that 40 years had indeed gone by. She looked exactly like she had stepped out of my algebra class. I checked the two others behind the counter with her. They were coifed as if they'd come off an assembly line.

The wait for a table was less than two minutes, otherwise I would have made a real fool of myself just gawking. The idea that I had somehow been thrown back in time, returned to adolescence was truly a scary thought. But as it turned out, things in Brigham City and Perry, Utah just didn't change. Fortunately I had. Now I had a driver's license.

The other worldly experience continued. A bubble-topped waitress took our order. She was busy but pleasant, another throw back to 40 years ago.

It didn't really matter if I ordered beef, chicken or buffalo. I was after the cosmic manna (divinely supplied spiritual nourishment) that Maddox does with flour. The basket appeared almost instantly. And it didn't take me long to empty it although I concentrated on savoring every morsel. On every exhale I could smell the butter and yeast on my breath. I just wanted to sit there and eat forever. Maddox redefines "hog heaven."

Howard seemed to enjoy his meal but he didn't appear to be in the ecstasy that I was. But then, I'm not sure you'd actually notice any difference if he were. Howard was like a clock in a thunderstorm. The world needs people like Howard or the rest of us would just dissolve in our own weird ideas and passionate emotions.

Ice cream came with the lunch order and I gave mine to Howard so that I could continue to dangle my fingers in the hot rolls. I would never be satiated. I knew it. Howard knew it. And pretty soon the waitress knew it. Before real separation anxiety between me and the bread basket took hold, Howard reminded me of 500 plus miles of eastbound travel required of the day. By now I was so full of lunch that I'd be a drag on the roadster's mileage.

The only thing that got me out of Maddox was the promise that I would return: Some Day. Put it on the list.

As Seno and I pulled out onto Highway 89 I took a last, loving look at the Maddox sign and noticed that is also read: FINE FOOD. *Wrong.* Carbohydrate utopia would be more accurate.

I-84 cut Salt Lake City out of the itinerary. This U.S. city led the nation in per capita consumption of Prozac and they recently passed a law saying that church members could pack concealed weapons when going to services. It was an easy short cut from Ogden through the mountains to I-80, bypassing the very clean and evidently very stressed city of Salt Lake. It was a good, fast road. Somewhere near Little America, Wyoming I heard Andy Williams in my headset singing, "Two drifters off to see the world, there's such a lot of world to see." And that pretty much summed it up.

I studied the pale green rock formations presented on both sides of the road and could feel the pull of increased altitude. Cake mixes require a little something extra when mixed here over 5,000 feet, I remembered from my days, weeks, months, years spent living in this area. The clear sunny sky of Utah became dappled with clouds in Wyoming. They looked like grey cotton balls. A prevailing westerly helped push us five hours across a state known (and proud of it) for having the fewest number of citizens.

The grey cotton balls were beginning to stick together and eventually blotted out the blue. Wind began to whip rather than just blow. I became aware of what looked like white pillows dropped in the range land. It was leftover snow from drifts probably two-stories high a couple of months ago. We pulled over in Wamsutter for gas and when I dismounted from the car, the wind nearly blew me off my feet. Without my helmet on, my hair would have been perpendicular to my body.

Howard jumped out of his truck and shouted into the wind, "No clutch!"

As a non-mechanical female I knew my place in this situation. I hung out in the ladies room removing grit from my teeth and admiring the marketing copy on the paper dispenser. Inside the tiny gas station was a safe place to peruse the pop machine offerings and come to the conclusion that mechanics would rather choke than drink anything sugarfree. My brain was willing to do almost anything rather than consider that my support vehicle was wounded. But was it terminal?

Howard walked from his truck to the garage bays and back again. I tried to read his facial expression for any sign of how bad things were but he didn't look any different than when he read the Sunday paper. But then, I could tell him his dog died and get the same expression.

There was no one tending the gas station. Wamsutter appeared to be a collection of three or four buildings all of industrial architecture inexplicably built here in the middle of a moon scape. The sky was growing darker and I didn't see a human form anywhere, except for Howard who was catorted half inside the cab of his truck. We were up over 8,400 feet; this time last week I was at seven feet in Pacific City. I was beginning to get "what's to become of us?" thoughts.

Suddenly Howard announced it was time to go. A washer, a cotter key, a few scraped knuckles and he had fixed the broken clutch pedal assembly. This was a relief but added to my anxiety when I considered that I didn't know a clutch from a klatch and without Howard around, was to become of me? If a person didn't have knowledge and strength then they'd better have an exorbitant amount of luck. What would have happened, I worried, if I had been all by myself? "Then you wouldn't have had the truck," I answered myself.

Big grey rain clouds filled the sky and they had brush strokes reaching the earth in the distance. There was more up ahead. It was as if we were in a dry trough while all around were shower curtains being drawn. If an art student had painted a sky like this they would have been flunked out of class. Who would have believed such obvious brush stokes?

What Wyoming lacked in population, it made up for in trucks and sage. Abundant trucks of all kinds--dualies, campers, pick-ups and a chain gang processional of commercial semis. Speed limit was 75 miles per hour and really *no limit* since there was no evidence of any law--county or state and since there were no cities, no cops anywhere.

Journal entry: April 12, 2002

Wyoming is like a piece of Antarctica right here in America. In April it is vast, humorless and intimidating. Lady Bird Johnson with her beautification campaign made billboards passé and I am here in Laramie to tell you that on some roads a billboard would be a welcomed visual addition. And I don't think I've seen a woman since we left Utah.

17

It was as if Laramie had been legally declared a glitz-free zone. There was nothing shiny in this bigger-than-average Wyoming town. Chrome didn't shine. Window glass didn't shine. There didn't appear to be a store anywhere in town that sold anything shiny. Several pawn shops in Laramie, but all were closed. What, I wondered, was in them? Lots of tools and tack, I wagered.

If I ever owned a coffee shop, however, I would want it to be like Muddy Waters Coffee Shop on Grand Avenue in downtown Laramie, Wyoming. Cotton dresses from the 40's hung along the wall like art pieces. Totally undisciplined house plants just "did their thing" in pots around the shop. Kitsch was everywhere and I was a believer that kitsch was nourishing--it must come from the same root word as "kitchen." The menu was calligraphed in colored chalk on a blackboard. There was a yellow bicycle in the bathroom and the walls were covered with record album covers including Flip Wilson's "The Devil Made Me Buy This Dress." Under the glass by the cash register was a collection of police patches and I noticed they didn't have one from New Hampshire. I took a shop business card and made a note to send my Manchester, New Hampshire police patches to Muddy Waters.

Outside a black lab dog sat on a wooden bench and watched two parked vehicles side by side, a blue Rolls Royce and a black Hummer. I overheard someone say that the value of Laramie just doubled by having these two vehicles parked in it. The Salvation Army store was having a half price sale and I paid 17 cents for a fork and another 17 cents for a spoon. I also found a yellow Big Bird head, a definite treasure. The only reason I could buy anything was because Howard still had space in the covered bed of his truck. When I filled that, I'd have to stop.

Hit I-80 eastbound and there wasn't a cloud for as far as you could see which was a considerable distance. The snow pillows, however, were even larger here. I wondered how big the snow drifts had to be in order for there to be so much of it still here. There were no shadows or trees to keep them cool...and yet, they hadn't melted. Wyoming gets the kind of snow that would bury a Freightliner and no one would find it until spring. All signs here, like FREE SHOWER WITH DIESEL PURCHASE, are on high poles lest they disappear in winter.

Wyoming put fear in me. For every mile east I was going, I'd have that mile to get back alone in my tiny roadster. The landscape was so vast that I began to mentally redesign my route home, shortening it. How could I possibly handle all this emptiness on my own? Surely it would take years to get back to Oregon. I couldn't drive hours and hours for days and days like Howard could. At 70 years of age, he made me look like a piker. It would take me five times longer on my own. Wyoming was frighteningly devoid of Subway shops, movie theaters or anything that looked familiar to me. Such expanse bothered me a lot.

April was National Anxiety Month and I was certainly doing my part. Then I noticed on the map: "Highest point in Nebraska."

It was hot and growing hotter. Dusty dry fields and an occasional whirlwind or farmer on equipment stirred up volumes of dirt. What trees there were seemed to have been treated rudely. Their tops were ripped off, limbs broken and resting in bigger limbs, bark split off, silver underskin exposed. What happened to these poor trees? What torture had they tried to endure and what would it have done to a human?

Along one stretch we passed lumpy fields with hundreds of tires weighing the ground down. These were acres and acres of sand dunes with stubble on top. The old tires were placed here and continued working. Their job description just changed from rolling on vehicles to holding the ground in place from erosion.

Of all the roadside attraction push pins I had stuck in my map of America, there was one pin on Nebraska that I was especially anxious to investigate. I'd heard about this place and read about it in tour books. Howard had brought me photographs of it from one of his Oregon/Illinois trips. Now that we were finally in Nebraska I traded my nagging fear in for anticipation. That was a good swap.

Alliance, Nebraska was at least 80 miles off of I-80, making it a detour of 160 very precious miles. I knew every town on the Planet was special and unique but Alliance appeared to be just like many Midwestern towns. A person would never have a reason to go here even for a last reading of a rich relative's will. If they were giving stuff away, I wouldn't go. This was country where announcements for Rotary Club meetings and "Elect Diane Linn country treasurer" signs were actually welcome visual relief. What I wanted to see, however, was officially located just outside Alliance. In fact, in 1989 the city officially excluded the attraction (they regarded it as junk) from the city limits, thus preserving it for pilgrims like myself. They wanted to bulldoze Carhenge! Unbelievable!

Carhenge was a "scholarly copy" of England's Stonehenge. Made up of 38 cars strategically planted in a circle, there were also three trilithons, the heel stone, two stations stones and the Aubrey circle. Jim Reinders, the creator of this huge (96 feet in diameter) monument, lived near the original in England. Carhenge was built as a memorial to Reinders' father who once lived on this Nebraska farmland. Reinders and 35 of his clan gathered in June 1987 and planted the cars, some of them five feet into the ground, headlights pointed toward heaven. They dedicated their work during the Summer Solstice and I've heard there might be Winter Solstice events held here too.

When asked WHY? Jim Reinders wrote, "Plane, loqui, deprehendi" which translates "To tell the truth, it's there to surprise people."

Does it ever! I was in quite a state of anticipation, like a kid sent off to his country grandma's for the summer, but I wasn't prepared for the abrupt sight of the site. It was closer to the road that I had imagined. We pulled into the dirt and gravel parking lot and I rushed to meet Carhenge as if it were a rock star, which I guess it sort of *is*, now that I think of it.

My glee turned to bliss when I realized that Seno would fit through the guard posts and I could put my little purple darling right in the middle of this amazing monument. I shot three rolls of film. My car in Carhenge! I was so thrilled that I told myself if nothing else fun happened in the entire coast to coast journey, that this was worth the trip!

It was so amazing to walk around this version of Stonehenge. The entire structure was coated in grey spray paint adding to the twin feeling of the place. On a top row was a Vega like the one I used to drive. Good use for that car. But there was a '57 Cadillac, a total mess but a good car at some point. A Gremlin, that deserved to be there, and a Valiant--sure, make a lead weight out of that one. (www.carhenge.com)

Scratched into the formerly chrome, now spray painted bumper of a Cadillac: DOUG PROPOSED TO CHERE 1-24-02. Did she say yes? How could a girl say no in the middle of such a great place? I love a guy who would think of proposing while surrounded by tons of junked cars. I personally would have broken Doug's fingers, however, for defacing such an honored site with graffiti. That wasn't cool, Dougie, don't do that again. A sign in the Carhenge parking lot warns, "If you vandalize, your dipstick will fall off!" I hoped Chere took note of that.

Many gas guzzling Cadillacs gave up their spot in a junkyard to be immortalized at this great roadside attraction. In fact, not counting museums and things you enter to view, just roadside, Carhenge gets my vote as the U.S. BEST--choice USDA prime (U.S. Department of Alyce).

The Sinclair Outpost station appeared to be the only place to buy Carhenge souvenirs. So I bought one of everything. Even Howard bought a black T-shirt with silver Carhenge graphic. Now I had coffee mugs from Stonehenge in England, Stonehenge in Washington State and Carhenge. There was only one left to get...

It was hours to Ogallala. As near as I could tell there were no internet cafes, no one-hour photo places and no video stores. I couldn't help but think, "How do these people live?" I'm sure they would answer, "Quite nicely, thank you."

There was one break in the mind-numbing monotony of the landscape. Along miles of fenceposts--fencing surrounding scrub brush to keep it from escaping, I guess--were shoes stuck upside down on the tops of the posts. There were tennis shoes, work shoes, cowboy boots and hiking shoes. I didn't see any high heels or slippers. What was the story here? In some places there was an entire uninterrupted row of footwear. I reasoned that no one would actually go out and buy shoes to mount on fenceposts. Even at the Goodwill a crummy pair of boots would be three dollars. So they must have just *had* them. Perhaps some rich uncle, the Imelda Marcos of Nebraska, left his estate to a disgruntled family member and after the estate sale there were all these shoes left. What to do with them? Well... There were miles and miles of shod fenceposts.

Journal Entry: April 14, 2002

Very dry here. But then that's an Oregonian talking. By my standards the entire U.S. is dry. Seeing Carhenge was a total highlight. It's very big and very, very funny. It hits my Delight Bone full force. I ran around through the cars like a puppy in a kindergarten class. It is the ultimate parody. Hundreds of years from now archeologists will study it and conclude that this civilization worshipped the Goddess of Internal Combustion and sacrificed cars to the Queen of the Gods: Mother Road. And they'd be right.

18

Howard wanted to stay in Ogallala, Nebraska so that we could have breakfast at Hokes Cafe where "Friends Meet to Eat." The inside of the restaurant on First Street was decorated like a 50's party. Rock and roll images were mixed in with car parts. There was a picture frame made out of '32 Ford windshield and a working clock that had been an air filter from a Chevy. The walls were solid with car kitsch and posters. While waiting for my poached eggs I enjoyed looking over the auto memorabilia that was everywhere.

"Hey, that's my car!" I said, pointing to a poster of Hot Salt II, a street rod event held in Utah in 1996 at the Bonneville salt flats. There was Franklin, my 1940 Ford coupe on the familiar poster with Terry Nish's record breaking rocket car. Riley Sermeno, the restaurant's owner, was summoned. He took down the poster and had me sign it. I felt like a celebrity right there in downtown Ogallala. I promised Riley I'd send photos of my coupe. But it would be awhile, I added, pointing out the window at my purple roadster. "I'm driving that thing across the country and I'll won't be home for awhile." His warm jet black eyes widened. Then he looked at Howard as if for confirmation for what he had just heard.

"Yep," answered Howard without being asked the question.

I-80 was to be home for the next 350 miles. Long and awful miles in 86 degree heat. A big Alyce raspberry to all those folks who told me that I was crazy for leaving "so early in the year" and predicting I'd freeze to death and be snowbound. The white heat in the cloudless sky cooked the road and we were basted top and bottom.

There was lots of rubber on the road, mostly exploded pieces of it. "When the rubber meets the road" was the phrase. In Nebraska some of it meets and *stays.* During one stop Howard pointed out the stretch of road that had nearly killed him less than a year ago. At 65 miles per hour, a rear tire blew on his 1940 Ford sedan as he was headed home from Illinois. The car went epileptic and airborne. Howard walked away with scrapes and bruises. The lovely maroon vintage car was totaled.

Seeing where it had happened was a sobering moment for me. Nothing could have foretold the tire's suicide on Howard's car. He'd done nothing wrong. It had simply chosen Nebraska's I-80 to blow up. Howard drove home from the accident in a rental car and then returned to Nebraska with a truck and trailer to haul the pieces of his classic Ford back to Oregon. Howard had walked away from this horrific scene because he'd been encased in sturdy steel. I didn't have that advantage. I had considered a roll bar for Seno but rejected the idea. (Later a newspaper reporter referred to Seno as a "tin slipper that could easily double as a coffin in the event of an accident.")

Now it was April 15th, Income Tax Day, and the heat was breaking records all across Nebraska. I could feel my brain cells deteriorating. I was like a Hersey bar in this kind of weather. I was so miserably uncomfortable that my paranoia for a potential accident was momentarily put on hold. If it had been normal weather I might of had the fear of God put in me by listening to Howard's story. I knew only too well that I would never survive a similar experience in my open car.

We took a break at Exit 279 and drove south on Highway 10 to Minden, Nebraska. I didn't much care where we went as long as there was air-conditioning soon. Alice Steinbeck wrote, "The word 'travel' comes from the Latin 'trepalium' which loosely translated means 'instrument of torture.'" Ancient Romans must have had a hot Nebraska day in mind.

Harold Warp's Pioneer Village was not part of the Smithsonian but it probably should be. Harold was interested in the progression of progress. How did we get from campfire to microwave ovens, for instance? He collected the interphases of stuff as it evolved.

Anyone who has ever misplaced something could find it or a reasonable facsimile of it in Minden at this museum. There were over 50,000 items all in order of how they developed. There were 12 historic buildings around a created town green. Even the trees here had descriptive identifiers. What did a real Pony Express station look like? See it in Minden. They claim that Harold's Pioneer Village was the largest collection of Americana anywhere. I don't doubt it. It was too hot to cover all 20 acres and all 28 buildings. (www.pioneervillage.org)

I was particularly interested in the amazing sod house because my grandmother had lived and taught school in such a structure. The walls were two and half feet thick! Outside there were sticks and leaves and grass clinging to the house but the inside walls were spotless whitewash and very finished. It was cool, dark and comfortable inside. Even the internal walls were two and half feet thick and the windows were set in giving it an old English Cotswold look. The roof was also grass. The place and the furnishings were 150 years old.

Car nut Howard wanted to see the 350 cars housed in several warehouses and he did, frequently saying things like, "I used to have one like this," or "My uncle wrecked one like this, only blue." I gave up after a hundred or so but I think Howard saw them all.

A very interesting display in one building followed the evolution of the American living room from 1850 to 1870 then 1890 and 1910 and 1930. Here you could see the linear progression of every single article--wallpaper, chairs, musical instruments, artwork, everything. In the next row was the same sort of display for kitchens. Then the same treatment for bedrooms.

My favorite environment was the 1890's era. There must have been a million dollars worth of furniture, clothes and hat pins in just this one building.

Remember the movie "The Graduate" when Benjamin was told to go into plastics? Harold Warp got the money for this independent museum from his plastic patents and products. Everybody's mattress came wrapped in Warp plastic. The business was family-owned and still doing well in Chicago.

Knocked off most of the heat of the day in the civilized cool of this museum and then suffered through the rest of Nebraska. I always thought it was just me, bored out of my skull with the state where even litter becomes interesting...but I measured it on the map and Nebraska *was* big. Wider than Wyoming or Colorado or Kansas or even Oregon. If it seemed like it was taking forever to get through it, it *was* taking forever.

Nebraska has a very long list of native celebrities. Johnny Carson, Fred Astaire, Marlon Brando, Sandy Dennis, Nick Nolte, Malcolm X, Gerald Ford and Darryl F. Zanuck all came from the Cornhusker State. Not one of them live in Nebraska anymore. Liz Winston wrote, "Nebraska is proof that Hell is full and the dead walk the earth."

We made it over the Missouri River and into Iowa just as the sun was setting. An American flag made of yards of fabric was whapping in the stiff hot wind outside the Council Bluffs inn. The sun's rays winked in and out of the weave and it made me sigh. Old Glory affects my tear ducts. What a great symbol for such a diverse nation, I thought. Nebraska farmers, Wyoming cowboys, cross country truckers, New York stockbrokers, Oregon writers, Michigan factory workers, grandmothers, rabbis, vegetarians, Air Force vets, gay performers, car thieves, Hawaiian bank tellers...we've all got a stake in this flag. How can we ever expect to hold it all together? Except for Carhenge's whimsy, I felt alien in Nebraska. "America is a geographic term," wrote Oscar Wilde, "it is no more a united nation than the equator."

Roadster Lesson #6: 'Tis better to have frost on your radiator than drive topless in 86 degree Nebraska heat."

19

Take a hammer and hit your thumb with it very hard. Experience that intense pain as it splatters and vibrates through your body. Now move the pain to your forehead. That was what my head felt like after an hour of wearing my motorcycle helmet. It was also rubbing a bald spot where my hairline used to be.

Gas nozzles and car clamps had broken off most of my little white lady fingernails.

My face was puffy. I coated my windblown skin with cortisone cream every few hours. Despite 32 blocker sunscreen, my nose was red and nothing else on my face matched it.

It had gotten so warm that I had to get into clothes I was saving for the June return trip back and found my sandals. I had covered plenty of miles in these leather sandals and I could count on them to be comfortable. I'd worn them to the top of the Aztec pyramids in Mexico. They lasted only one day in Nebraska. A strap broke and now I had them held together with red duct tape. I duct taped the other sandal so that they'd match. Heat must have caused me to be delusional enough to think that the tape would be mistaken as intentional decoration.

Not fussing every morning was a delicious plus of the trip. I rather enjoyed looking like road lint in my baggy pants and Mel Fisher's "This is the day" T-shirt. But I was going to be up on stage in a few days and I needed to get over my casual highway hag look and be perfectly beautiful for Friday's arrival in downtown Chicago. More than anything else I needed an especially good night's sleep.

At 4:30 a.m. I was awakened by someone, right outside my door, saying, "I wonder what's under here?" And I heard another male voice say, "Maybe a dune buggy." I was instantly awake and hit the door like a rabid German Shepherd. I knew they were talking about my roadster, covered in the parking lot and as close to my room as I could safely park him. I needed to make sure that curiosity did not get the better of someone. I pressed my eye up against the door hole. Two men with gym bags were simply walking by the car. Returning to sleep was impossible.

I did my yoga routine and that popped all the kinks out of my back and legs. I showered and folded and packed things. Then I choked down a small tin of tuna and stepped out of the room to walk to the

Pilot truck stop. An ancient memory from 30 years ago, when I used to live in the Midwest, hit me. It was a distinctive smell--an odor with a threat. The message was, "It's nice now but you are going to *get it* today." The morning air felt fresh, like it was being breathed over honey, but the memory of five Missouri summers came flooding back to me. We were in for a hot one.

There was a coin-operated internet machine at the Pilot truck stop. I attempted my first contact with my web site. There was a button called UPDATE where I could post my travel journal. I wrote the description of traveling across Oregon including the wonderful send off at the Columbia Gorge Hotel. Then the machine erased the entire message. The keys were sticky, as if coated with sugary pop and not all of them were in the same location on the keyboard as my office computer. An ashtray full of cigarette butts was at my elbow and it was not removable from the little booth. I started typing again, shortening my description and sent the first installment. Then I wrote about Wyoming and sent that. I sent David, my web guy, three emails because I was afraid the machine would eat my communiqués and I'd have to start over. This little adventure into truck stop cyberspace cost me thirteen dollars.

Council Bluffs, Iowa was listed in the *Roadside America* book as the place to see black squirrels. I didn't see one but maybe the Iowa rodents are smart enough to stay away from the interstate.

I was anxious to be on the road before it turned into an oven again. Or rather, to get as many miles as possible behind us before it became the inevitable oven. This was not road tripping. This was power tripping. This was the "Get There" mode of traveling that was no different than the pressure of my office. Once on my own, after Chicago, it *had* to get better or this trip was one big hairy mistake.

I-80 lay like an exhausted flattened snake across Iowa. This poor land. Trees were bare, grass was grey-brown. Everything was still in winter mode only now it was hit with a surprise oppressive heat. I could see the rivers were down when we crossed on hot concrete bridges. The temperature shot up to 92 degrees by noon, breaking records going back as far as records were kept. The plants must have thought they'd been transplanted to Hell. I know that's how I felt. Just four days previously I had been wiping blobs of snow off of Seno's windshield.

In my Iowa message to David and everyone reading the website, I told them about a great book sale going on at the Des Moines library on Euclid Street. I bought six books and didn't see any of my old titles in the sale. And I also wrote how they could get Egg Nog French toast mix at Todd's on Northeast 14th Street. With help from Alissa who worked at Todd's, I found a one-hour photo place and had pictures in the mail for the web site in record time. Howard and I reluctantly got back on the interstate and continued east.

Somewhere near Conroy, Iowa there was a sign for an outlet mall. In the Iowa sun this Oregonian was like an earthworm left on the sidewalk. I was fading fast. The sign was enough to get Howard to pull over--otherwise he would have continued on to Illinois and I would have become worm jerky.

The outlet mall parking lot radiated heat off the black asphalt like a waffle iron on high and met the bleaching heat of the air. I performed a cold water bird bath in the restroom and felt my brain cells coming together again. Slightly revived I could not get back on Mother Road--she had turned into a crematorium consuming everything.

The only use I had for outlet malls was: they drain people away from places I want to be. If I found an actual bargain in one of these extended "strip mauls," it was a lucky accident. But in searing heat, this Iowa mall had something I really, really wanted and it was free: air-conditioning.

The duct tape didn't hold my sandals together so the alleged mission was to replace my old friends. My leather buddies and I had gone beachcombing in Sarasota, bar hopping in Key West and they performed the ultimate travel function--they packed flat. We had even walked High Street in Oxford together in England last August. My sandals were, of course, irreplaceable but I needed something on my feet.

I went into a teeny bopper store, one of those places where they sell fuzzy diaries with "Princess" on them and tube tops with labels like 90 per cent Angel. They also sold lavender flip flops for three dollars. But I didn't stop there. I had to get a plastic ring with glitter lip gloss inside. There were 800 different hair items--clamps, clips, scrunchies, barrettes, mini hair extenders, bows, ties, wires, elastics, bun covers, snoods, rhinestone hair pins, marabou and flower clips--and I wanted all of it. If I had five heads I couldn't wear all the stuff I had now. What a great diversion on an impossibly hot day. It was the right outlet mall at the right time. I laid down my Master Card and wrote "supplies" in my expense log. Now if found on the highway dead from heat exhaustion, my hair would look wonderful pulled up in red marabou feathers and purple rhinestone hair pins.

Journal Entry: April 16

The weather has got to improve. I'm feeling very intimidated about having to get back across this vastness. If it is this hot now, imagine what it will be like when I try to get home in two months! Seno and the truck are taking the heat much better than I am. I feel like a cowpoke whose horse has brought him in and all he can do is hang on. Our vehicles brought us into Illinois but I am riding very low in the saddle. We've made it to Princeton, Howard's original home town. I've been here before and I know it's a pretty town but right now the only thing I want to see is the inside of my eyeballs.

20

On this month in history Lincoln was assassinated, the Titanic sank and to keep up this April tradition, my money was stolen.

How did this disaster happen?

We were staying in Room 209 on the second floor of the Bird's Nest Motel in Princeton, Illinois and we called down to the desk clerk and asked if there might be any rooms now available on the first floor. One had been vacated and we agreed to take Room 112, thus necessitating a move of our stuff down one floor and around a corner to the east side of the motel. That seemed simple enough. Check out was 11 a.m., I had the room key for 209 and it was locked. Howard and I flitted back and forth like moths between the vehicles and these two rooms, rearranging stuff to make life easier for our descent into Chicago. We had costumes, brochures, hats, a banner, my Big Bird head, thank you gifts, an ice chest, make up, books, boxes of power bars and file drawers full of maps. We really had three separate piles for three distinctly different parts of the trip. The truck/trailer plus Seno part, the Chicago (convention) part and then the trek that Seno and I would make alone. Every item fit one of these three parts and a few things belonged in two or more sections. It was time to sort it all out and arrange it in the covered area of Howard's pick-up truck.

At 10:00 a.m. I headed back to our original room on the second floor and by 10:04 I was rushing out the door toward the manager's throat. The motel staff had stripped the room, the mattress was naked and my money belt (a thing called a "leg safe" actually) was gone. It had my car keys, credit cards, six checks and my cash. The manager examined the room, pulled the mattress off the bed and checked the bathroom. We hurried down to the laundry room hoping that the cleaning staff had inadvertently tossed my valuables in with the linens down a laundry shoot. We rifled through sheets and pillow cases. We stopped what laundry was being washed and examined that too.

There were two motel workers besides the manager. The woman claimed she hadn't been in the room. That left the guy. He just shrugged. The manager asked to be left alone with him. I honored that and went to Room 112.

Soon the manager arrived and asked if I had misplaced my things and might they possibly be in my possession somewhere. Howard and I had already ransacked everything but I knew I wasn't having a senior moment. After the manager suggested this three times I finally told him, "You can look through everything in this room and if you find any money, I'll let you have half of it!"

This was a filthy, stinking nightmare.

I had no choice at that point. I called the Princeton Police Department. Two boy-next-door police officers arrived in a squad car. Sergeant Barry Portman and Patrol Office Scott Underwood asked all the expected questions, took notes in a small pad just like on TV and grilled the manager and his workers. They searched the vacant rooms in the motel and left.

I sat down and listed all the items that were missing. I had six checks, two from each of my checking accounts. A call to the bank would solve any attempt to get funds with those checks. I was missing one credit card. I found the telephone number to cancel it. A call to these efficient folks and they arranged to have a new card (with a new number) waiting for me at the hotel when I arrived in Chicago! The bank ATM card was AOL but the bank didn't want to do anything about that one because the PIN number was still safe in my head. The car keys were missing but I had an extra set on a chain around my neck, a precaution that I blessed my efficient Past Self for. I'd easily make another set. I could take a little comfort knowing Seno had two kill switches so even if someone tried the key in the ignition, the car wouldn't start. The only thing left in my "leg safe" which, by the way, has to actually be *on* your body to function correctly, I guess, was the cash. American greenbacks.

The manager who was not capable of appearing pale, looked quite sickly. He told me to use the phone and fax long distance all I wanted. I took advantage of that.

Before the trip I had pondered how much cash to take and consulted friends for opinions. I don't usually go with much cash because most of my travel involves credit card transactions and reimbursements. I only need cash for tips. But this trip was longer and vastly different. Hostels, for instance, frequently want cash only. And I pictured car repair places in Tennessee that might not know what a credit card was and would laugh at the concept of an out-of-state check. With more than ten weeks ahead of me, I was advised to have between $3000 and $4000. I took $2800. I had poked $200 of it in Seno's emergency kit. I also had some left over grocery money. The motel employee had stolen $2610. And there wasn't anything I could do about it.

I had logged hundreds of thousands of miles of travel, international and domestic miles, and I had never lost one dime, one franc, one kroner, one peso, one yen, one lire.

The Dali Lama says, "When you lose, don't lose the lesson." In my defense I'd have to say that I was only separated from that stash for a few minutes and it was in a locked motel room with the key in my hand. But I *was* separated from it and that was my error. So what was the lesson? That question began to grind away at me.

I had planned my expenses knowing this trip was a huge financial risk. I was cutting out two and a half months of earning. Not only would I *not* have any income, I wouldn't be doing any marketing or running my business at all. I was walking (or driving, rather) away from my business for 71 days. And I had no sponsor, I was on my own. I'd gone over my finances and it looked like I could swing it OK. But with this set back, the financial planning part of the trip was thrown out of whack. This was a beating I could not afford. Should I continue after Chicago or cut my loses and head home, safely under the wing of Howard and his truck? I'd just come 2,000 miles and had 6,500 more sketched on my map. But now, how could I afford it?

I pondered the questions along with the big spiritual one: learn the lesson. All day in Princeton, going to pick up the cash my daughter wired to me, having new keys made, buying a new padlock for Seno's bonnet, all day I picked at the questions like scabs. Finally I heard, from deep down in my skull, "You don't get it now but the lesson will be revealed to you and it will be worth it."

One of the things I wanted from this trip was to "road test my philosophy." The stuff I say and think I believe, the methods I teach for handling Life, was it real or cliché?

This rotten thing has happened!
So what? NOW what?

I should have known better.
So what? NOW what?

I was an idiot!
So what? NOW what? Are you ever going to do it again? Did you do it on purpose? Do you think anything like this has ever happened to a careful person before? Do you suppose you can shut up about it and get on with life?

I don't care who you are or what kind of a mess you've just gotten yourself into, you can ask yourself the above questions and you'll work your way out of it.

Just found out that your spouse has not been the faithful little sweetheart you expected? So what? NOW what? Do you think this has ever happened to anyone before?

You just got a speeding ticket? So what? NOW what? Are you ever going to speed again?

You just locked yourself out of your house or apartment? So what? NOW what? Do you suppose anything like this has ever happened to a careful person before?

I got outside myself and analyzed my behavior bit by bit. Alyce systematically listed each loss and assigned solutions to each one. She met all sorts of obstacles especially from the Western Union employee who announced loudly in a busy truck stop that $900 had arrived and proceeded to count it out on the same counter where he sold beer. He might just as easily have given Alyce a T-shirt to wear that read: "Hey, this lady's got CASH!"

Alyce did not do bodily harm to the clerk, the motel manager or his employee although she engaged in harmless fantasy that systematically annihilated each one from Planet Earth in a most distressing way. Alyce was all-business with the cops and although stressed, was still nice to Howard who did a superb job of staying out of the way.

Best of all, there was no panic. There was no "why me?" There was no "woe is me." Alyce said "So what? NOW what?" This formula went instantly and easily into place.

"Wow," I thought. "it really works."

But it wasn't until later that afternoon when I began to breathe more normally that a couple of insights found their way into my scratchy mind. While Howard and I were in the hardware store having new keys made, a cat came ambling down the aisle through the bins of bolts and nails. Cats seemed to come in two varieties. One kind was the Robert DeNiro-style of cat that looks around and says, "You talkin' to me?" The other kind of cat was the Miss Piggy variety of cat that says, "Attention, attention! I just love attention..." The cat coming toward me was one of those friendly shop cats that go to work every day. I got down on one knee to pet the jet black cat and get comfort from her soft fur.

She had only three legs. She didn't seem to know that. She was playful, sweet, animated and acted like she adored me. The message I received from the cat: losing a hind leg was an accident, losing your spirit was optional. Thanks, cat, I needed that. Losing my money felt like I'd lost a large part of what would make the trip possible, a leg, for sure. Could I afford to continue? With the weather trying to fry me alive, did I even *want* to continue?

The second insight. I was riding in Howard's truck and we were headed to the town square in Princeton. My gaze was just drifting, noticing the street signs, the newspaper office, a cafe. We were stopped at a light and I glanced over at the newspaper box and read the large headlines on the front page. April 16, the Princeton newspaper lead story: BABY LEFT ON HIGHWAY. I turned to Howard and said, "I don't *have* a problem."

Journal Entry: April 17

When I start looking at the details of today, I like the person I have become. I held my ground even when the motel manager repeatedly expressed his disbelief. In my younger years I would have gone ballistic at his questioning me, a throwback to a childhood trauma of being falsely accused. It was especially sweet, however, when he found my credit card and two of my checks in his filthy dumpster, thrown there by the thief, his employee. Never found the keys or the cash, of course.

This experience has been a great appetite suppressant, although I wouldn't recommend a diet of it.

I have to continue to Chicago and complete my speaking assignment with all the energy and fire I ordinarily would. But what then? Howard has agreed to go with me to Michigan to see the Henry Ford Museum (you wouldn't be able to keep him from it once I said I was going to Dearborn!). Do I watch Howard drive back toward Oregon without me? Or do I let practicality prevail and convoy home with him?

Something to consider though. Nothing has physically changed. I am still healthy and the car still runs. It is money and nothing else. AND the psychological dent which I can accept or reject.

Roadster Lesson #7: Leg safes aren't.

21

Paramount Studios could not construct a more picturesque Midwestern town than Princeton, Illinois. Large homes with turrets and wrap around porches, brick streets, town square, collies in the driveway, plastic pink flamingos on sale at the feed store, porch swings, multi-level bird houses, American flags. Everything was clean and neat, picked up, clipped, trimmed. Old library, war memorial, angle parking on Main Street. One penny gets twelve minutes of parking in downtown Princeton and if the meter expires, there was real trouble. The fine was one dollar.

People left their cars running while they went into the bank or the convenience store. I saw it myself. One big, black muscle car sat parked, engine purring outside a gas station mini-mart and even I was tempted to drive off in it. Outside of Citizens First National Bank I met Mike Moore who told me that 150 years ago Princeton had 7,300 citizens. Howard said that when he was a kid here 60 years ago there were 7,200 people. Evidence suggests they are the same 7,200 people here now. The population has not changed by a single person.

What an unlikely place to be stripped of my cash.

We left Princeton once I had a chance to read what happened to Baby John, left in his car seat along a highway by his 34-year old mother. The police said he was fine and bubbling and laughing despite his half hour of abandonment. This act, in Illinois, was called a Class A misdemeanor. If you steal more than $500 from someone, however, it was a felony. What was *wrong* with this picture?

It was, thankfully, only a few hours drive to Berwyn, a very close in suburb of Chicago. We were lucky enough to be guests of Howard's sister Phyllis who lives on Maple Street not too far from a White Castle. Those of you with a hamburger interest will know why this was particularly advantageous. They sell these steam-grilled, flavor-filled, five-holed little burgers in batches of ten. And you don't find any White Castles out west. OK, in the grocery freezer but that doesn't count. (www.whitecastle.com)

I wiggled out of the "remember when" chat between Howard and his sister and found the library only a block away. Using the internet here was a vast improvement over the truck stop experience. On the walk back I noticed brown bunnies nibbling grass. What a homey touch! Bunnies seem to have adapted quite nicely to city living in Berwyn. Phyllis said that she had a deer in her yard once that wandered over from the park.

The next day I had the great experience of having lunch with an Oxford chum, Chicago Polish firecracker Peter Morrison. He was kind enough to drive to Phyllis's house and save me floundering around in the streets of the Windy City trying to find him. Less than a year ago we were dining in the 14th century dining hall at Magdalen College of Oxford University. Now we were enjoying white dumplings and dill sauce at Klas restaurant on Cermak Road in Cicero, Illinois. I learned about fencing and bees and language and how to say "grandmother" in Polish.

Central casting would select Peter to act the part of an Irish Chicago cop. But Peter also had a passion for classic languages and parrots, how's that for a combination? He coached an amazing fencing team and even judged fencing matches at an international meet in Italy. He was enthusiastic and animated with his stories and I enjoyed being his audience. He had done so many different things and had so many different interests that listening to him was like watching a tennis match conducted in a phone booth. Peter had been all over the globe, Oxford was just a hop for him and he wasn't afraid to go anywhere. I was lucky to find him in his hometown. He was soon to be off to South Carolina for a blue grass fiddlers' festival and taking his beloved birds with him. I asked how long the drive would take him and he said he would do it in one haul. I was envious. Didn't he get tired? What did he do then? He said he would pull over at a rest stop, drop his car seat back and sleep. His constant, longtime companion, this parrot, would sleep head down on Peter's chest. I tried to picture that in my mind and I thought he might be mistaken for a dead guy in a car wearing a stuffed bird. Peter was so packed with life, just like I had seen him in England, that he seemed barely able to keep his energy inside himself. One of my favorite pictures, still on display in my kitchen, was one of me and Peter our last night in Oxford. He was wearing a black hat and my beaded shawl under the lapels of his dark suit. Peter was opinionated and definite about things and after days of road travel, he was just the jolt I needed.

That evening Howard and I mapped my route from Berwyn to the Westin Hotel in downtown Chicago across the street from the John Hancock Building. I was going to have to get into my roadster and drive this by myself the next morning and I didn't want any surprises so Howard was good enough to do a dry run for me in his truck. I took careful note on the map and memorized the street names and familiarized myself with the buildings at important intersections. Over 25 years ago I had lived in Evanston on the north border of Chicago but I had never driven into the heart of the city which I never figured was a heart at all but more like a devouring stomach--I'd be digested if I entered. Phyllis thought I was completely crazy to attempt it.

The evening had barely cooled to 80 degrees and the humidity all day long had me feeling like a White Castle hamburger bun, quite moist and collapsible. It was a good idea doing this trial run to locate and circumvent the ongoing construction sites of downtown Second City. On the way back to Phyllis's home, Howard took a different route and my liberal west coast naiveté got a double dose of the big city projects. Hundreds of people roamed the streets on this Thursday evening, shuffling through litter, sitting on wrecked cars and the steps of boarded up tenement housing. This scene was just minutes away from Marshall Fields department store, Chicago's Miracle Mile and Oprah's penthouse. My mind couldn't grasp it.

I was restless all night.

22

OK, this was it. My mantra for the morning was: Riverside-Cermak-Ogden-Chicago-State-Deleware. I repeated it over and over. My nervousness jangled my resolve reminiscent of when I first started my speaking career. I held my hands in tight fists to keep them from shaking. I could address an audience of 3,000 with less anxiety than I felt that morning. At 9:30 a.m. I was going to have to get in my open car and drive through some of the most frightening streets of my life thus far. I did the only thing I knew to do to calm myself. I called Gracie, my 4-year old granddaughter. We chatted a bit and then I said, "Gracie, I've got to get into Seno and drive him to downtown Chicago. Do you think I can do it?"

Her response was flat and immediate: "Yeah."

Sometimes all anybody ever needs is for someone to say "yeah." Just a little faith on the part of anyone, even someone who didn't know what a Chicago was or what might happen.

I remembered the helicopter business owner who was interviewed in the newspaper and asked, "Does being an entrepreneur still give you butterflies?" She said, "Yes, but now they fly in formation."

Just to keep my fear factor under control, if I didn't look up and see how huge the buildings actually were, I could pretend I was driving through Portland. After all, it was just asphalt and stop lights. Cars weren't any bigger in Chicago. The speed limit was the same. What was there to fear? I backed the little car out of Phyllis's garage and turned onto the street.

School children, passing in groups and holding hands, broke their grips and waved. Construction workers stopped, stood, gawked and smiled. The roadster magic was working again. After a mile or so I became a one-car parade with pedestrians cheering from the sidewalks and people in passing cars whooping. I tried to gratefully acknowledge the greetings without inviting additional contact. Shopkeepers came out to point at the odd purple car. Utility guys dangling from light posts gave me "thumbs up." With each positive gesture, I felt like the whole city was saying, "You go, girl! You can do this!" Those people will never know how much their encouragement meant to me that morning.

I made every turn correctly.

I arrived a few minutes ahead of schedule, always a relief to me. I kept away from the hotel to wait for the appointed minute for Seno's arrival at the Red Hat Society convention. I parked two blocks away in a ten-minute zone. A young excited woman rushed up to the car and said, "I have to paint you. Stay right here! I'm going for my camera." I replied that I'd stay six minutes but that I had to get to the Westin. She took off. Two hard hats approached the car. One was very chatty with an Eastern accent and the other was quiet and dumbfounded. Then a creepy guy came up, kept touching Seno and asking questions. Just when I thought my nervousness was going to cause my soul to leap right out of my body, I fired up the roadster, made a right at Delaware, crossed Michigan and got me and Seno finally to the front of the Westin Hotel. A huge goal met.

Several newspapers and magazines reported that the roadster's arrival in downtown Chicago stopped traffic on Michigan Avenue. I couldn't say. I was surrounded by women in wind-whipped bright purple dresses and holding their red hats on their heads. Sue Ellen Cooper, the Exalted Queen Mother of this tiger phenomenon known as the Red Hat Society, greeted me in her royal sash and red gloves. We had met in California on a Red Hatters train ride and shopping spree to San Juan Capistrano that was covered by the Today Show film crew. Legend has it that Sue Ellen had accidentally started this craze by wearing a red hat and getting her women chums to also wear red hats and follow the advice of Jenny Joseph's poem about "When I am an old woman, I'll wear purple and a red hat."

I had over 40 years of history with purple. The Alyce-as-a-teenager bedroom was painted orchid with curtains, carpet, bedspread and even furniture in shades of lavender and deep violet. My big, old Portland home was painted four shades of dusty plum and purple. I sleep on purple sheets, eat on purple plates and burn purple candles.

Red had always been my business color. I wore a red suit when I did my presentations and my red logo always scored hits. My big red "A" was emblazoned on letterhead, business cards, press kits, my watch and even embroidered into my clothes. Of the fourteen books I had written, twelve had red covers. My shoes were red, even my glasses were red.

So when I heard about the Red Hat Society and its dress code, I thought, "Hey, these people are singin' my song! Let's play!"

Sue Ellen had already undergone her elaborate coronation ceremony the day before and I was sorry I had missed that historic event.

There was a riotous red and purple pajama breakfast party. So when Seno, the purple roadster with red wheels made his appearance, this was all part of the show. He set off a firestorm of camera clicking and even the lady artist followed me to the hotel to get snapshots.

When I Am An Old Car (with apologies to Jenny Joseph)

When I am an old car, I shall wear purple
with pretty red wheels
which some say doesn't go and doesn't suit me.

And I shall demand fuel additives
and engine repair
and say we've no money for sausages.

I shall rev my pistons at SUV's
stopped at stoplights,
and refuse offers to drag with Mustangs.

I will smile and wave at drooling young men
and park in motorcycle
parking spaces.

And I will make up for the stock appearance
of my youth...when suddenly
I am old and am painted purple.

The Red Hat Society skyrocketed from Sue Ellen's little group of friends to over 3,000 chapters in less than three years. There wasn't a religion around that didn't envy that kind of growth. The only qualification for membership was to be a woman over the age of 50, wear purple (could be a purple bathrobe, purple tuxedo or purple dress, your choice) and put on a red hat. Thousands of women heard the call and boom! the RHS went coast to coast and then overseas. This was their first convention and hundreds of women flooded the Westin Michigan Avenue to flaunt their wild purple outfits and amazing red head gear. One woman from Scranton, Pennsylvania wore her husband's red fire engine helmet. Well, it *was* a red hat. Unlike most conventions, nobody seemed interested in what you may have done or may be doing for a living. Instead, they wanted to know where did you get that fabulous brooch? what brand is that gorgeous purple nail polish? where on earth did you find that awesome hat? did you make it yourself, dear?

The Chicago Tribune printed a picture of Seno across one full page of the paper. *People Magazine* was rumored to be there. *Modern Maturity* set up a backdrop for Seno in the hotel's parking structure and had me pose in my purple and red regalia. When I wore my velvet Victorian dress to the afternoon tea with my over-the-top red satin hat, I was photographed more times than I have been *in my entire life!*

That Friday evening there was a Red Hat Society version of The Amateur Hour and I attended wearing a furry neon purple bunny suit complete with huge head (with perky red felt hat) that kept me blissfully incognito. It was a funny luxury to look out through two rabbit eye holes and see people come up and try to have an exchange. The bunny didn't speak. Again it was pose for photos and wait while friends tried to use their cameras, re-remembered to open the lens cover, re-posed, traded places and then did it all again. The Red Hat ladies wanted their pictures taken with *anything* that was red and purple. I could have been dressed as a red and purple septic tank and they would have lined up to be photographed with me. It was delightful to be a celebrity without even opening my furry mouth. Perhaps, it occurred to me, my pearls of wisdom were not necessary. Maybe all I needed to do was show up in costume.

Steam was building up in the bunny suit and I stepped out onto Delaware Avenue around 9:00 p.m. I thought it might be fun to walk around downtown Chicago and cool off. I couldn't even make it to the corner. The wind had whipped into a frenzy and the cold penetrated the bunny fur. I scampered back into the safety of the hotel.

Who knows what the weather was like on Saturday? I was busy preparing for my part of the program and signing books while manic women swirled like crazed fairies all around the hotel. The carpeted halls were littered with little purple and red feathers from all the flouncing boas. Camera flashes went off continually like indoor fireworks. Who would have believed that grown women, some of them in their 80's, could have so much fun playing together? (www.redhatsociety.com)

I performed "The War Bride" for the RHS's Saturday luncheon. The War Bride was a stand up comedy character who reported on Life in America, in particular, the War Between Men and Women. With comic material right off of the pages of daily newspapers and from actual research reports, this "journalist" character of mine went right into the trenches of male/female gender messes. (One of my largest and most difficult research projects was gender differences and gender communication. I swallowed facts that nearly choked me to learn. From this I created a business seminar for many conferences, credit unions, the FBI, and the National Guard. But I could also see a lot of humor in the situations between the sexes and eventually I came to realize that laughter was our most important common denominator. So I created the War Bride character to elaborate on male/female snafus.) Dressed a torn wedding dress and a WWI army helmet, my War Bride character said things on stage that I couldn't say. She had more attitude and sarcasm than I allow myself. She appeared to be a cross between Geraldine (crossdressing Flip Wilson) and Bella Abzug.

Standing up on stage, under my metal helmet, looking out over a ballroom ablaze with red hats was a remarkable moment. Each head nodded and wobbled slightly and since there were several hundred out there, the movement was very much like the ocean. A sea of red hats was a very accurate description.

The Red Hat Society rewarded the War Bride's efforts with a standing ovation and cheering.

It was an honor to be chosen as a speaker at this first conference and the participants paid me over and over, hugging me in the hallways, giving me their business cards, asking if they could be photographed with me and buying all my books. One woman asked me to autograph her hat. A dozen women handed me their addresses and phone numbers if I needed help or a place to stay on my way across the country.

On stage as the War Bride, I had quoted Truman Capote who said, "The most dangerous thing in the world is to make friends with someone from Vermont...because he'll come sleep in your closet before he'll spend $10 on a hotel room." A Red Hatter from Vermont with a great smile gave me her card and invited me and Seno to come stay with her.

I was preparing for the evening's dinner speech when Howard called from his sister's place and informed me that our scheduled leave time Sunday morning included snow and sleet! What? Howard was not given to exaggeration but how could a 92 degree Thursday turn into a 32 degree Sunday?

John Steinbeck refused to write about Chicago in his cross country *Travels with Charley*. He would only say, "Chicago broke my continuity. So I leave Chicago out, because it is off the line."

Carl Sandburg wrote, “Here is the difference between Dante, Milton and me. They wrote about hell and never saw the place. I wrote about Chicago after looking the place over for years and years.”

Early Sunday morning Seno roared up out of the bowels of the hotel’s parking garage and begrudgingly climbed the ramp onto the trailer. The sharp cold wind was whipping freezing rain into the loading area as we strapped him down. Even the bell captain was wearing foul weather gear. The object of this morning’s game was to get out of Chicago before any significant traffic made things worse.

Lake Michigan looked like a shipwreck in progress and there wasn’t a living soul along State Street. Sale banners over head became sail banners flapping against street lights. The truck’s windshield wipers were nearly pulled off in the wind. Metro boulevards turned into turnpike and all was grey-grey heading eastbound.

This was the antithesis of the bright red and purple laughing women back at the Westin. It was quiet in the truck and stayed calm all the way to New Boston, Michigan. Wet and windblown we pulled into Betty’s youth hostel, a private home with guest rooms. I climbed down from the truck and into the arms of what appeared to be a carbon copy of Howard. His brother, slightly younger and without the moustache had agreed that yes, he needed to see the Dearborn museums too. Bud had driven up from Virginia to meet us and I was very happy to see him. And as I thought it would be, the country youth hostel was a safe place to leave the roadster while we three browsed the museums.

The main reason I wanted to come to Dearborn and see the Henry Ford Museum was because I could then say “YES!” when asked by a member of the Ford V-8 Club if I had “been there yet?” Then they wouldn’t have to tell me how fabulous it was and what I was missing and why I should go there.

23

Dearborn, Michigan was a true vacation for me. My roadster was secure and happy at his country kennel. My official work had been completed in Chicago. And I was bookended by two brothers who were both crazy about cars and as ready to see what Henry Ford had to offer as I was. We had three days to see it all and three days were not enough.

But it was a start. The sky was still ominous so we elected to spend our first day touring indoors.

The centerpiece of the Henry Ford Museum was a classical brick building that resembled a college. The emphasis of the museum was on *innovation*, not just Ford products. Well, this widened the subject substantially. A living tribute to American ingenuity, the displays included aviation, transportation, agriculture, jewelry, home products and historical oddities like the chair Lincoln was sitting in when he was shot, complete with stains.

It has been said that no two people ever read the same book. That also means that no two people ever see the same museum either. Howard may tell you about the progression of engines, Bud may remember the wild prototype cars. I thought the most remarkable exhibit was Buckminster Fuller's Dymaxion House.

Only on display since October 2001, this one-of-a-kind round aluminum house never went into production. It still seems workable to me today and I'd buy one. Bucky thought of almost everything. Based on a design as simple as an umbrella, this efficient house could have been manufactured for $6,500 in 1946, the cost of a new Cadillac. I was enthralled with the extremely unusual and practical house.

Every now and then I'd come across a coin-operated make-your-own-plastic-toy machine. I could put in a dollar and watch the metal molds come together, see the nozzle squirt the hot plastic, then poof! the mold popped apart and my toy was pushed into the waiting drawer where I could reach in and get it. I made an Oscar Mayer Weiner Mobile, a Model A Ford and Mickey Mouse.

I didn't know that President Kennedy's Lincoln was retrofitted after the assassination to the tune of $1,000,000 and put back into service for Johnson, Nixon and Carter. Didn't they feel sort of creepy using it? The infamous convertible was parked in the line up of presidential limousines that started with Wilson's carriage.

I saw an incredible student-made solar-powered car that resembled a sheet of glass on four tires. There was Charles Kuralt's RV and the very famous Old 16, the first American car to win an international auto race and to serve notice that the Yanks were serious about cars.

I had my picture taken with a crash dummy.

I got to see the only Bugatti Royale in the United States. Six of these cars were produced and their target market was royalty. They were two expensive even for royal tastes. One ended up in Japan and was the subject of an article called "The Most Expensive Car in the World." It was up for grabs: $5,000,000. I saw the one in Dearborn for a lot less.

It was a lot of walking, a lot of pointing, a lot of reading and learning, a lot of "look-it this!" Anything that Harold Warp missed in Nebraska, Henry Ford had picked up and installed in Michigan. (www.hfmgv.org) We were three tired little touristas that night and slept well in our simple digs at Betty's hostel.

Betty Johnson was like a relative you'd actually like to have, instead of what you usually get. She had a long braid down her back and a warm, wonderful smile. We had emailed each other a few times and she knew the odd little car was coming. Her American Youth Hostel had room for six people so I was relieved when all three of us, using half her available bed space, could call it home for three days. We had plenty of room and the use of her ample kitchen. Betty's sweetness and quiet place were exactly what I needed after the frenetic celebration in Chicago.

Greenfield Village was up next and we were there at the opening along with several thousand kids who were there to see Thomas the Train. When we all poured through the turnstiles, the three of us headed in the opposite direction and had the better part of the village to ourselves for many hours.

Henry Ford wasn't content just to have a building full of stuff (the Henry Ford Museum). He dragged buildings from all over the place and arranged them like wooden Monopoly pieces into his own view of a village. His modest birthplace was one of the first installations and right next door he placed the Wright Brothers' shop and their home.

I was a fan of Orville and Wilbur Wright and I looked over every inch of their home; to me it was a shrine. After a visit to Dayton, Ohio I had read *The Bishop's Boys* by Tom Crouch (W. W. Norton, ISBN 0-393-30695-X), the recommended life story of the brothers and I found myself truly in love with Orville to the point of dreaming about him.

"Not within a thousand years would man ever fly," said the discouraged Orville Wright in 1901. In 1903 they lifted off at Kitty

Hawk. This important story illustrated to me that the winner with unshakable faith in her/his project was a myth. People who succeed must frequently doubt their endeavors. I know I did. I never really thought I could make it around the entire route of my sketched trip. Surely a mechanical failure or a mishap would occur and I'd have to ship the car home and get on a plane for Oregon. I believed this to be a likely outcome. And I told myself, "No point in being a damned fool about it. Quit if you can't stand it any longer." Seeing the home of my heroes, the Wright brothers, refreshed my belief that even with a rotten attitude, and both Orville and Wilbur *had their moments*, success was still possible.

The buildings that were Thomas Edison's laboratories in New Jersey were moved to Ford's village. The first house ever lit with electricity, Sarah Jordan's simple boarding house, was here. The H. J. Heinz house was extremely interesting architecturally and was used as the horseradish factory that evolved into the world-famous food processing company. There were 81 acres and over 300 years of history created around pleasant streets and interesting shops. Nothing was reproduction. If they said it was Noah Webster's house, it wasn't a replica. And no, that wasn't a copy, that's *the* dictionary.

We saw a Cape Cod windmill, a covered bridge originally built in 1832, a southern plantation house, a train station, even 400-year old English Cotswold buildings painstakingly taken apart and put back together, stone by numbered stone. There was the Illinois court house where Lincoln practiced law and the spartan quarters of William Holmes McGuffey, creator of the 1800's McGuffey readers. All of this was punctuated by horse-drawn wagons and Model T products going puckety-puckety up and down the streets and all the while being circled by the whistling steam engine.

These were not dead buildings either. There was fudge and muffins to buy in the old John Bennet store, moved from London. There were workshops and mills for textiles, pottery, printing, glass blowing and tin smithing. A person could walk their legs down to nubbins in this place. Bud and I climbed into an empty stone horse trough and pretended to bathe. It just seemed the thing to do at the moment and it felt good just to sit down.

It was possible to ride a horse-drawn omnibus, a Model T, a train, a steamboat, a 1931 Ford Model AA bus, a wagon or the carousel.

Oddly enough we three agreed on a favorite house! It was Robert Frost's residence. The four-time Pulitzer Prize winner lived in what looked like a colonial doll house moved to Dearborn from New England.

There was an interesting letter to Henry Ford written by Thomas Edison in his backslanted, elegant handwriting, dated 1914. It read: "Friend Ford...The injurious agent in cigarettes comes principally from the burning paper wrapper. The substance thereby formed is called 'Acrolein.' It has a violent action on the nerve centers, producing degeneration of the cells of the brain, which is quite rapid among boys. Unlike most narcotics this degeneration is permanent and uncontrollable. I employ no person who smokes cigarettes. Yours, Thos. A. Edison"

Henry Ford must have been Thomas Edison's biggest fan. There was a massive sculpture of Edison in the center plaza of the Village and the museum was originally named The Edison Institute. The two would travel together and camp, calling themselves the Vagabonds. The photographs taken of Henry Ford give the impression that he was a calculating, serious fellow but Edison must have had a sense of humor. He was an admirer of Morse code and named his daughters Dot and Dash.

The Automobile Hall of Fame was across the parking lot. It was a long walk. We actually got our weary bones into the car and drove over to this next museum.

In his life-sized candid picture in the Hall of Fame, handsome Louie Chevrolet looked like a starter kit for Robert Redford. He was all about racing and I stared at his image a long time. He looked so happy, so thrilled! He had that Teddy Roosevelt grin and aura about him that said, "To hell with everybody, I am doing *exactly* what I want!" This museum wasn't about the vehicles, it was about the people. I learned, for instance, that the guy who invented cruise control was blind.

I received an unexpected and warm greeting from the President of the Automotive Hall of Fame who, when told of my cross country journey, asked me point blank: "How drunk were you when you thought of this idea?" Jeff Leestma and volunteer guide Jerry Steinard gave us a personal tour through the Hall of Fame and made special note of one particular inductee, Alice Huyler Ramsey.

In 1909 Alice became the first woman to drive a car across America. An Alice! Her car was also an open car although the 1909 Maxwell did have a flimsy pull up canvas-type cover. She left New York City and got as far as Iowa when roads just ceased to exist. With no maps, she followed the telegraph lines. She did it in 59 days, a record. The idea was the marketing scheme of Carl Kelsey, the P. T. Barnum of the Maxwell car company. The tires on her touring car had no tread! I bought two books in the museum's great book store about Alice's amazing adventure. What problems did she have? How did she cope? Did she have help? Was she alone? Did she ever want to give up? I wanted to know all the details of her trek. It was worse than that. I wanted to hire a medium and have Alice channeled for information!

On the way back to the youth hostel Bud pulled his car into an open air market and the three of us went in three different directions collecting goodies that we wanted to eat for dinner that night. Unlike most men who think that high cholesterol might be a Jewish holiday, Howard and Bud paid attention to what they ingested. It paid off. They were both trim, fit and both looked more my age than their own. Bud had ridden a bicycle solo across Canada and Howard didn't know what the inside of a doctor's office looked like. They both must have had their faults but they were about the best traveling companions a person could ask for.

We hauled bags and food cartons into Betty's kitchen with just enough energy to fix dinner. Nobody seemed to be orchestrating our activity, it just somehow naturally came together at the dinner table. A new guest had arrived at the hostel, a Canadian. We invited Jonathan Makepeace to join us. He entertained us with stories about his unusual name and about how French Canadians practiced what they called "revenge of the cradle" which meant having lots of kids in order to get the message across, "We're not going away." He translated a letter written to Betty in French. When we asked him where he was bound, there was a shocked silence. He was traveling to his ancestral home of Princeton, Illinois!

Journal entry: April 23

Amazing coincidences seem to be common in hostels. It's not likely that a conversation like the one we had this evening with Mr. Makepeace would have occurred at a Hilton or a Holiday Inn. Betty and I were the only two people in the house, it seemed, not from Princeton, Illinois!

Hosteling allows a traveler to enjoy either privacy or comradeship and I never know which one I want until I'm there.

After dinner I asked Howard to attack my motorcycle helmet. I gave him a hammer and told him that he couldn't hurt it. It wasn't much good to me in its current condition which had been putting a permanent dent in my forehead. He slammed the brass hammer into that helmet so hard I thought it would surely crack the shell.

I have the book about Alice Ramsey's drive across the United States in 1909 and I think I'll carry it on my trip for good luck and inspiration.

The next morning the brothers and I went back out to meet Mother Road and she arranged for a cloudless sky and dry pavement. We convoyed southbound on I-75 until Toledo when Bud waved and made his exit to return to Virginia. Every time I've had a visit that involved Bud I always missed him for days afterwards.

Traffic in Ohio was serious. I got the impression that the truckers were a "take no prisoners" sort of people. Several times I saw massive diesels with 42 tires hauling what appeared to be steel and probably to Detroit. 42 tires!! I own six cars and I don't have that many tires. You could send a kid to college on the cost of those wheels!

Howard and I wandered around Bowling Green, Ohio searching for the elusive propane for his truck. His truck and trailer wouldn't fit just anywhere; we had to pick our streets carefully. The rear ramp fell down once, frightening a fellow traveler in a pick-up truck. When Howard's truck took $103 worth of propane I began to look forward to seeing this orange monstrosity disappear from my roadster's rearview mirror permanently.

Roadster Lesson #8: He who travels fastest travels alone. Security costs you *something.*

24

Despite having to find fuel for both our vehicles, we still made it with enough time left in the day to take in the American Packard Museum, The Citizens Motorcar Company in downtown Dayton, Ohio.

What can be said about two people who could spend days at the Ford Museum, leave and go the very next day to still another car museum.

Two things make this possible: a) vehicles were just a small portion of the Dearborn museums and b) these two people were gear heads. And this place was the only restored Packard *dealership* operating as a museum even though Packard stopped manufacturing cars in 1956.

Of the hundreds of cars I saw across the United States, the one that really lit my fire was the speedster I saw that afternoon in Dayton. It was a good thing the Devil wasn't around offering trade ins for this beauty. What would I have traded for that car? Let's see... I would have traded my purple roadster for it. I would have thrown in Howard's truck and probably Howard. Could you blame me? It was a 1928 black Packard speedster with red wheels and red leather interior. This was a real steel automobile with breathtaking lines. If I could *be* a car, I would want to be this one. I got a headache just circling it and lusting.

Howard found Al Capone's dark blue Packard and posed with it. It seems that Al bought cars in identical pairs so he could send one in a direction while he slipped out in another direction.

The entire place was a time capsule..."a time when dealerships were outposts of elegance and Packards were presented under chandeliers and graceful palms." It was not a stretch of the imagination to picture Clark Gable ordering his next Packard here. (www.neighborweb.com/details/1351.htm)

Packard's slogan was, "Ask the man who owns one." I found an ad from 1937 that read, "Ask a *woman* who owns one." And I do.

Despite my heavy breathing over the vintage iron on Ludlow Street, I had come to Dayton for another reason. I had been blessed with two speaking assignments here the year previously and those two trips were not enough to see and do everything available in this mid-sized American city. If a person couldn't find something of interest in this town then go ahead and bury them.

More patents came out of Dayton, Ohio than any other U.S. city. What is it, the water or what? Between the National Cash Register Company and the Wright brothers and the guy who invented pop top cans, they make the rest of us look like mere vacationers on the Planet. Even Erma Bombeck was from Dayton.

I visited Sun Watch Indian Archeological Park (uncovered in a muddy Ohio field) and saw their wooden version of Stonehenge and how a prehistoric community charted time. I regressed even further to the largest conical earthwork of its kind built 3,000 years ago, the Ohio Miamisburg Mound. I climbed to the top and wondered how they did it. (A feeling reminiscent of the Eiffel Tower, the Statue of Liberty and when a group of students put a Volkswagen on the roof of the student union building at Oklahoma State.)

Perhaps one of the best sited art museums anywhere, the Dayton Art Institute was its own billboard; it overlooked the city and the river, impossible to ignore even at 65 miles per hour on the interstate.

People even remotely interested in aviation, eventually find themselves here. I particularly enjoyed the commentary by national park ranger Bob Petersen at Wil and Orv's other bike shop on Williams Street. He was the one who got me sufficiently interested in the Wright brothers as human beings rather than just legends and to plow through the book, *The Bishop's Boys.* (www.nps.gov/daav)

Senator John Glenn said, "The observance of Inventing Flight can only truly be commemorated with mammoth proportions. Dayton will be the place to be." So take that, North Carolina. (Ohio and North Carolina duke it out periodically on coins and license plates for the title of "Birthplace of Aviation.")

Dayton was significant for a couple of reasons--there was the largest military aviation museum in the world, the United States Air Force Museum *and* the birthplace of Alyce! There were no words big enough to describe this hugely significant place. At least in *my* life.

Here I was in the USAF Museum book store, which was larger than most city libraries, wandering through the startling array of esoteric aviation books and feeling like an interloper. I didn't even like to fly, what was I doing here? The full color books (aisles and aisles of them) can short out your brain with their flashy photography of flying anything--blimps, kites, biplanes, jets, rockets. I steadied myself and rounded a corner and came face to face with a splashy book about The Flying Wing.

This odd aircraft, designed/built/tested and then scrubbed, reinvented itself as the stealth bomber, the plane that you could see but somehow the Air Force convinced us that non-Americans could not see. I wasn't interested in that delusion. I was more interested in the infamous grandfather of the stealth, the experimental Flying Wings of more than half a century ago. Because my dad was one of the test pilots.

Some said that the plane, just a big wing with no fuselage, flew like a maple leaf and usually in a down position. When I asked my father about that, forever a man of fewest words, he replied, "I didn't have any trouble with it."

I picked up this heavily illustrated book that was the size of an encyclopedia and started to leaf through it when my thumb snagged a page. The photograph, staring back at me, seemed to radiate off the paper. Reproduced life-sized was the certificate given to my father for having flown The Flying Wing. His name was in type as big as a headline. I recognized the paper instantly because the framed original hung over my dad's desk. Zap! A little lightening bolt suddenly connected me to aviation, the Air Force, World War II and Dayton. It was not a particularly pleasant sensation but sometimes your history is not of your making and defies rejection.

So ground-loving pacifist that I was, I was still the colonel's daughter. Imprinted like a salmon, I couldn't outmaneuver my heritage, no matter how long I stayed away from it. My father would never be featured in the Dad Hall of Fame but he certainly deserved his spot in aviation history. All he ever wanted to do was fly. There was no room for three kids in any of his cockpits.

But I hadn't come to Dayton, Ohio for this either. I closed the book and headed south of Wright-Patterson Air Force Base to a more human-sized air field, the one on Springboro Pike. The large illustrations of Orville and Wilbur on the side of the hangar let aviators know when they've arrived at the Wright "B" Flyer.

I had been in contact with these people for months. It was one of the few destination spots on my journey. For a $10,000 donation I could receive a one inch square of the original fabric wing covering from the 1903 Kitty Hawk plane. Or for $150 donation I could go up in the 1911 Wright "B" Flyer, a replica of the first mass produced airplane in the world. I had a reservation for this flight.

The Wright "B" was a step above a hang glider. There was just a little bit more to it but not much. The pilot and one passenger sat on little butt holders about the size of a salad plate and positioned their feet close together on a toilet paper tube-sized pipe. There was nothing else there, no walls, no tray table, no windows. All parts of my soft tissue would be hanging out there in the air. A person would feel more confined and protected on a carousel horse. Behind the "seats" was an engine that looked vaguely like it came off of a go-kart. Except for the two thin wings held apart with wires and poles, and two old car wheels, there was nothing else of the plane. Still, I was looking forward to a flight where I didn't have to be frisked, x-rayed, insulted or get harassed about too much stuff in the overhead compartment.

Most of the guys who tinkered inside this hangar were in their 70's and 80's, my dad's age if he were still alive. They were lovers of preservation and machines. A black Model T Ford restoration, designated as the "staff car," was one of their pet projects when they weren't in parades with the float, a small version of the famous biplane, complete with stuffed Bishop flying with one of his sons. The real star of the Dayton General Airport, however, was the meticulously crafted Wright "B" Flyer, a unique and historical sight. (www.wright-b-flyer.org)

I arrived early but not "two hours before flight time" as recommended by highly irritating airport authorities. Nobody asked, "Has your luggage been under your complete control at all times?" I love this question. When I hear it I have to admit that yes, I am indeed responsible for my travel pookie, the lobster, and the Mickey Mouse ears are also mine. And yes, I packed that feathered fan too. "Has anyone asked you to carry anything for them?" No, I haven't accepted stuff for anybody else. Where would I put it? And do I look like somebody who likes to schlep stuff? No one in their right mind would voluntarily ask for the pseudo-security measures in U.S. airports and I felt like I was defying the whole stupid system by booking the one flight that would circumvent this nonsense.

The day had finally arrived and I chucked my fear of flying as if I'd never had it. I wore my leather flying hat and parked my 1927 roadster next to the 1911 airplane. Wind gusts were making the volunteers nervous and I'd have to wait. This was an airport after all, so no surprises.

Like a good little airport traveler, I bought one of every souvenir in the gift shop and when the wind sock outside still wouldn't cooperate, I settled in to watch the video about the Wright bothers, a PBS production. With things not much calmer, I was advised to go have lunch and check back. I did that. The pilot, a grandfatherly guy named John, told volunteer Ed Logan to have me sign the papers, we'd go up as soon as he finished his sandwich. I signed the waivers that I was sane (OK, I fudged) and if I ended up with my head buried in the Ohio sod and my butt in the sun, my pieces would be sent back to Oregon and the bill would go to my daughter.

The wind sock would not go down and the plane would not go up. I wasn't going to be "slipping the surly bonds of earth" that day. Judging from the stern look on John's face, begging wasn't going to work either. My dad used to say, "There are bold pilots and old pilots, but no old, bold pilots." It didn't take a genius to see what kind of pilot John was.

My Internal Financial Director was not disappointed with this outcome. There was $150 that would live to see another day...and so would I.

When I climbed in my roadster to leave Dayton General Airport, a quick blast of wind shook the car sideways. The wind gusts would have made flying in the Wright "B" seem like a ride in a blender.

25

Friday, April 26 marked a completely new era in my saga of crossing America.

I stayed in the same motel room as the previous night, ate at the same breakfast place as I had the morning before, did my back-popping yoga routine as usual but there was going to be nothing usual about this day. I was about to disengage myself and Seno from the Mother Ship. It was time for Howard and his beastly, propane-guzzling truck to head westbound and for me to strike out on my own.

I needed my alone time like I needed air. My desire to live alone included even the exclusion of house plants from my environment. If I had any other living thing in my house they were there uninvited--slugs, bugs, butterflies, squirrels. After a business trip, I approach and think, "Thank God no one is home." Sometimes sharing the details of a business trip was akin to living it all over again...and I only get paid to live through it *once.* I was a solitaire by natural inclination.

I was beginning to understand why my dad had picked the P-40 as his favorite military plane. "So I could fly alone," he had said. A genetic predisposition? Perhaps. Likely, actually. I suspect this sort of thing may be hereditary.

People who prefer the lone path were not necessarily anti-social. In fact, they may be, like I was, very intensely social...in prescribed doses. We solitaires frequently loved people and didn't have intimacy problems, we just enjoyed the insides of our heads as much as listening to others' heads.

"God created the heavens and the earth in just seven days...but then, He had the advantage of working alone."

This intense itch to be off on my own propelled me to April 26. It had been growing steadily like a black cloud so thick that it blocked out any rays from the financial sun issue. I was so focused on getting out on the road alone that I forgot to have the discussion with myself about the missing money.

From the novel *The Prodigal Women* by Nancy Hale (Charles Scribner's Sons, 1942): "One of the things she found a private pleasure in was driving her car alone. All the country was dead, sad and tired. She felt hopeless too, but in the car it was not so bad. There was the feeling of being snug within the body of the car; the top and sides of the car shutting her into a little ambulant house that she could direct at will. From her little moving box, she could look at the passing country. It made her feel free."

There's a reason they call it JOY RIDE.

I would not have a Charley, as Steinbeck did, to be my co-pilot and open doors of communication for me as all good dogs do. I would not have the advantage of a camper equipped with kitchen and bathroom either. I would not have the male advantage of being able to punctuate my miles with little conversations in roadside taverns over a beer as both Kerouac and Least Heat Moon did. I would not have the backing of a car company and three women friends as Alice Ramsey had. I would not have the delicious safety net that only $2610 could provide.

"Here, you'd better take this," said Howard as he handed me the national Early Ford V8 membership directory, referred to as "The Roster."

I didn't want to pack anything more. I was wearing most of my clothes just so I wouldn't have to pack them in space that didn't exist. I reluctantly took the paperback roster and squeezed it in between the radiator shell and my Red Cross emergency pack.

I had one more thing to do before I left Dayton. Bessie, the motel manager, needed a picture of herself in the car to show to her grandson. How could a grandmother refuse another grandmother such a request? She did especially well getting into the roadster despite her artificial knee. One needed to dismiss all pretense of grace in order to get behind the wheel of this awkward little car. With no doors, the only choice was up and over. She was a jolly lady as she practiced gloating, saying what she planned to say to her grandson as I took her picture. Seno would develop a guest list of people who would sit in his drivers' seat and just glow. Who would have suspected that a chunk of purple fiberglass, four tires and some gears could make so many people that happy?

Now it was *my turn* to be happy behind the wheel. While the early morning commuters reluctantly hit the two big interstates that clog Dayton, I was looking forward to getting in it. No, I was chomping at the bits to be on the road on my own. Whatever whiney little fears I had were obliterated by my sincere desire to be alone with my roadster.

Mark Twain: "Twenty years from now you will be more disappointed by the things you didn't do than by the ones you did do. So throw off the bowlines. Sail away from the safe harbor and all orange trucks. Catch the trade winds in your sails. Explore. Dream. Discover."

OK, he didn't say that part about orange trucks.

I pulled my helmet on over my hair, clicked my seat belt, turned the ignition key. It was Monte Carlo, the Indy 500, Daytona, Oscar night, Wimbledon and Carnegie Hall all rolled into one moment. I shoved the stick into first gear and left the parking lot, crossed the freeway and dropped down onto the curling on-ramp. The grille of the orange truck still filled my rearview mirror. The maps, tour books and video camera stowed in my passenger seat started collapsing on me as I made the tight right hand curve. I held the junk in place with my elbow while gripping the wooden steering wheel and cursed out loud to no one in particular and myself in general.

The interstate straightened out and at the next exit I read that great big sweet sign that said: EAST. It might just as well have read: "Adventure, this way." I glanced quickly at my rearview mirror and watched the orange GMC as it made its exit: WEST. "Whew! I've done it!" I thought. "If I only get one mile, at least it will be one complete mile all on my own, all 5,280 feet of it!"

The Universe had a great sense of humor. It occurred to me that 55 years ago I had extricated myself from the confines of my mother, I was born, and there I was in Dayton, Ohio (courtesy of the base hospital at Wright-Patterson AFB). Now, of all places to begin the solo portion of my trip, through no conscious advance planning of my own, I was again, free of the umbilical cord of a support vehicle...and once, again in Dayton. I had to laugh at this and think, gee, I haven't made it very far in 55 years. I had no more attachment to Ohio and my birthplace than I had to Wal-Mart. Ohio was just a word I wrote on bank account applications. This was typical military brat behavior.

The 202 Exit appeared and I took that to Highway 40 which was to be my lifeline across all of Ohio. Unlike the countryside west of Chicago, Ohio was fully green with spring life. I passed cats in windows, old cars in back garages, lawn chairs as if in conversation, white marble mile markers that looked like little gravestones and a kids resale clothing store called "Once Upon A Child." The temperature was roadster perfect and the high clouds looked like flowing white hair in a pool of horizon-to-horizon blue sea. I could not have designed a better day for myself and Seno.

SLOW DOWN FOR HARMONY, the sign read. Good advice, I thought and so authoritatively presented. Then I realized, it was a road sign for Harmony, Ohio. "Oh," I thought, "well, I liked the first interpretation better."

The word Ohio means "great" to the Iroquois. A white interloper, looking over the rich, fertile Ohio landscape said, "It will be our own fault if we are not the happiest people in the Union." Sounded like a guy who must have cleared a few rocky acres in New Hampshire. Every time I'd come here on business more and more of the Buckeye state revealed its treasures. I was thrilled to visit the Serpent Mound two years ago. This bizarre snake effigy was best viewed at seven in the morning and from the tower. Why would native people, who had to concern every waking day with food and survival, spend thousands and thousands of man hours constructing this unusual mound? It was the largest and certainly one of the most elegant native images in America. The design seemed contemporary and it was 3,000 years old. (www.ohiohistory.org/places/serpent)

Highway 40 went straight toward Columbus. Farmland turned into roadside feed stores and then into strip malls. Then skyscrapers loomed in the distance like the monolith in *2001: A Space Odyssey.* Before I knew it I had passed the I-70 sign and the opportunity to avoid downtown Columbus. I figured, I've done Chicago, how bad could Columbus, Ohio be? There's nothing quite like getting one thing done to make a person believe they can do another.

My idealized fantasy of my journey was sunny, blissful back roads. The reality was, I couldn't avoid both cities *and* interstates. If I took the blue highways, they eventually led right down into the heart of a big city. To avoid the city, the 400 or the 200 series of interstates circled the American metropolis. So there was the choice: human-sized streets with 50 to 100 stoplights and the potential of seeing something interesting or 70 miles per hour "Get There" with the trucks and commuters on cell phones.

Seno and I went right through the middle of Columbus. I heard my own voice inside my helmet exclaiming, "Oh, look at *that*!" Such interesting architecture. Men and women in suits looked startled and occasionally someone would come to and realize that yes, a woman was driving a purple roadster through downtown and they'd smile and wave. Hmmmm, more conservative group here.

Columbus had James Thurber and the *Santa Maria* but I needed to make tracks. I was charmed, however, and finally had to circle a block and park to get pictures of a wonderful sculpture of life-sized people playing with alphabet letters.

On Broad Street with its high buck estates, I sat at a stoplight next to a school bus full of teenaged boys. It began to rock as the entire group leaped to the windows.

"Nice car," one shouted to me.

"Nice bus," I said back.

"Can I drive it?"

"In your dreams."

And I really hoped he *did* drive it in his dreams. I know I had been driving it in my dreams for 18 months.

Somewhere east of downtown I lost Highway 40. America doesn't have nearly enough road signs. I was to discover that repeatedly. I backtracked two miles. Sure enough, 40 jogged south then east again. I went south and found what seemed to be a main road confirmed by Fireman Hooker, the handsome uniform at the

Reynoldsburg Fire House. Why do fire guys always look like the wholesome Boy Next Door from any 50's movie? They just make me want to go home and throw a cat way up in a tree.

Time seemed to be rolling too fast and 40 tried joining I-70 at several points. Finally I just went with it all the way to the bridge and the WELCOME TO WEST VIRGINIA sign.

I had my directions for Prabhupada's Palace of Gold and I hadn't read them thoroughly. It did not escape me that this trip was a microcosm of my life--complete with ignoring clear direction and surrounding myself with too much stuff.

Thirty years ago I had traversed this state and I remembered myself describing it then as "one big bunch of mountains," but by golly, as soon as it became West Virginia, the road immediately turned into a galloping snake.

When I stopped in a parking lot to finally read my directions, a creepy *Deliverance* sort of guy pulled up in a trashed car. He got out and approached me until I could read his baseball cap "Miserable? Try Jesus" and see the spaces between his teeth. I answered two questions, snapped his photo, hoping it wouldn't have to be used as evidence later, and took off. I reminded myself that in 1997 West Virginia made it legal to eat road kill. This appeared to be a state at the lower end of the economic food chain. And unless I wanted to see Seno rotating on a spit, I'd best not take my chances.

Highway 88 was aptly named because the road number illustrates the path of the road. When they say 15 miles per hour in West Virginia, they don't mean 16. Tight curves, up, down, shift, shift--each turn I had to take as if someone might be coming from the opposite direction. Because sometimes I was right.

Just when I was about to give up on the improbable notion that the Palace of Gold existed, I started seeing little road signs for it. I had read that the there was only one Hindu holy site outside of India and it was in the United States. That seemed very unlikely but what was even more unbelievable was that it was located in West Virginia.

New Vrinbadan was such an unexpected shock. I could expect to find a 22 carat gilded Hindu temple in the sacred Cascade Mountains of do-your-own-thing Oregon (have a rahneesh, anyone?) but out here in the high hills of West Virginia? Getting 254 tons of marble up twisting dirt roads was probably easy compared to adjusting to Life

Among the Dentally Challenged who were their neighbors.

I was asked to put paper footies on to tour America's Taj Mahal. I was still reeling from the impact of seeing the sun hit all that gold on the palace dome. Equally striking was the sense of humor of the guide who chided me and the other two touring guests, a giggly Hindu couple from Chicago. The guide was dressed in a grey pull-over sweater and grey Docker-type pants and had a perpetual grin. He questioned us as we walked the inlaid marble halls and looked out through the stained glass peacock windows. He joked and laughed, hardly something I expected on a tour of a sacred site. I couldn't place his accent and he played mental tricks with us on that subject. It took me awhile to grasp his level of humor and to join in the game. His simplicity was a sharp contrast to the complicated designs that completely encircled us.

Walls, ceilings, floors were all thoroughly, painstakingly coated with pattern and design. Ten elaborately decorated rooms held treasures and unnervingly real sculptures of Shrila Prabhupada, the holy man responsible for the fervor to build this place. His Divine Grace was seated writing in his study and crowned, life-sized on the altar. Although he dressed in simple traditional Indian garb until he left this mortal world in 1977, his devotees prefer to honor him in a manner befitting his position as a representative of God. What appeared to be a marble Catholic confessional was the spiritual man's shower and toilet. The orange marble sink weighed 300 pounds and had gold faucets with rose quartz handles.

Large Marie Antoinette crystals hung in a massive French chandelier surrounded by Renaissance paintings of Lord Krishna. Teak, onyx and silver all worked overtime to glorify the "home" for the memory of an obviously highly successful communicator. Even ABC Television announced, "You have to see it to believe it." A virtual tour on the internet, although valuable and well done, cannot do it justice. Even my own eyes could not completely take in the intricate details of this holy place. (www.palaceofgold.com)

A terraced garden outside the palace featured 34 varieties of water lilies and over 3,000 rose bushes, named All America Rose Selection Award Winner and "Outstanding Rose Garden in North America" for a decade. I couldn't keep four rose bushes healthy and I live in the designated City of Roses where they grow in back alleys. Imagine succeeding at the delicate art of rose growing in the Appalachian hills!

"The magnificence of the Palace of Gold would be hard to exaggerate," understated CBS in a news magazine show.

The visual impact of gold embroidery, thousands of hand painted flowers, carved lotus and 35,000 feet of inlaid marble shorted out my brain. The guide's accent was Russian and I bent my reality around what I was hearing. He encouraged us to visit the temple grounds just a little further down the road. I found him to be one of the most intriguing people on my entire cross country tour.

I eased Seno cautiously down the hill but nothing could have prepared me for the pristine little lake with three onion-topped gazebos, two story-high dancing figures, a kneeling life-sized elephant and sacred cows. The elephant dwarfed my car. Laughing people carried on their version of monastic life here which appeared to be anything but somber. The temple and the lodge were modest, large dark wood things and I saw a "Retreat Center Office" sign.

My take on religion is: either everybody's right or everybody's wrong. I spent the night at New Vrindaban.

I attended the evening services in the pew-less temple, putting my aching hip joints directly on the marble floor and learning to chant with the irresistible drumming. I wanted to observe and not detract from their worship, and not insult them by trying to blend in, which would have been impossible anyway. Bells, incense, chanting, singing, candles. It could have been a Roman Catholic service from 40 years ago. There were four extremely elaborate altars (this is Alyce, the Glitter Queen reporting this!) with gilded dieties, flowers and bright Mexican colors--the antithesis of Garrison Keillor's Lutherans. The community's happy displays of joy were reminiscent of the Red Hat Society convention.

All exchanges with devotees were spiced with a joyous humor and verve that welcomed me whole heartedly. Outside I sat on a curb with a woman from Michigan who had been at New Vrindaban 25 years. She was still recovering from a hysterectomy but she looked relaxed and was full of quirky humor too. My only disappointment was that the vegetarian restaurant was closed. I heated a cup of lentil soup in my dorm room, thanked my good fortune for steering me here and gazed totally spellbound from my second story window at a full moon. Rippling silver disks reflected in the lake. White light shown on one of the gazebos where I had spent an hour writing. My roadster, moonlight on his car cover, sat just beneath my window. Now I could say I had had real West Virginia moonshine.

If this first day was any indication of what my trip was going to be like, I was truly in for The Drive of A Lifetime.

Journal Entry: April 26

How does it feel to finally be doing the dream? I asked myself that as the hay bales, front porches, car lots and highway signs went whizzing by today. Feels a little unreal. To have been the Dreamer for so long and now to be the Doer, inside the dream instead of outside it, still it feels like a dream.

I learned that when asked how did you find out about Prabhupada's Palace of Gold, the correct response is, "Krishna sent me."

This is magic. This is why I came.

26

Getting Seno down out of the West Virginia mountains was a task much more suited to the morning. There was a vast expanse of green hills and a pink morning sky but I would be risking frostbite to videotape it. I needed all hands and feet to get the car around the hundreds of tight turns and there were no turn outs. In West Virginia, turn outs were for wimps, I guess. I recited the Hare Krishna chant all the way down to I-470 and found that my anxiety went from intense to pastel.

Howard had indeed pounded my helmet to its betterment. I could wear it without feeling like my cranium was being drilled for brain surgery. Under 35 miles per hour I had to keep the visor on my helmet half way up to avoid fogging. At higher speeds I could close it completely but only as a last resort because I had to remove a glove to lift the visor. Putting the mittens back on at 70 miles per hour wasn't easy and it certainly wasn't safe. The cold was getting through to me. Once into fourth gear when I no longer had to shift, I could warm one hand by putting it under my thigh and drive with the other hand. After a mile or two, I switched hands.

I did about 40 miles of I-470 which looked like I-Anything and we officially arrived in Pennsylvania. I noticed that purple seemed to be a popular truck paint color and I wanted a photograph of Seno parked next to one of these behemoths. In Washington,

Pennsylvania I had my chance and took it...a sleeping Kenworth in a corral of trucks near a Hardee fast food place. I positioned the roadster next to the semi's front fender and climbed out to get the shot. What a contrast of big and tiny and both vying for lanes on the road! I noticed that my head came up to the top of the truck's lugnuts. If I had the feeling that I was being eaten alive by these highballing transports, it was no wonder. It was comparing a closet to a living room.

Seno and I found the hospitable and historic Lincoln Highway to take us across Pennsylvania. It was built as the first attempt to unite the country, with roads anyway. It was established before the era of blasting their way through things so the ribbon goes up and over amazing hills. Then it starts to twist. Trucks are allowed to go only 20 miles per hour on much of it and there are pull outs where trucks must stop. Saw at least three runaway ramps, inclines where brakeless rigs can save their lives if they need to. There were flashing lights, arrow and limit signs on curves, guard rails and a simple warning: STAY ALERT.

What a wild ride! I shifted so often my right arm grew tired and there were some places that no gear was exactly the right one. I was either lugging the engine or too highly rev'd. Stopped to photograph a castle restaurant in Stoystown and totem poles at the Lamberts-ville turn off. Buckstown, Reels Corner, Wolfsburg, Breezewood and past the turn off for Graceville.

That last one got me to missing my little Gracie far too much and I stopped in Chambersburg to call my daughter-the-attorney who had been left in charge of my "normal" life. Kelly had, thankfully, volunteered to sort the formidable amount of mail that arrived at my front door and passed through the house to the recycling bins in the back alley. It was this pipeline of postal garbage that camouflaged my bills. Although I'd paid them in advance it was critical to my trek that Kelly bird dog my finances for me. It made the trip possible; without this kind of support my Internal Financial Director would never have permitted me to go. It was Kelly that had wired me the money in Illinois and Kelly who worked full time for federal court and Kelly who sloshed through my mail and Kelly who rode herd on The Warthog, my granddaughter, Gracie. Yes, together they are Grace/Kelly.

My daughter bought a colorful carpet, a map of the United States so that Gracie could follow my progress. As a result, Gracie was getting interested all sorts of maps. During my call, Kelly told me that

Gracie had bit a cookie all around and said "See, I made Australia!" At four and a half years old! That's my grandkid! What a sweet warthog.

Near Mount Union, Pennsylvania I turned left on State Road 233 and made a mental note of a motel. I might need that place, I told myself, since the youth hostel wasn't answering their phone and I didn't know if they would have room for me. I followed the directions carefully this time but was creating a Plan B in my mind as I drove up 223 which looked more like an Oregon logging road. Dense forest came right up to the edge of the road and private little cabins dotted the back woods. I read the funky wooden signs people put out for their cabin retreats: Jack's Frost, the Peterson's, Lost Weekend and Place With No Name.

I was about to give up trying to find Pine Grove Road when I saw "Pine Grove Grocery" and I turned to the right. Seno stalled. I started him but could *not* get him into reverse! After several minutes I gave up, wiggled the stick into first gear and pulled forward and there was a building with the youth hostel flags flying from it! The roadster knew where the Pennsylvania AYH was all the time! (Note: The roadster had never refused to get into reverse before and did not refuse after this incident.)

I drove around to the front, parked, went in, rang the cow bell and guess what? I'd be staying at the Ironmaster's Mansion, a 12,000 square foot historic home built in 1826 and now an Allegheny Mountain youth hostel!

One of my goals for myself was to be able to carry in one hand everything I needed for an overnight stay somewhere, anywhere. I wanted to become like one of those Australian travelers who can be away from home for an entire year and live quite nicely out of a pack no bigger than a bowling ball. Perhaps in another life. With cameras, both still and video, motorcycle helmet, essential gloves, security devices and maps, I could leave all my so-called toiletries and all my clothes in the car and still have to haul gear. Because the cockpit part of the roadster was unlockable, I couldn't leave anything there that I couldn't replace. And nightly I had the end-of-the-day task of zipping/snapping the tonneau cover and then wrapping Seno in his cover, slinging a bungee cord under the car and hooking it to the other side of the cover. I developed an efficient system of rolling and folding the large cover so that I could make short work of this effort in the evening, never having to turn it or wonder which end was which. Slowly the car was teaching me how to travel with it.

I was anxious to get my bed secured so I could explore the mansion and its history. I had a room with six beds all to myself (just on the other side of a brick wall from Seno's front fenders) but the rest of the building was bustling with a group just back from "caving." They were the Venture Crew #13 from Bridgeton, New Jersey and had as many adults as teenagers. The whole place was rocking with laughter and running, people exhausted and happy. Seno's arrival in the parking lot got me an invitation to join this group for spaghetti dinner, a group project in the hostel's big kitchen. I loved being able to say "yes" to Shirley Sever and her bright-eyed crew.

At long rows of tables we discussed everything from the terrorist attacks to tourist traps. When I told them that one of my goals was to go from Pacific City (Oregon) to Atlantic City (New Jersey), I got a flood of advice about their home state. I hadn't intended to go to the southern extreme and see Cape May but they would not hear of such a remiss. And they were well acquainted with the Ironmaster's Mansion because it was an economic jewel for their various adventures.

I learned that the Appalachian Trail was literally right outside the east door of the hostel. Called the "AT" by those who hike it, care for it and love it, you'd think they were discussing a living, breathing thing when you hear people talk about the Trail. It is a continuous footpath that covers 2,160 miles from Maine to Georgia. Some of it was a good walk and some of it was a strenuous climb. Most people hiked it in sections, taking weeks of vacation each year. Any way you did it, hiking the entire trail was a major accomplishment. Just listening to what was involved, I felt like Slug Bait.

Over 150 years ago, the Ironmaster's Mansion was owned by a family who participated in the Underground Railroad. Neither underground nor a railroad, it was a system of sympathizers who moved slaves running from the south to safety in the north. This stop in Pennsylvania, just north of Gettysburg, had been an important link evidently. The high ceilings, wide baseboards and trim, steep but graceful stairway was all the evidence from the interior of an older time. It seemed a perfectly designed building for a hostel. There was a baby grand piano in the large entry room and a wall-sized open hearth. All the floors were bare wood. It was large and functional and hopefully water tight. The wind had whipped up a thunderstorm. I think everyone in the house was too tired to care.

When I went into the communal bathroom I hardly recognized the face in the mirror. My skin was red and dry and wrinkled.

Appearance was obviously not this person's top priority. I rather liked that.

My dorm room was very cool--no, I mean it was cool like being in a meat locker. I didn't undress for bed and added blankets from the other beds to my own. When that wasn't enough I put on my parka and dug under the stack of heavy wool blankets. With the roadster not visible even from the lonely forest highway, I relaxed and slept.

Journal Entry: April 27

Another one of those "who-wuda-thunk-it" moments that are becoming typical of the hosteling experience. I told this band of adventurers from Bridgeton, New Jersey that I knew only one person from their state. And I wasn't sure I was going to be able to see John because he has been wrestling with a medical problem involving his thyroid and the scary "C" word has been bandied about. So here I was in Pennsylvania with a small group of eastern folk and we discover that two of them have had John as an instructor at Cumberland Community College! It was enough to make you think that the census people have it all wrong--there are really only a couple of hundred Americans max!

I met John traveling in England and frequently people have a travel persona much different than their professions. John was puns and parodies and mischief and a terrific entertainment. We all agreed to that but Becky added that he was tough and really "got you prepared for university." I was a bit relieved that the one person I brought up in the conversation was not a jerk.

*I'm very grateful to have this group not only prepare dinner but carry most of the load of talking because I am too tired. Like Niles said of Maris (*Frazier*), "She tires easily under the pressure to be interesting."*

27

The New Jersey contingent had coffee for me made from bottled water and fresh ground beans. It smelled so good I wanted to dab it on my wrists. I was ready to follow them anywhere because everything seemed to go easier for me with them around. Shirley and I talked about the challenge of travel packing in small spaces. She told me about a bike trip she and her husband took when they ran into a wine tasting/sale. She said, "I took my stuff out of my bike pack, put it in my husband's gear and then loaded my bike up with blackberry wine." It occurred to me at that moment what men were really for: they're purses. We women load their pockets with lipstick, their brief cases with feminine products, their packs with our extra shorts and their trucks with dolls and furniture and lawn ornaments. At last! That mystery solved. Men really *are* excess baggage--just waiting to be filled with treasures and hauled away!

The rain dripped, splopped and splashed outside on the long porch. Under ordinary circumstances this would have been the time when I pulled over and happily read a murder mystery and waited for a weather change. That was the fantasy. It never happened.

The Ironmaster's Mansion would have been that idyllic setting for the rest of the day but, like many hostels, it closed from 9:30 a.m. till 5 p.m. That meant everybody had to leave the building. The adventurers were scrambling, packs appearing at the door. Despite the rain, they wanted their pictures taken with Seno and they anxiously awaited my uncovering the car.

The car cover was soaked and sagging to the ground. I rolled it and strapped it and stuffed it in the leg space of the passenger side. The good news was that wet, it took up less space. I put on my snazzy purple rain pants that matched the car, put on all my coats, put on a red rain poncho on top of all of it. With the helmet to complete the ensemble I looked like a gay hazardous material handler.

I photographed the New Jersey group as they stood in the rain around the dripping car. Shirley gave me her card and they all wished me luck (as everybody does while shaking their heads). I waved a mitten, lowered my face shield and climbed the hill northbound from the safe, dry hostel.

The next six hours were driving hell as I had my first submersion baptism in the roadster. I got tangled up in the confusing forest maze of roads trying to find my way back to something resembling a highway. My only navigator was my memory and I thought I had the map and my route numbers thoroughly memorized. When I was confronted with a 174 sign, it wasn't on my truckers' atlas and I had to go to my Pennsylvania official highway map to find it. I figured out what to do next as the rain soaked the map.

Passed old farms, mail boxes, gravel driveways. It was Sunday morning and few people were out. The wind buffeted the roadster.

It was pouring rain and collected on the clear oval serving dish that was Seno's windshield. Blobs of water arranged themselves on *both sides* of this piece of glass. Unfortunately the same thing happened on the face mask of my helmet. Now I had three layers of water blobs.

To keep the helmet from fogging at these lower speeds, I cracked the face shield a tad. With enough rain and wind, water dots were flipped on the inside surface as well. This made for four layers of water blobs.

Eventually raindrops made it to my glasses and began to collect there. Now that's five layers of water blobs.

I know that the human brain can still function on very limited visual information but this was getting a bit much. I learned that I could eliminate the water from the face shield by leaning my head to the right and taking the full brunt of any wind. The rain would at least run off the curved clear plastic of the helmet.

I considered unscrewing the windshield and pushing it forward, out of the way. That would have eliminated two layers of dots. But it was called a windshield for a reason, I figured, so I muscled on.

Gripping the wet wooden steering wheel was actually easier barehanded. The big waterproof mitts made my hand muscles work harder. I found Highway 74 and finally 94 and elected to take the four lane Highway 15 rather than risk the curves and hills to Seno's soaked brakes. I skidded once while trying to stop, steering right while we kept heading left. I didn't need to experience that again so I took it slow, pulling over whenever I had a native on my tail.

I saw the familiar red of Texaco through the thick grey rain and I think Seno pulled over without my asking him to. He had accepted the cheap gas at a Brand X station the day before and I don't think he liked it; he seemed to long for familiar food.

Stress, cold and coffee were collecting in my lower regions and I bolted for the station's cafe ladies room. That was when I discovered that my snazzy purple over pants were not waterproof, despite my testing them on an Oregon hike. My jeans, my tights and my not-tonight cotton briefs were all as wet as dish rags. Getting out of a wet bathing suit was difficult; this was impossible. My zen-like composure, at this moment, took a flyer as I panicked, struggling under the weight of three jackets, my down parka and the wet poncho. Water was flipping everywhere in the stall and I was hopping around as if stung by a bee.

I really couldn't tell if I was totally successful when my backside hit the toilet seat with relief. At this point I was panting, shaking with cold and about to cry. Being lost on forest roads hadn't added to my confidence either. The rain was socked in from horizon to horizon and I wasn't entirely sure where this Texaco station was on the map.

"Man's inability to stay quietly in his room is the cause of his unhappiness," wrote Blaise Pascal.

Even my Internal Critic took pity on me and did not point out the impracticality of my topless adventure. Instead, my Internal Pollyanna noted that I was indeed inside of a dry building and I was beginning to thaw. Seated like a top heavy Buddha, I began to peel the layers off and drape jackets on the stall walls.

What was so horrible about my office that I would subject myself to this rather than stay home?

It took awhile but I finally warmed, pieced myself back together and entered the cafe. Everybody looked and everybody pretended not to see. I must have appeared sort of crazed and if anybody had seen the car, they weren't the least bit interested in asking the driver any questions. Two eggs were $1.25 and I made mine disappear quickly, left two grateful dollars and sloshed out, dripping little puddles as I exited.

My beloved Lincoln Highway was the next off ramp and I was once again on it and eastbound. Just a little rest and I was what? right as rain?

Now the rain pelted my helmet so hard that I suspected it was turning to hail.

I noticed pentagrams on Pennsylvania barns and signs that read "America Bless God" instead of the other way around. The smells were strong. A sudden rush of floral but there were no flowers around, the reassuring smell of very wet freshly tilled acres of dirt, then suddenly a belt of fertilizer and cow pastures. Whew!

I passed up opportunities to see Amsterdam, Donegal, Berlin, New Oxford, Derry, New Paris, St. Thomas, Scotland, Nashville and even Paradise...and I hadn't left Pennsylvania!

Outside of York the rain began to lift and my spirits with it. I was almost back to my old self when I flew by a donut. I had to go back. I wheeled around the parking lot of a little group of businesses and pulled along side an upright chocolate sprinkled donut as tall as the roadster. It had a rural mail box stuck in it that opened on the street side. While I was photographing this funky donut a couple arrived in a red car with their sun roof open. They asked about Seno, I asked about the donut. Turns out that a friend of hers built the thing 15 years ago and it was made of fiberglass. I said, "So's the car!"

I went to the historic town of Lititz where I had earned my certificate for learning to twist pretzels several years ago. The certificate from the Sturgis Pretzel Factory hung in my office next to the Who's Who in American Colleges award. But, being Sunday, the pretzel place was closed and so was the American Candy Museum. I treated myself to the large bathroom at the Subway shop and stood naked until my skin dried. I blew my undies on the hand blower. Getting back into my semi-wet clothes wasn't as awful as I thought it would be and the experience of no vibration for awhile was reviving me.

Outside in the street Seno was drawing people leaving churches and enjoying an after-rain walk. I met a handsome bald guy with a silver feather earring and two young boys. Caleb, David and Steven said they liked my car and I told them I liked their town. There was an historic train station park nearby complete with three kids fishing in a too perfect stream and a lady walking a straining back and white dog. Everywhere I looked was a picture post card in Lititz. The town had been around since 1756 and a lot of the buildings looked every minute of 250 years old. Before Mickey Rooney popped out of somewhere and began to sing, I left.

Lancaster, Pennsylvania was where the Amish met the outlet stores. Handmade quilts were sold next to the Gap and Samsonite. There was a string of Texas food joints, big fat hotels and an amusement park that featured a castle and a dinosaur posing as a mountain dragon. The water slide was closed but the Amish buggy rides were going strong. Horse-drawn black-wheeled carriages with orange triangles on the back tootled around amongst the SUVs and family vans. One store doing a brisk business had a plastic sign reading: "Amish Stuff." This town was a dizzying array of contrasts. Does anyone besides me see the irony in "See our dramatic 3-screen feature 'Who Are the Amish?'"

I found the Railroad Museum of Pennsylvania in Strasburg (just follow the tracks) and their Sunday parking lot was full. Every kid from Philly with a divorced parent was there buying wooden train whistles and waiting to get on a real steam train. "Miss the train and you'll miss Lancaster County," the brochure read. Thomas, the blue train with the grey face, the same Thomas belting ear-piercing squeals in Dearborn, was scheduled soon. (www.phmc.state.pa.us)

The sky was opening up now and real sunshine was warming and drying the roads. I motored on to the Red Caboose Motel and Restaurant. Not content to have a funky caboose as a natural billboard or even as a diner, this guy bid on a collection of old cabooses after being dared to do so by a friend. (Oh, let's hear it for testosterone!) Imagine his surprise when the railroad called him six months later and said, "You've got until this afternoon to move these 19 cabooses." Donald Denlinger, with more naiveté than seems possible, adopted the dirty, window-broken, rusty, kerosene-soaked hulks--all 950,000 pounds of them. The call came in January in the middle of a snowstorm. Picture Donald as he turns to his wife Lois (who was probably enjoying a cup of tea or her favorite soap opera) and says, "Honey, you won't believe this but I..."

Journal Entry: April 28

There must be more than 30 brightly colored cabooses lined up in a horseshoe pattern outside and Seno is parked next to N-9, mine at least for the night. I am surrounded by wet clothes hung in the shower, on lamp shades and on chair backs. Tomorrow may be a repeat of this morning's BATH ON WHEELS. Outside my caboose's door is a huge coupling mechanism and the caboose's platform, sort of a miniature porch. The excursion train from the museum screamed by all afternoon making its historic steam noises. It's ten o'clock now and I'm nestled in my laundry room caboose and things are dark and quiet. A few minutes ago a horse clip-clopped in the roadway just a few feet from my window. I peeked out and saw the dark outline of an Amish carriage with a tiny yellow light swinging merrily as it went. This is amazing! As much as I rely on the internal combustion engine, it is most agreeable to have a night without the sound of one. Here I am in a caboose in Pennsylvania with the soundtrack from 100 years ago. Is this a great life or what?

A classic sign on the Lincoln Highway: DAVE'S HUB CAP CITY AND ESCAPE REALITY, MASSAGE, TANNING, BODY WRAPS AND WAXING. What gets waxed here? Me or my car? And are we talking car bodies or people bodies? Would I *want* a massage from someone with over 100,000 hub caps and wants to escape reality as a result?

The wind was blowing the cotton ball clouds around but it was much more conducive to roadster travel than the day before. The clouds were threatening but not following through.

In another pass through Strasburg it seemed like everyone, religious or not, was trying to sell something. After several days of passing thrift stores, garage sales, flea markets and church rummage sales, I was clearly suffering from retail withdrawal. Sometimes I actually whimpered out loud when I passed a particularly large Salvation Army store or worse yet, an estate sale. Without Howard and his ugly truck, I couldn't buy anything! I had wanted to break myself of this compulsion but I didn't realize how painful it was going to be. My Internal Healthy Person told me about how much more time I would have now for truly educational pursuits like county museums. I told this person to get stuffed. I wanted to buy Amish bonnets, little wooden lawn bunnies and jackets made of quilts. My Internal Space Director (the one who said things like, "Don't bring another *thing* into this house!') and my Internal Financial Director were performing gleeful square dance maneuvers in my head. I slowed up to look at a farmyard full of wooden hex signs for sale. Surely my property should have its own hex sign. If there were things to be hexed in Pennsylvania, of course there must be things to be hexed in Oregon. How had I lived this long without my own hex sign? But Seno didn't stop and part of me wailed like a banshee.

I got along well with the rest of rural Pennsylvania, amusing a small town postmaster by parking the roadster outside his door and mailing a stack of postcards. Part of the reason to travel was to gloat and send messages back home to those still chained to their desks or shops. Post cards are like miniature versions of smarmy Christmas letters. Which prompted me to buy a rubber stamp that reads: "Spare me the details of your disgustingly wonderful life." No one, in the history of the world, has ever mailed home a post card from Europe saying, "It smells funny here, the people are grouchy, they won't give me what I want, they won't speak English, the weather sucks and I want to come home." No, you paid a lot for that

European vacation and by golly, gloating privileges come with every transatlantic air fare. And I hadn't come 3,000 miles across the United States to write home and tell everybody that I had to dry off in a Subway sandwich shop restroom.

I steeled myself against the inevitability of another big city, Wilmington, Delaware. My navigating was dead on but I was unprepared for the freaky bridge across the Delaware River. It was high, well-humped and trucks hemmed me in going 70 miles per hour. The bridge curves to the right so I could see its uplifting assault on the sky, points jabbing the clouds. We all hit the metal grating and Seno's tires shimmied. I began to chant, "Hare Krishna, Hare Krishna, Krishna Krishna, Hare Hare..." The bridge felt like it was redefining the curvature of the earth and that soon I'd leave its gravitational pull. The wind, probably the jet stream, blew the little roadster into the lane of trucks. "Hare Rama, Hare Rama, Rama Rama..." I gripped the steering wheel so hard that my hands turned white from the knuckles to my elbows. For the first time on the trip I really, *really* wanted to be somewhere else. Once on the other side I had the additional challenge of the correct exit which I found thanks to the advice of the New Jersey-ites from the youth hostel. "Take the last exit before the toll" they warned or I would be lost forever, like Charlie on the MTA.

Seno racked up states number 13 and 14 in a matter of minutes.

There was no rain but it stayed overcast and I zipped along Highway 40 again, my old friend from Ohio. Turned south on Highway 55 and was blown left and right for miles. My shoulders and hands ached as I traded hands back and forth to relieve the strain.

Saw a sign for "Bohemian Collision." What do you suppose that was? Poets who violently disagree with each other? I think perhaps it was a car repair place but "bohemian"? Does that mean they use unconventional methods to fix your car dents?

I also passed a stack of huge tires arranged like a kid's toy, large stacked to small, a tower of rubber, a monument to the God of Rubber. People here appeared to like lawn ornaments because I saw several roadside stores with inventory all set out front--wooden people, concrete angels, glass balls, bird houses, wicker arches. The funniest one was a group of wooden lighthouses, all sizes, clumped together like a family reunion; they were fenced in with chain link fencing as if they might try to escape.

I missed the turn off for Vineland and accidentally got the right one for Cumberland Community College. I drove to the campus like I did that every day. Asked a student where the English department was and he said "right there" pointing to the closest building. I parked, wandered in, prowled the halls, found "J. Adair" on an office door with his schedule posted next to it. For that day he was at F8.

I asked a school secretary for the location of F8 and she looked reluctant, reaching for the phone to call security. I still had my motorcycle helmet on and my three layers of coats and my eyes had become permanently blood shot. I promised not to disturb his class and she glowered at me, "See that you don't."

I waited nervously until students filed out of the classroom and John appeared, thinner and serious in crisp white shirt and tie. He, of course, didn't recognize me and I walked along next to him while a student chatted.

John had spent a lifetime creating the persona of a curmudgeon. What a failure! I enjoyed him so much when we met at Oxford and wanted to tell him so and also relay the compliment from the student I met at the youth hostel. John couldn't accept a compliment if it meant world peace. When he was named Professor Of The Year, he posed with his head in a toilet seat and called it the POTY award.

He reluctantly posed in the drivers seat of the roadster but said later he was spotted by a student and asked, "Who was that?" He had replied, "That was my twin sister who stopped by because she's off her medication." John was understandably distracted with his medical situation. I felt like Belushi in *Animal House* trying to raise Flounder's spirits by crushing beer cans on my forehead. Unfortunately I also looked like Belushi and the last thing John needed was a visit from some nut case on his campus. He had a black belt in wordsmanship, was a master punner and was obviously a respected teacher. Just don't tell him.

John's immediate dream was to a) resolve his heath crisis and b) take a course at Cambridge in England. What can you say to a person whose life was being held for ransom by "tests" and the medical profession? I left dissatisfied with my ability to connect with the John I'd shared so many laughs with just nine months ago.

What was supposed to be only 50 miles to the Jersey coast seemed to take forever. It never rained but it didn't clear either. The wind kicked up and would move the car sideways. It required mental concentration and just plain muscle to keep Seno in one lane or the other. Eventually my right foot started to cramp horribly. I tried straightening it and using my left foot on the accelerator pedal. My left foot seemed to weigh more so I could only use this maneuver as a last resort and then just for a few minutes. My eyes were dry from the rushing air and I tried alternating closing them but I was losing depth perception with this idea. I had to just let them burn. I was getting very tired.

When we arrived at the edge of the Atlantic I was too sore and too exhausted to be excited or even relieved. I looked at the stormy sea and I looked at Seno. I could only manage a little, "Well, we did it."

To the beach towns it was still winter. Most motels and inns said "no vacancies." "Closed" would have been more accurate. I had an address of a place to stay on Maple Street, I found it and if I had been alone with a normal car, I might have risked it. But the layout and parking on the street...I don't know...it just didn't feel quite like the place to leave a roadster overnight. Trash cans banged like thunder and paper swirled in the streets. The collection of beach-tacky buildings was precisely what Oregon did not want for their shoreline and why the entire Oregon coast belonged to the people, not private enterprise. A hurricane could do some improvement to sections of New Jersey's coast line. This one town was like an old lounge singer with make up cracking at the wrinkles and a voice like Selma Diamond from 40 years of smoking.

The wind surged in great puffs. It seemed to come from different directions. When I took my helmet off, I had to face the wind to get it back on because it blew my hair like a manic hair dryer.

One beach town was more like a ghost town with all the buildings still there but no lights on. Few vehicles and even fewer people were out braving the cold wind. At one intersection a huge 600 pound stoplight swung and twisted over my head dancing in the wind. What a dent it would have put in Seno--or my head! I took the hostelers' advice and headed south for Cape May and the promised Victorian-style atmosphere.

I seemed to be lost, went over a toll bridge, left at a light, I was all over the place and finally came up Trenton Avenue and telling myself, I had to stop soon and eat. The next place, that was it.

Never did find a place. But what I did find was the elegant Peter Shields Inn, one of the finest examples of Georgian Revival architecture in the United States. The 1907 mansion had one of Cape May's gourmet restaurants but it also had what I really wanted: off-street parking for my little car.

The check-in lady tried not to say, "Who let the riff raff in?" when I stood before her asking about rates and vacancies. She was actually very gracious and told me I could look at a few rooms on the second and third floors and have my pick of those. I definitely couldn't afford anything as fine as the award winning inn with an unobstructed view of the sea but I hopped up the carpeted stairs to enjoy a look anyway. I was doing fine until I hit Room 6, a Victorian room done in burgundy. I'm sure I let out with an audible "ohhhhhhhh!" The roadster was parked for the day; that was *it*.

The place was dripping in good taste. I wanted these people to come and redo my 1910 house too. "Tea is at four," she explained as she ran stretchmarks through my Master Card. I was anxious to shed my road warrior look. I had 15 minutes to go from parka to perfume. I grabbed my room key and was out to Seno's bonnet like a shot, getting into my good stuff. An older couple with matching luggage was preparing to go in.

"It's a Morgan," he was telling his wife authoritatively as she admired my car. He wore a golf shirt from his club and she looked like she'd stepped from the pages of Neiman-Marcus. And these were their beach duds.

"What year is it exactly?" he asked, retired CEO in each of his tones. It wasn't a question so much as a demand for information.

"1927," I replied, respectfully.

"It's just darling," she said, as if we were discussing a hat. She was cute.

"Thank you," I said looking full-face at both of them.

Why didn't I straighten him out on the "Morgan" thing? I have sort of a policy that when a guy who thinks he knows it all comes around with his lady and starts spouting off information to impress her, I don't bother to correct him. He'll only take it out on her later over dinner because nobody likes to be wrong and have it pointed out. There was a price to be paid for the slam to his ego and she'd be the one to pay it. So as long as I liked *her*, I didn't correct *him*.

I secured the tonneau cover, figuring I'd save the car covering operation for later. Soon I was humming and wiggling around my room, swathing my face with make up and tossing my layers of quilted nylon and down. Um, what to wear? This was the east coast, wear black, they all just do black until someone invents a darker color. I slithered into my long black jersey dress that announced the fact that I was female instead of camouflaging it. I yanked the hair scrunchy from my ponytail and redid my long hair into a classy side do. Instead of walking like a male orangutan, I took the antique hand rail and side stepped, gliding one foot over the other down to the second floor and I was ready to take tea.

Several couples sat primly in parlor chairs holding saucers and tea cups. A coffee table supported a silver tray full of sweet things, red raspberry somethings and miniature scone hummers. I greeted everyone quietly and walked to the table to pour myself a cup of tea. Thin delicate cups were set out and a sterling silver tea pot with an ornate handle was polished to a fairthewell. I got the tea cup all right but when my right hand gripped the heavy silver tea pot, the thing shook like there was an earthquake. My driving hands couldn't handle the gentility of tea service. I got a little tea in the cup and had to concentrate on holding the thin saucer and sit down. After days of griping Seno's steering wheel, my hands seemed to be useless at doing much else. I didn't take cream with my tea because I knew my hands couldn't handle a spoon.

The others were in conversation so I didn't interrupt. No one acknowledged me and I concentrated on getting sweet sticky things to my mouth. This was definitely not a youth hostel. Finally the guy in the golf shirt asked one of the other couples if they had seen the purple roadster in the parking lot. They began discussing what a fine classic, vintage car it was, the older man explaining to the couple about my ride. The arrogance of the old guy was staggering. I looked directly at him and he at me. There was no recognition on his part. I took another bite of scone to keep from blowing my cover. His wife left to go prepare herself for dinner although she certainly looked like perfection to me.

How deliciously fun it was to hear someone discussing my car! It would have totally ruined the guy's day to tell him that he probably spent more on insurance and tires for his car than I had on my roadster. He knew less about cars than I knew about brain surgery.

When he began elaborating on just what it took to find, drive and maintain classic automobiles, I'd had my fill of the game. I leaned forward to set my cup on the coffee table and I smiled at the man. "Bugatti," I said in my sexiest Lauren Bacall imitation. "It's a Bugatti."

"It's *your* car?" the younger man asked.

"Um-hm," I purred and walked to the head of the stairs feeling my butt swing just slightly left and right. It would have taught me a lesson if I had tripped, fallen down the stairs and made a complete fool of myself but the gods in charge of nyah-nyah were working in my favor. I made an superb exit.

I picked up a spare jacket in Seno and walked across the deserted street to the tall beach grass. I found a stick and headed straight toward the waves. There was still plenty of sun but the chill wind kept everyone off the miles of perfect sand. Cape May had all the drama of the ocean but all the charm of acres of Victorian houses and shops. What a heady combination! The place next door was the Angel of the Sea, two grand pink landmarks built in 1850 that were named "Best Seaside Inn in the USA." If you want to stay there on the Fourth of July, you'll pay around $1,000 for a room. The pink Painted Ladies were sisters to the Peter Shields Inn, operated by the same folks. (www.angelofthesea.com and www.petershieldsinn.com)

When I got to the water's edge I looked back at the white Georgian mansion and located the window that was my room. I waved at the Alyce that would be there later in the evening. Then I did my ritual that I love to do when I am especially happy and feeling totally blessed. I took the stick and in large letters I wrote in the sand, "THANKS!" Thanks to Krishna or God or the Universe or Creative Intelligence or Quan Yin or Pale Hecate or Lady Luck or to myself. Someone needed to be thanked for this fabulous day, this fabulous moment. So, just thanks, a great big *THANKS!* written in the sand. I touched the writhing Atlantic sea water with a finger and then my lips. I had made it 3,200 miles. My thanks was only two and a half feet high; it could have been two and half miles high.

I wandered around the Peter Shields like I had wandered around the Ironmaster's Mansion. I noticed things like window hardware and floor vents because my own dear Craftsman-style house was always in need of a good role model. Lacey palms were on the veranda along with a life-sized zebra sculpture. The woodwork, the Venetian mirrors, the center stairway were all making me swoon. I loved this stuff. There can't be enough antimacassars, marble tops, brass beds, stained glass, flowered wallpaper, fainting couches or velvet pillows.

There was a gorgeous Gibson Girl painting in a fat gilded frame. I looked at her blue hat with the 12 inch plumes and I said to the picture, "Give me that hat."

What on earth was a delicate flower like myself doing on this cross country trek that had me reduced to eating canned tuna for breakfast and pumping my own gas?

They called it appetizers, I called it dinner. Cherry tomatoes, cut celery, baked wheat munchies, cashews, five different kinds of cheese, three different wines were served on the second floor parlor. There were more couples this time for the early evening do and the average age was a tad lower but the stock portfolios were probably just as high. Caution was afoot. Not too much would ever be exposed in settings like this. "Stop screwing around with people," I said to myself and the subject magically came around to cars. One of the men said that he'd give anything in the world for a 1940 Ford coupe. That really headed the conversation in my direction and I hauled out my baby pictures of my '40 Ford and had a fine old time with the guys talking about 283 small blocks and glass pack mufflers and four-barrel carburetors. Eventually the women got bored, wandered off and then came back to drag their husbands to dinner and left me with several bottles of wine ("it's open and you know it won't keep") and all the munchies. The guys asked when I planned to leave in the morning and I said I'd stay for the 8:30 a.m. breakfast and then I would take the cover off and they could have all the pictures they wanted of the roadster.

I absolutely wasn't leaving the Peter Shields Inn that evening. I paid for the luxury of the room and I was going to wallow in it, celebrating my arrival at the Atlantic Ocean. I sashayed up the stairs, wine glass in hand, stopping to admire the frames and the prints and the porcelain on the third floor landing. The place was a museum and we were all going to get to sleep in it! Was I the only one who knew what was involved in restoring and maintaining a massive house like this? Was I the only one who felt that staying here was an overwhelming privilege?

I was drunk on the antiques. The white wine probably helped. The heavy exhaustion of the drive from Strasburg enveloped me like a down comforter and my success tucked me in.

Roadster Lesson #8: Everybody loves old cars. Especially if they don't own one.

29

People were in the parking lot for Seno's unveiling the next morning. By now I knew the questions as well as most of the answers.

"1600 single port, 57 horsepower, 4 cylinder engine."

"75 miles per hour with a great tail wind. 100 miles an hour if it's dropped out an airplane."

"About 9,000 miles...hopefully. And two and a half months to do it."

"Regular gas. I don't know what kind of gas mileage it gets and I don't care. It weights about as much as a piano, so it can't be too bad."

"Pull over and park or wear rain gear. Look, folks, you won't melt in the rain unless you have flying monkeys as pets."

As I was wrestling with the car cover, folding and strapping, my key fob broke. A tall, sweet old duffer offered one of his. I was strangely reluctant until I saw his wad of jail house keys and collection of key rings and then gratefully accepted. He insisted that I take the small pocket knife attached to the ring. The Universe was providing for me instantly, perhaps my old luck was back. I was very much impressed with his simple generosity and he even put my keys onto the ring.

The clouds from the day before were long gone and nothing was left but crisp clear blue sky and intense blue ocean. I took an early morning drive down Beach Avenue until it dead ended with the famous Cape May lighthouse in the distance. I got Seno's inevitable portrait. The sun was already high in the sky at eight a.m.; it felt like 10 a.m. A guy on a sandy park bench watched me photograph the car.

"It doesn't get any better than this," he sighed.

Drove back along the my-house-is-more-Victorian-than-your-house drive, parked in front of the Peter Shields and looked up at my bedroom window. I had been awakened at two a.m. for what I didn't know until I looked out that same window. I don't think I had ever seen the full moon on the sea before. The whole world seemed to be made of sterling silver. There were no clouds, just clarity and moonlight. I folded my arms on the ledge of that window and rested my chin for a long, long look at the gentle Atlantic and the radiant light.

The cardiologist came out and I took his picture with the white mansion electrified by the eastern sun. We joined the group for breakfast of berry French toast, melon, warm tapioca and coffee and we all jabbered a bit more. The side conversations became a group conversation when I got them going. We'd turn this place into a jolly hostel yet. If you want to get someone from New Jersey to talk just ask them for a route suggestion. They won't shut up after that.

I had one more person to photograph with the car, a vacationing cop, and then I was off, up the Parkway to Atlantic City. Everything felt perfect and I was in a good mood doing about 55 miles an hour. A grey car appeared in the left lane as if to pass, but instead it just hung there awhile. Then it sped up just a bit and the passenger's right hand window went down. A little disposable camera appeared and then poof! a flash. A hand came out, waved and then the window went back up again. I waved back. I hope they got the shot they wanted. Kodak should hire me just to drive around in this purple roadster!

The guy at the toll booth was beside himself to see Seno. He would have kissed the car on the lips if there hadn't been 12 cars behind us.

At last, Atlantic City! Was I really going to make it?

I went straight into downtown and kept going straight through the towering hotels and casinos, straight until I literally had Seno's tires up on the ramp to the boardwalk. NO MOTORIZED VEHICLES ON BOARD WALK.

I parked the car, pulled myself out to videotape the moment and also to see what was up and down the famous boardwalk. Millions have seen it but I hadn't so it was new and exciting to me! A white cop car appeared and the uniformed police officer stopped. I asked him for directions to the Chamber of Commerce office. He said, "Probably City Hall and don't leave your car."

He didn't mean "don't leave your car there," (in that 10 minute zone) he meant *don't leave your car.* He slowly rolled away and instantly two creepy guys were at Seno's fender. "How much is it worth?" one asked. I hopped back in, chucked the video camera and fired it up. "Oh, not much," I said and hit the throttle.

All I got to see of the famous boardwalk was a few feet of what appeared to be decking.

I had a color brochure about Pacific City, Oregon and a stack of Cape Kiwanda post cards and my mission had been to deliver them to the Chamber of Commerce in Atlantic City, New Jersey.

They had less space here than Las Vegas so everything was jammed together like too many rolled socks in a drawer. Ceasar's Palace went up instead of out like its desert sister. Trump appeared to have won the Gaudiest Developer of the Decade award hands down. I found the municipal building but more importantly I found Vincent Brown in the parking lot who showed me where the Chamber of Commerce offices really were. He was jiving me there in the parking lot when I took his picture, the only shot I took in Atlantic City that day.

The Parking Gods were unbelievably benevolent and I found a parking spot on one of Atlantic City's busiest streets right in front of the Chamber offices. I met Alice with the cutest head of blond curls since Shirley Temple. I said, "I just drove from Oregon in a topless roadster." She came out, did not contain her astonishment and called the newspaper.

Before I handed it over, I stared at the cover of the little Pacific City brochure. The contrast was numbing. I was looking at the antithesis of Atlantic City. If you left your car in Pacific City, the waves might take it out to sea. If you left your car in Atlantic City, it'd be taken out, see? The amount of concrete in Pacific City could probably fit in a bucket, I don't remember seeing a sidewalk. The amount of concrete in Atlantic City could probably pave over all of Iowa.

Some Oregonians felt that even walking in the woods was environmental terrorism. Their approach to forest management was "don't touch it...*EVER!*" Spotted owls had become the little demigods of the Pacific Northwest and loggers had become the endangered species. I had a more Rodney King view on these issues; couldn't we all just get along together? I donated to conservation causes and wrestled with voting issues over the environment. I tried to be a responsible Oregonian. I was not quite so militant on these issues and if someone described a place as "commercial" or a "tourist trap" then that's right where I wanted to go. What interesting little tschotske might be there that I absolutely couldn't do without? To some, Atlantic City was an abomination. To me it was something to explore and I wasn't going to be able to do that because I could not leave Seno's side. Another police cruiser cautioned, "Stay with the car or lose the car."

My idea of gambling was writing two pages on my computer without hitting the save button, so I wasn't horribly disappointed that I couldn't leave any money here.

The sun was warming things up, I was down to one jacket and getting thirsty. Ben Fogletto, news photographer for Atlantic City's *The Press* had me pose wearing my leather flying hat and hugging the car.

After that the only thing left that I could do in Atlantic City was "cruise the gut." I drove down Atlantic Avenue with my video camera on automatic and just pulled it out and pressed the red button. Stopped at an intersection, two shopkeepers came out to the sidewalk pointing and I aimed the camera at them and they went wild.

A city bus, big tall thing, pulled up to my right and the driver, way up there said, "How fast will it go?"

"Want to drag?" I asked, fully eight feet below him.

"Sure," he grinned.

Atlantic City's blocks are fairly short so it was a quick and uneventful race and I took my victory humbly, exchanging "thumbs up" with the bus driver. I doubled back at the Tropicana and started up Pacific Avenue to complete my tour. Workers, pedestrians, people cruising, everybody was in a party mood so Seno got lots of attention. At one stoplight, a man was standing on the corner with a cell phone to his ear and I actually heard him say, "Forget about it." Yeah, *that* fo-geta-abou-tit. Hah! My New Jersey experience was just about complete!

I found Highway 30 easily enough and got away from the din. In New Jersey they pump the gas for you just like they do in Oregon--much more civilized. I pulled into a station and thought I'd arrived at the set of the old Jack Benny show. Two fellows were actually dressed in clean Texaco uniforms with ties and hats! What an impression! And they were the only ones on the entire trip who knew exactly the secret of where Seno's gas tank was located.

I spent hours crossing New Jersey farm country in my attempt to avoid Newark and the tangle of highways that showed on the map. I came to Hammonton, the Blueberry Capital of the World and turned onto Highway 206.

One of the Peter Shields guests had told me, "Trenton is the only state capitol that doesn't have hotels or motels." Why? "That's because nobody wants to stay there."

I don't know if that's true but I never saw one. What I did see was squalor. And loads of people sloshing through it, noise, debris, traffic, kids. How sheltered I was from all this. This wasn't Bangladesh, this was America. I was sure that I was lost and dead about 140 times trying to stay on the path of Highway 206. Some of the stoplights were 300 years long. "Roll up your windows and lock your doors." Well, I had no windows and no doors. I had only the element of surprise. Who on earth would drive that car *here?*

Almost as instantly as the slum appeared, it disappeared. Just like in Chicago. As if a magic wand had been waved. If I hadn't been sitting in a pool of my own nervous sweat, I would have doubted what I had just seen. Now all was green and orderly. What caused this phenomenon? What was the explanation for this? I was baffled. Next thing you knew I was in Princeton the township, then Princeton the boro. What's the difference?

Here there's landscaping, no litter, few people and cars that lack dents and rattles. Even the garbage truck was quiet. What on earth was going on here?

Clouds had covered the blue but it had looked like this before. I stopped and called my friend Irving in New York to tell him that I was on my way. When it started to sprinkle, I pulled into another gas station and put on my rain gear. Barely made it back to the car before the rain started. No biggie, I thought. I've plowed through rain before in Pennsylvania.

This was different. Slower traffic, and the rain wasn't running off of my windshield and helmet. My seat began to feel wet. A construct-ion zone slowed traffic to a stop and thick patches of mud lay on the asphalt. Soon it was like sitting in a shower. A sheriff's car in front of me stopped short and I did too, skidding in the mud. Then the lightning started. But Seno was fiberglass, nothing to worry about. The traffic was thick and slow and eventually it was so dark and raining so hard I couldn't see past the car in front of me. I could barely make out a small yellow and red Motel 8 sign and I ended the lunacy of trying to progress any further. This game was officially called because of rain. I don't think I could have gone another mile. I spent the night once again surrounded by drying clothes but I thoroughly enjoyed watching the first television I'd seen in weeks. I called Irving and reported my surrender to the elements.

Journal Entry: April 30

Very tired. Sure doesn't feel like I got very far today. Going back to Cape May is a must, I think. Many tours and Victorian events. Whatever it is there sets off a vibration on a string of my heart-harp.

I'd like to go back to Atlantic City but I'd have to either: a) drive a junker I wanted to lose or b) take a bus in.

Observation: Some New Jersey politician must be in bed with the manufacturer of stoplights. They proliferate here. You'll be tootling along at 50 miles per hour and there's a bloody stoplight with nothing and no one else there. They seem to have more stoplights than anywhere else!

30

I wasn't even sure where Somerville, New Jersey was but that was where we spent the night. My next piece of the mosaic was to get me and Seno from this Motel 8 to Chestnut Ridge, New York and Irving's house. I knew that if I wasn't on the road by six a.m. I'd have to wait. I also knew I needed a rest, roadster miles being twice the length of regular miles. So I took my time, enjoyed the Soap Opera called the morning news and found the freeway entrance about nine o'clock, hoping traffic would lighten up.

Fat chance. Things didn't ever lighten up on the East Coast. I was surprised they didn't all vaporize in their own stress! When they were not having it, they were giving it.

It was nerve wracking, high speed, heavy traffic, lots of trucks. There was a jammed two lane exit for New York City and this poor van in front of me wanted into the exit lane. He kept driving slower and slower until we were both stopped. The lane to the left of us was thick, fast and unrelenting. Finally the van just inched over. Nobody was willing to make room. He must have had a very important reason for wanting to go where he was going, I thought. I would have given up, changed my route, my phone number and my name and just forgotten about it.

I exited at 14A, nerves jangling but done with New Jersey. I parked Seno in a small lot next to a bagel shop. I was reading my map when an older fellow pulled in next to me and asked if he could help. I told him I needed El Dorado Street and he offered to lead me there. He was a guy with a bagel in his hand, how much of a psycho could he be? I glanced at the map and knew the general direction but I followed this guy in his car. Pretty soon he pointed to the right and waved and left. I was where I needed to be, personally escorted by someone more than making up for the selfishness of Interstate 287. I parked in front of Irving's house and called him on my cell phone.

Irving was having breakfast on his deck and reading his *New York Times*. He was flabbergasted to get my call even though we'd been in contact for weeks. He came across his lawn to meet me. He was amazing! He looked like Cary Grant and sounded like Tony Curtis. His wife Christina also bounded out the front door. She was up front, beautiful and you just knew she was creative by looking at her.

They both marveled at the car, shaking their heads. "How did you ever do it?" And I felt like I was just getting my journey started. Christina had me posing in a knitted cowl in the roadster, a photo for her upcoming sequel to *Knitting in the Fast Lane*, before she left for work.

I barely had my land legs when Irv suggested that we go have lunch downtown. I thought he meant downtown Chestnut Ridge. I hopped in his car and if the ride didn't keep me riveted, his stories about his midlife crises of a few decades ago did. Irving grew up in The Bronx, thus the Tony Curtis impersonation and he had been a bicycle messenger in Manhattan. There could be no greater luck than having an experienced former messenger boy as your tour leader for downtown New York! And much to my surprise and complete delight, that was where we were headed! I'd been to the Big Apple before but this was just so unexpected. There I was petting Chris and Irv's cats and the next moment I was standing outside the Demarchelier on East 86th Street with my hand on the door just about ready to pull it open. I stopped.

"I expect to see Woody Allen at any minute," I said.

Irving looked stunned, like I'd hit him with a cattle prod. He said, "I was eating here by myself one day when I saw Woody Allen!" After that, Irving was convinced I was psychic. The place just looked like the set of a Woody Allen picture.

Vegetables. I needed veggies, greens, anything that didn't seem dead. My food plan had been shot for weeks gyrating wildly between the low carb, the low calorie and the I-have-only-one-life-to-live diet. I'm sure my stomach was getting food and saying, "What am I supposed to do with *this*? Oh, sure, the hips, now there's a place. No, the thighs. Even better. What *is* this strange food? Has she lost her mind?"

It was a great lunch and we finished with a cappuccino. We had to. The last day of our Oxford course, Irving and I had treated ourselves to cappuccino at the Grand Cafe on High Street. Here we were, only a few months and thousands of miles later. I photographed the table where he had seen Woody Allen. Irv said that he almost didn't recognize him because he wasn't wearing his signature glasses. Despite Mr. Allen's rather horrendous personal life, I separated that from his wonderful movies. *Zelig* was a course in neuro-linguistic programming. I think there are two different kinds of people in the world: those who like Woody Allen movies and those who don't.

We walked to Central Park, down a path and up to a mini-mountain of rock. It was a perfect ten day by anybody's standards. People were tossing balls and Frisbees, walking every variety of dog, skating zigzags between tottering oldsters, pushing prams, giving advice to each other. I perched on the rock with my Cary Grant look alike friend and enjoyed the sun and the show. I had no idea I was going to be in Central Park. I could not bring my roadster into the City. "It would cause a riot," Irving said. So even if I had the guts to do it, the scene would have screwed up Manhattan and not in a good way.

It seemed so odd to just pop downtown for awhile and see the Metropolitan Museum of Art. The sculpture in the Rooftop Garden was new to Irving too. (You always hope the natives aren't bored out of their skulls showing you things.) I don't think Irv gets bored. There was a big red trowel, a safety pin with a blue head, a waving handkerchief and slices of blueberry pie. (Why not peach?) These sculptures were huge and the works of Oldenburg and van Bruggen. The garden trowel was perhaps 24 feet high and the view from the top of the Museum, on this day, was a jewel. So near closing Irving and I had time for only one exhibit and we both chose the surrealism display with Dali plastic lobster telephone and nightmare-like art, a man and woman with clouds in their heads, a dramatic Greta Garbo image.

The next day our adventure wasn't nearly as dramatic. I needed to get my rain problem solved and Irv needed a travel vest because he, like John, was going back to Europe for more course work. I could sigh with envy but my travel was wrapped up with the roadster and if I couldn't drive to it, I wasn't going this year.

So I was in this sporting goods store and I was trying on caution yellow rubber bib overalls. What am I *doing*? I thought. Is this the fashion accessory I think I should have? Where was the person who liked to dress in glitz and lace? Was she gone forever? I had been reduced to yellow rubber!

"I feel like an idiot," I said to Irving.

"You'll be a dry idiot," he pointed out.

I was also a person who didn't like sitting in wet jeans. This had better work. I selected a large size to fit over my big feet and the extra wide straps should help seal me in like a ziplock bag. I looked like I was ready for an Alaskan fishing boat. I hoped that after this trip I wouldn't have need for these awful pants. I hoped I'd settle down and not create any more adventures for myself that would cause me to wear these things again. Had anyone ever worn a pair out? I think a construction worker could be run over by a D-9 Cat and they'd peel the yellow pants off like a banana and give them to somebody else to wear.

So for $24.99 perhaps the rain problem was solved. As long as the traffic wasn't too fast or too heavy or the road too oily or too muddy and the visibility was still good, the sun still up, I could drive in the rain with my Super Pampers.

For two days I questioned Irving about the Tappan Zee bridge which had me in an anxious state. Between the intensity of I-287 and the horror of the Delaware bridge, I was most reluctant to even imagine what the bridge across the Hudson River to Connecticut was going to be like. I was very scared. Irv and Chis said that I should hold back until after ten a.m. and then attempt it.

I wanted to be in Arkansas by Memorial Day, away from all heavily touristed areas and it was already May 2. I had such a distance to cover. I poured over my maps every morning and decided and redecided the various routes. Mileage charts didn't apply to Seno. I was learning that one good down pour and my schedule was a joke.

Irving had joined a local writing group and wanted me to come and visit the class as his "show and tell" project. I promised to make my loop of New England and be back in time for his Monday, May 13 class. My loop could be tightened to accommodate weather and weariness.

Christina gave me a Reiki treatment in their kitchen. I just sat in a chair and she rested her hands on my shoulders and then a couple of places on my head. While she was doing this I checked in with my internal cast of characters, the parts of myself that discuss my life in interminable detail. I recognized the internal director who loves a project and a deadline, my Internal Teddy Roosevelt, the militant go-getter that, when riding into the Valley of Death, would say, "Stiff upper lip now, lads!" This guy voice was responsible for getting me into things that made me very uncomfortable. He would forget that I was a 55-year old grandmother who used to outweigh Arnold Schwartzneggar. He completely ignored my past history, the seven years it took me to get over my fear of driving and the 15 years it took for me to earn my first college degree. Caution annoyed him and he regarded any complaints as whining. "We need to hit the bridge at 10 a.m.," he insisted, as if we were going to blow it up (Alex Guiness implied). He regarded my Internal Financial Director as "a paranoid" and would run rough shod over my Health Director. He was messy, seemed to think someone would pick up after him (he has much more important things to do), would get impatient even with a microwave oven and would forego sleep altogether if he could. He thought most social functions were a colossal waste of time. He only wanted to watch television if there was a murder mystery or a documentary available. When I checked in that morning, with The Gang of Bandits that live in my head, Commandant Ruff Rider was pacing and grumbling, jangling the car keys, anxious to get started.

Then another character approached. A saffron robed Buddhist monk with classical shaped nude head and only black for eyes (no white) under tight, flat eyelids. He had the air of some sort of authority, like a master of a school. He walked up to the Commandant, took the keys and said, "I'll drive today."

Chris took her hands away and I told her my little experience. She looked amazed and said she was giving me "alert calmness and control free of stress." I said I thought she hit the mark. When people think in words that describe abstract things, my mind translates them into images that bring it into some physical manifestation--in this case, characters. Without some expression of the concept, for me, there is no concept.

Chris drove Seno around the neighborhood. When she returned she was obviously reluctant to release the steering wheel. I had been standing with Irv telling him how possible it was to have such a toy. When he saw Christina's face, he said to her, "What color do you want yours to be?"

"Periwinkle blue," she replied.

It occurred to me that perhaps I should be selling these roadsters. I told them that if they bought a car from Matthews Memory Lane Motors in Portland where I had found Seno, I would deliver it myself to New York. Ho, ho, funny joke. We all laughed but many of my crazy adventures start with some remark like this! (www.memorylaneclassiccars.com)

"See you a week from Sunday!" I called and zoomed off in the direction of Dreaded I-287.

The morning traffic moved but not too aggressively, everybody driving in a civilized manner and speed limit an intelligent 45 miles per hour for crossing the Tappan Zee. What a fabulous piece of aerial filming that would have made--the purple roadster crossing the blue Hudson River on such a bright day. Instead of being terrified, I enjoyed it! What a surprise. What a *relief.*

I kept focused, made it through the concrete maze and popped out on the Merritt Parkway. This was more like it! It may be the perfect roadster road. Also known as Highway 15, it paralleled the shoreline in Connecticut. It went up and down but not steeply, there was a little curving but nothing too drastic, enough to keep it interesting. Trees lined both sides blocking any annoying wind. All exits were well marked. There was no commercial signage or businesses but the road was serviced by an occasional gas station. The Merritt was like a poem in the middle of America's highway war novel. I didn't want it to end.

But I needed to get off in Bridgeport. *Finally* a town smart enough to put up signs assuming people may enter their space who didn't actually grow up there! Please! The rest of America, take note! Give us some signs! Halleluia! Amen!

I was on Main Street following the attractions signs when, on the left, I saw this really insane-looking building. As red as Oklahoma clay, this stone thing was a hybrid of at least four architectural styles. It was as if Gothic and Romanesque and a couple of others just collided, compressed and a dome popped out the top with a bird on it. Surprise! I was exactly where I wanted to be! I was at the Barnum Museum.

Phineas Taylor Barnum had the reputation of being the grandfather of public relations, the "Shakespeare of Salesmanship." How would it be to have the job of PR person for the Barnum Museum? Well, I met Arvis Westmoreland, P. T.'s PR person and alter ego of Ruffles the Clown. Staff had called Arvis when the purple roadster arrived and parked right out in front and now I was getting the museum's personal touch. She told me about clown college, the national clown association and clown chapters. So the next time I thought my professional organization was a bunch of you-know-whats, I would consider what a meeting of *real* clowns must look like! The gavel to bring their meetings to order must be one of those plastic ones that squeak.

There were three floors of exhibits and the climb to the top was worth it to see Tom Thumb's carriages and furniture. He and little Lavinia, both shorter than yardsticks, charmed the world, literally sprinkling joy globally, especially with their historic wedding.

I confess I didn't know that much about P. T. Barnum before coming to Bridgeport. His image in my mind was of brilliant ad man who occasionally visited "the truth." As usual, when you get to know somebody (why should an historical figure be any different?) your perceptions change.

I didn't expect to be inspired by Mr. Barnum's life.

In the mid-1850's the only family form of entertainment was museum going. P. T. had a go at retail, got restless and bought a dull, little museum, pumped his brand of swashbuckling promotion into it and voila! Barnum's American Museum, complete with hoaxes and oddities. He had musicians play outside his museum to attract attention but had them play so poorly that people would go inside to get away from it. He called himself the "Prince of Humbugs" and practical jokes were his forte after his grandfather conned him over a piece of swamp land.

Barnum experienced truly horrific set backs and he would somehow bounce back, rebuild and go on. Couldn't we all use more of this ability in our lives? This was one of my expressed reasons for taking this trip! What was his secret? P. T. found his direction from the Universal Church. It was one thing to say "all things ultimately are for the best" but it was another to actually live that concept. How can a person come face to face with tragedy and still say well, it must "ultimately be for the best." This man was clearly tested in harsh ways and yet walked the walk. I found myself wanting to know him, know his motivations.

Today, of course, P.T. would have to contend with being grilled and skewered by Mike Wallace on *60 Minutes*.

When was I going to be too old to start something? After one year of retirement, at age 60, Barnum got involved in CIRCUS which, of course, his name became synonymous. He created a "traveling museum" that evolved into his version of what a circus could be and became the Greatest Show on Earth. I promised myself right then that I would never use age as an excuse, only as a key to open some new possibility.

I learned that the first person to be shot out of a cannon was a woman, Mademoiselle Zazel. I couldn't imagine being talked into this stunt! There were galleries and exhibits here to inform and entertain *everybody*. That was just what old P. T. would have wanted.

Eventually James A. Bailey joined Barnum. He was a logistic genius, a man for whom my trip would be child's play. He shipped elephants, people, tents--an entire functioning village--town by town, around the world. He must have had the patience of a soccer mom and nerves of an air traffic controller.

The Barnum Museum, a national treasure, received presidential congrats when it stabilized itself, its mission and its finances on Main Street in Bridgeport, where, by the way, P. T. Barnum was mayor. I watched the special film about Barnum's amazing career and soaked up his inspiration. Like Tina Turner, P. T. didn't do anything "nice and easy." I felt like I would later need what Barnum's life was trying to teach me. (www.barnum-museum.org)

Ken Blinn, Director of Programs and Avril jumped right on the PR possibility with my roadster and soon the *Connecticut Post* was there taking pictures and reporter MariAn Gail Brown was grilling me for answers. Here was a take-no-prisoners kind of reporter with a bushel basket full of dark hair sometimes half hiding a pixie face. The questions were rapid fired in a Queens, New York accent and the good news! a media person who actually listened and built another question on your answer. She kept digging for the "why's" of my trip.

Ken served coffee and the three of us camped around the boardroom table with our mugs like drinking buddies around a campfire. Ken had a natural radio voice, which I commented on and sure enough, he also did a radio show. MariAn was psychic and could predict what songs would play on the radio next. Ken's wife Stacey was an award-winning academic who (no surprise anymore!) MariAn knew.

MariAn was in downtown Manhattan September 11, 2001 and had to run for her life as the third building collapsed at what would become Ground Zero. She said she wouldn't have made it if she hadn't just *that year* gotten fit and lost 78 pounds. Alyce, I said to myself, are you *listening*?

I could have spent hours talking with these two very interesting people and gathering their life stories. It was a bit difficult to leave. Ken presented me with a silver whistle engraved with the Barnum Museum building on it. I could start my own circus with it or call for help. It was an important momento of the trip. It helped anchor Barnum's inspiration.

Wind gusts whipped down Bridgeport's Main Street and rocked the roadster just sitting there. It felt like being in a wind tunnel and I told myself it was just buffeting coming from the ocean. I took Highway 8 up to I-15 but eventually got off at the slower-paced Highway 5 when the wind exhausted me. This road dumped me, unsuspecting, onto I-91 just in time for Hartford rush hour. I needed two things: I-84 and the exit for the youth hostel. I made one but not the other. When I finally caught on that the exit numbers were going up instead of down, the hostel exit quite behind me, I didn't want to fight my way back. Before I knew it I was half way between Hartford and the Massachusetts line.

I was watching intently for the exit to little road 197 because I wanted off the damned interstate and over to Dudley and a second chance at a hostel. If there was such an exit, I doubt it. The wind was tossing me back and forth like a cat with a stunned mouse. I urged myself on one mile at a time. The wind twisted my helmet as if a large deity was trying to screw it off my head. Driving became like quilting, one awful stitch at a time. There were signs for historic Sturbridge and I was spent. I rolled off determined to take the first opportunity to just have everything *stop*. The roar in my ears was now permanent.

(Note: Headlines the next morning read, "Winds pound region; gusts knock down trees, power lines. Howling winds gusting up to 55 miles per hour wreaked havoc. Police officers were out all afternoon directing traffic around fallen trees." *Metrowest Daily News*, May 4, 2002)

Just off of frontage road and behind a row of trees, nothing around it, was a motel. It was a quiet, neatly cared for spot. The fellow minding the desk looked like the brother of the motel manager in Princeton, Illinois. I concealed my cash and handed over my credit card. When I tried to fill in the blanks on the carbon pack registry form, my right hand couldn't hold the pen. The muscles in both forearms twitched from their hours of strain. He filled in the information for me and I got my right paw to make zigzag marks that in no way resembled my usual signature.

I was way out past exhaustion and I was learning that it didn't hit me until I stopped and pulled myself out of the car. I needed to quit before I got in this condition. I needed food and I needed somebody else to fix it. I needed pampering in the worst way. In spotty English the desk clerk advised me to go up the road. "Very historic," he said. I felt like I'd just made history myself surviving the wind and I wasn't up for any more history. But I took his advice, got back in the car and wearily pulled the stick.

America was just an English colony when Colonel Ebenezer Crafts opened his tavern, the Publick House. The same hearth that warmed a cavalry company in 1771 was going to warm me and a bowl full of French onion soup. What really enticed me, however, was the sign outside in the parking lot with my two favorite words on it: BAKERY OPEN. General Lafayette enjoyed the Yankee cooking here over 200 years ago. With that kind of a track record, they could certainly appease me. Since I was half dead, I'd be an easy customer.

The restaurant with its wide floorboards and beamed ceilings, was the centerpiece for a 60-acre resort with wide green lawns, sheep and apple trees. A person could evidently stay here, snuggle up in big, fat pillows in rooms full of antiques. They had a list of holiday activities that had me scrambling for my "must-come-back-here" list. Just arrive for a weekend in January and they'd fix me a hot buttered rum after hauling me around in the snow in a horse-drawn sleigh, complete with velvet blanket, I'm sure. On St. Patrick's Day they'd warm the cockles of my semi-Irish heart with soda bread and meat pies. In December they promised to have costumed dancing wenches serve me wassail. There wasn't a holiday I could name that they weren't ready to spoil me rotten for. These people obviously had pampering down to an artform. Jog, they said, or play tennis or swim or hike or cross-country ski or golf or canoe or just sit in a lounge chair under the Colonel's elms. That last part had a real appeal. That and the plush canopied bed with the brocade pillows pictured in their brochure--the *only* brochure I have ever seen in my entire life that was actually suitable for framing because of the Grandma Moses-style cover by artist Ed Parker. (www.publickhouse.com)

I had no business showing up looking like road lint to have dinner at this splendid chic chic Shaker place. It was not for the faint-of-purse but the road had put a dent in my appetite and I didn't need much. The cordial waitress asked me what kind of motorcycle I had when she saw my helmet occupying the other seat at my table. "I don't ride a motorcycle," I answered. But that was all I said. No explanation, no attempt to be civil. What a jerk.

By the time I left, however, I'd become a minor celebrity for the second time that day. The parked roadster was a little magnet for attention.

After a few spoonfuls of cheesy soup I was infinitely more civil. I gave Kim, the waitress, Seno's photo business card. She was genuinely enthused and told me about the classic cars her dad had in *his* garage in Hudson, Massachusetts. Kim was beautiful and sweetly attentive, probably sensing that I was feeling like warmed over panther poop. Next thing you know Brad Arcoite, one of the managers, was almost beside himself with glee as he had just come in from circling my purple roadster in the parking lot. He shared stories about his '57 Chev and talked to me like I was the only other car buff in New England. Then Albert Cournoyer, godfather of this whole complex who modestly had the understated job title of "innkeeper," was at my table checking out my baby pictures (photos of my cars) and telling me about his trick '62 Corvette! We had a fine old time jawing about iron and fiberglass.

Now if you were sitting in an upscale historic inn and saw some female that looked like she'd been rolled out of a demolition derby walk in and sit down and then watched as two managers both wearing suits surround her and talk to her, wouldn't you wonder if maybe she was dealing drugs or had parked illegally in the parking lot or *something?* Nobody was going to give me eye contact after that!

Albert and Brad, without any close second place winners whatsoever, got the award for Best Dressed Men in America on the Alyce Trek!

Albert looked like an actor whose name I don't know. He was as well turned out as the lawns outside. With a bag full of cornbread sticks from their bakery, I was now equipped to collapse for the night and have a piece of the Publick House for breakfast in the morning.

Journal Entry: May 3

Note to Alyce: Get a lot more money and come back here as soon as you can.

31

Part of me wanted to sit in that nice motel bed propped up with pillows eating cornbread sticks and sipping coffee for the rest of the day...or go back and visit the historic town of Sturbridge. That had been a great stop a few years ago. But when I consulted the calendar that I had brought from home to predict and guide my possible progress, I could see I was days behind. So much for a schedule-free trip!

When I climbed into Seno's cockpit I noted a notch in his left rear fender. Evidently that grinding noise I heard while driving in that high wind was the fender being pushed into the body of the car. It found a metal place in the rolled leather thing that surrounded where I sat. The leather pad was eaten away and there was a half inch bite in the inside of the fender. I was tossed around so thoroughly, I had no idea this was happening.

There was a special place in Maine that was calling to me. "The best is yet to come," described how I felt about this little coastal town. It was the reason that I had risked driving north and doing a New England loop instead of chopping off this leg of the journey. Like a siren singing in my brain, the Lobster Republic of Ogunquit wanted me to visit.

But I'd have to get out bed to do it. My fear of returning to the asphalt had kept me in the sack rubbing my sore muscles and slathering myself with sympathy. But my Internal Commandant read the newspaper story of the damaged wind with glee and observed, "See, it won't get any worse than that. Let's move it!"

The traffic was thundering outside and I just didn't want to get back into it. When I did finally get on the interstate it was surprisingly light. But I couldn't take jockeying with Mayflower van lines, Consolidated Freight and oil tankers at 75 miles per hour so early in the morning. I'd have to warm up to it today. I took Highway 20, the slower more gentle eastbound route.

Linda's Breakfast, Tony's Used Cars, Chuck's Auto Repair, the Purple Rose Lawn and Garden Gifts, The White Mansion Banquet Facilities. Everyone was lined up along the two lane highway. This stretch had obviously broken the chains...or the chain stores and enterprises hadn't discovered this area yet. I enjoyed the mom and pop independent businesses along Highway 20. I knew there was going to be an interstate in my day and I just wanted to put it off as long as possible.

It was cold and crisp as any November morning in New England. The trees here hadn't budded yet adding to the November look. Only it was *May*.

I-495 took a big wide bend around the metropolitan mess known as Boston. Fred Allen said, "I have just returned from Boston. It is the only thing to do if you find yourself there." It was a fine city and I'd logged many hours of historical touring there. But it was the only city that AAA actually advised against driving in and the traffic wasn't a condition, it was a war in progress. I took the outer ring that radiated around Boston and took a short side hop into New Hampshire.

My hands and legs were getting cold despite the layers of insulation. I imagined what it might be like to have a little heater in the car blowing warmth on me. The mind was a wonderful thing and if Tibetan monks could sit in snowdrifts in wet sheets thinking warm thoughts until steam rose from their shoulders, then I should be able to raise my body temperature a few degrees.

On the other hand, just stopping for awhile might not be a bad idea. And I had just the place! Off of SR 111 was another "henge," the third one in this story. There was Stonehenge in Washington State on the edge of the Columbia River, there was wonderfully irreverent Carhenge in Nebraska but this was to be the most mysterious Stonehenge of them all...and I'll include Britain's in the mix too.

Formerly known as Mystery Hill, now called "America's Stonehenge," this site is a vortex for controversy and heated debate. I wandered around in the maze of man-made chambers, walls and corrals surrounded by upright stones with accurate astronomical alignments. Did Irish monks build it, or a Civil War farmer with too much time on his hands or did native Americans suddenly decide to deviate wildly from anything they had ever done before? Indications are that this site was over 4,000 years old making it *older than Stonehenge on England's Salisbury Plain!*

There were no trilithons and no blue stones. The site doesn't look like any "henge" I'd ever seen before. But there was plenty there to chill a person's backbone and set grey cells to wondering what on earth might have gone on here. The stone placements show the site to be a large calendar for equinox and solstice and eclipses. I was free to walk all over the site without the annoyance of a tour guide and on this day, I had the intriguing grounds to myself. Without the road wind, the walk was pleasant and the sun lit the details of this amazing site.

The thing that would creep a visitor out the most was the Sacrificial Table with a groove cut deeply into solid rock making it resemble a Thanksgiving turkey platter. Underneath it, in a chambered rock room, was the Speaking Tube. If one person talked into the tube, another person, standing above would perceive the Table as talking. A complete oddity in America, this rock holy place would be completely at home in Ireland or Scotland or England. Research continues but the best money was on Celt-Iberians creating the site. (www.stonehengeusa.com)

I thoroughly enjoyed the book store with information on over 300 unusual rock sites in New England. Harvard professor Barry Fell's *America B.C.* covers an amazing array of myth-shattering facts that indicates America was visited by Phoenicians, Egyptians and Celts long before Lief Erickson was a sparkle in his daddy's eyes. There were books and information here that I had not seen anywhere else.

It was a neat little jab in reality to come to New Hampshire and get my fourth and last commemorative coffee cup and complete my set of "henges."

New England states were so small, they were like bedrooms that Seno and I could zip in and out of. We were back in Massachusetts and interstated over to the coast and once again over the line into New Hampshire. I thought it would be scenic to follow the shore but instead got stuck in Saturday shopping traffic on Highway 1. I was chomping at the bits to get to Maine. Patience, patience. I passed rummage sales and still I wouldn't stop. I wanted water but I wouldn't stop. I wanted to unkink my back but I wouldn't stop. "We're this close, we're not stopping." I had officially become my father.

A kid memory: I remember once when my family was packed into a Rambler station wagon and crossing Kansas, that my brother actually ripped the keys out of the ignition in desperation to get my father, the man with a long range bomber pilot's bladder, to stop. The black and tan car limped to the side of the road and family members exploded from it like popcorn from a hot pan and all pee'd in a field forsaking modesty completely.

I crossed the Piscataqua River into Kittery, Maine and the welcome sign: "MAINE, THE WAY LIFE SHOULD BE." No argument.

I still wasn't "there." Past the outlet stores, the greasy fish and crab smells, past the signs for "beaches" and ever northward we went.

Eleven days ago the idea of making it to Maine seemed an staggering impossibility, a Christmas wish that wasn't going to happen. I was intimidated by the expanse of Wyoming and Nebraska, robbed of my cash and facing problems only money could solve and remembering the predictions of the runes that I'd have a hard journey, "slippery slopes, unsure footing." But there had also been indications that my usual Life's good fortune was smiling on me again. The surprise of the Palace of Gold, the vacancy at the Ironmaster's Mansion, the Victorian glory at Cape May, the amazing lunch in Manhattan. The rain had nearly drowned me twice but it hadn't really rained on my spiritual parade. Now that I was getting close, a General George Patton variety of compulsion was urging me taking over.

Finally. Ogunquit.

Off of Highway 1 and through the startled pedestrians, I headed to Perkins Cove. Only one parking space left in a tourist-choked Saturday noon parking lot and it was next to the restaurant's front door. I parked, shut the engine off and felt the relief of *no vibration* for a full two minutes before I could unbend my body and climb out of the car at Jackie's Too.

A Maine native greeted and seated me. Martin, a man of normal height and build but a polished sparkle to his eye...and how did I just *know* he was from Maine? The canvas baseball cap? The I'm-comfortable-and-I've-been-here-forever body language? If there was any doubt about his New England heritage, that disappeared with the accent.

The veranda was enclosed in a white tent that whap-whapped in the stiff sea breeze. The sun was fully out and brilliant and warm enough for some people to show their white bird legs and wear shorts. I sat there trying to convince myself that I was there, really *there.* The black cliffs of rock were gently pounded by the intense sapphire blue of the Atlantic. I sipped a quart of iced tea with extra lemon and the physical sensation of doing that helped to jolt me. It was not a dream. I was not only in Maine, I was in some sort of Alyce Nirvana. I had such a jolly time at Jackie's with the staff and enjoyed the crab cakes so much that I bought the only T-shirt of the entire trip, a purple embroidered Jackie's shirt. (www.jackies-too.com)

There was something, and I asked myself *what specifically*, about this little town that had drawn me like swallows to Capistrano, butterflies to Pacific Grove or vultures to Hinkley Ridge. This was my fifth visit to Ogunquit. How can a mom penguin find her kid penguin in a convention of identical tuxedoed birds? She just gravitated to the right one. Just like I gravitated to Ogunquit.

"The best is yet to come."

That was this day.

Jennifer, also working at Jackie's, and Martin posed next to the purple roadster in their purple shirts and sent me on my way, like a happy seagull, tummy happy with crab. Martin had been generous enough to call around for me when I had asked him about a secure spot for Seno and off street parking. I left to find "Nellie" because she, they said, would provide safe haven for my traveling billboard.

I considered not telling anyone about Ogunquit and it may be a big mistake to describe it because the place was getting thick with visitors. It was like packing the Osmond Family Reunion into a double wide. The streets were narrow and the cars were doing a procession as if they were a carnival ride. For me there was just the right amount of stained glass, perfumed candles, embroidered wind breakers and stuffed toy lobsters. Charming bed and breakfasts, old inns, well kept lodges lined the twisting street that went back to "town," an off-balanced little intersection of angled streets with galleries, hand packed ice cream, emporiums and
Carpe Diem Coffee.

Yes, I made it to Atlantic City and delivered the Pacific City postcards, but for me personally, a greater accomplishment was reaching my old friend Ogunquit.

The fictional Cabot Cove was alive and well in dozens of incarnations all up and down the Maine coast. One just expected Jessica Fletcher to pop out of Barnacle Bill's nautical supply store and announce another murder. I seriously thought about renting a place here for a month in the winter as I read the ads on an October visit. Everyone said I was nuts to consider it, but could I think of a *better* place to escape and with any better reason to stay indoors, sleep on flannel sheets, wear sweats and write?

White porches with white rocking chairs, white picket fence and white columns, the Nellie Littlefield House was every fantasy of a Maine bed and breakfast, only better because there was no weird owner to assail you with stories about her cat and try to get you to drink herbal tea. "Two nights, please."

From the recessed lighting and sprinkler heads in the ceiling, I knew the renovated 1889 house had been a major gut job. The photo album in the library documented the down-to-the-studs effort. Oh, my. My house should be this lucky. "Nellie" was resplendent in all new everything. Doors, latches, bathrooms, furnishings, paint. She was an old shell completely redone new, like a '40 Ford with tilt, air and cruise. Eric Haselton was literally up to his ankles in house ash in the photos. Looking vaguely like Benjamin in *Good-bye, Columbus* (only better looking), Eric even stripped the roof tiles, cleaned and then reused them. We discussed the spirits that seemed to occupy our houses. He also wrote poetry, played guitar and was an accomplished photographer. The breakfasts of raspberry French toast and an egg concoction with fruit were his doing. Evidently he didn't sleep. Ever.

I settled in and watched the world go by from one of the white rockers on the second floor balcony. There were grandpas pulling red wagons with quiet kids, trike and bike riders, couples dressed alike (!), an old duffer with a prissy little dog, two handsome trim men with flying hand gestures, plump women with shopping sacks. I enjoyed a doughy thing from the Bread and Roses Bakery while rocking and gazing. (www.visit-maine.com/nellielittlefieldhouse/

My dad had a phrase for moments like this. He would say, "I wonder what the poor folks are doin' right now?" I heard him say that in a $5-a-day rented row boat out in the middle of an Ozark lake. I heard him say it while watching 4th of July fireworks with Jim Beam in his hand. He didn't have to be in a luxurious place, just a luxurious state of mind to say that. And I thought to myself, "I wonder what the poor folks are doin' right now?"

Roadster Lesson #10: If you keep going, you get there.

32

Marginal. When something was "marginal" that meats it could barely make it, could just barely keep up, right? A Marginal Way would mean the path taken for least effort or perhaps mediocre.

Didn't make sense. Marginal Way was anything but marginal. This footpath hugged the edge of the rugged coastline and would take me all the way from Nellie's to Perkins Cove. A two foot wide black asphalt ribbon showed all the jagged cliffs, tidepools and unusual rock, everything that met the wide expanse of electric blue and on this day, calm waves. And it was called Marginal Way.

It was as perfect a day as a traveler could pray for and I joined the strolling people for this early Sunday morning walk. All manner of humanoid was on the trail. Even one power walker who appeared oblivious to any life form in her path, wires in her ears, baseball cap pulled tight, fists clenched. I thought to myself, I used to go through life like that.

Then there were sitters. Some stopped by a momentary path elevation and enjoyed the rest on a park bench but most because the stunning view said to stop. Couples photographed each other on promontories or walked the walk hand in hand. Any long hair untied blew romantically in the soft breeze. A Yorky stopped and let me pet her silky fur.

Some people started their walk at the cove and were walking north. I started at Nellie's and was walking south. As people passed, engaged in conversation, bits of it was overhead by the opposite hikers. I heard words like "entrance exam" when two college kids passed wearing Dartmouth sweatshirts. I heard "Florida" mentioned between two tanned and withered oldsters. I overhead "cancer" spoken between two women.

"Be here now," I told myself. At the end of their morning walk, would they remember the sound of the sea or the smell of circulating freshness in the air? How about the light on the daffodils or the water in the tidepools? How much would I remember of the same path, of my trip or of my Life? Always pondering the next mile of highway robbed me of the now street. Be here now. Be here now.

What happened to the Ogunquit lighthouse? Was it the victim of a budget cut or did it sink into a sandy sink hole? What appeared to be *only the top 20 feet* of a normal lighthouse sat about halfway along the path. It was too big to have been stolen from a miniature golf course. Where was the rest of it? Or are all the other lighthouses just erect and this one didn't get its Viagra? It was Greek isle white, blinding white when hit with full sun and it was best photographed with someone next to it for scale. There were no artists perched on wobbly easels painting this lighthouse and I had never seen it on a postcard. The Ogunquit lighthouse was just, well, *short.*

From the curved "C" shape of the cove, I started my more inland walk back. It was getting quite warm and I drained my water bottle. I walked by the quaint pet store, a cottage dress shop, a jewelry and glass shop. Each had its own unique carved wooden sign. Ogunquit was known for these signs, many lavished with gold or embellished with 3-D things like lobsters or coffee pots. I passed the cemetery and stopped to get a snapshot--someone's underwear was neatly draped on a fencepost. "I wouldn't have expected this in Maine," I heard myself reacting aloud to no one around. But it *was* Sunday morning and that comes right after Saturday night.

When I arrived full circle back at Nellie's, I had a message. Impossible, I thought. Nobody on earth knows where I am!

It seemed that the bright ladies at the Ogunquit Camera Shop had told a newspaper reporter about the roadster when he stopped to have his film developed. I remembered them well, they had processed my recent pictures and I had met Kitty Carlisle, the saucy shop cat who had her own photo business card. When I thought about it, who better to know what was new than the pair who run the film processing for the town?

So I met Stuart Nudelman at the lighthouse and we had more of a party than an interview. He treated me to butter pecan ice cream at Marguerite's after photographing the car. What a sweet vat of Life niceness Stuart had fallen into! A refugee of school administration from New York City, Stuart retired to his beloved Ogunquit but now carried three business cards and wondered when he ever had time for a full time job. He had the enviable position of art critic, newspaper story finder, photography instructor and performance board member. Then there was serving on the governor's art commission. Stuart was a happy camper and when he described his life, his round eyes lit up. He also knew cars and like everyone in New England was a good source of route advice.

Ogunquit was to be my most eastern. My Alyce heart had a sore spot in it because I wasn't going to be able to see my friend Irene in Orono, Maine. She was pregnant and was certain to become the Best Mama in Maine. We met at a youth hostel in Burlington, Vermont and had kept up the connection for five years.

I quietly wrote post cards and packed in my room while half watching *Young Frankenstein* on television. I looked at Gene Wilder's hair. Mine was beginning to look a lot like his, like filament wire.

I crammed a red lobster hat into a mail bag for its trip back to Oregon. It would arrive there before I would. I walked out of the Post Office and I slowly went up to the roadster, the top of the Nellie Littlefield House visible just over Seno's shoulder. I knew I was going to have separation problems here. I was running short of days and it hurt like hell to be making a smaller loop of New England. How could I leave my favorite old friend Ogunquit?

For the first time since Wyoming, I snapped a tape in my portable deck and screwed the earphones into either side of my head. Up until now the only soundtrack had been the blasting of wind and roar of trucks and the car's engine growl at my back. I had to smile as I heard Jerry Reed doing *Lord, Mr. Ford* and "my smokin', chokin' automobile," a good driving song. I couldn't look in the rearview mirror or I would have lost the courage to leave. I set the course for Highway 1 southbound.

Somewhere near the turn for the interstate *Flashdance* came on the tape and with it all of its gutsy power and I teared up. For months before leaving for this trip I would blast this theme out across the bare floor of my attic and dance in front of my map of the United States with the pushpins in it. "What a feeling! Make it happen!" It was such a farfetched dream, such a stupid idea for anyone, much less a potato like myself. I didn't really believe it would ever happen. But I kept doing things as if it might. Everyone I talked to humored me and listened patiently and then changed the subject. So when I heard that familiar music and those no-holds-barred lyrics I had to bite my lip to keep the tears inside. I was in it, in the dream. Why do it? You don't *ask* for your dance, you're given it. Because this was the dance for the Alyce Life. I was dancing for my Life.

The opportunity for I-95 appeared and I took it, wanting a situation that would require my undivided attention, the interstate. Again I saw the thumb of a trucker as I curled onto the freeway. No eyes or face, just a thumbs up. If I could I would personally thank all the people who beeped, smiled, waved, hoo-rah'd, thumbed, whistled and cheered. They will never know how sore I was physically, how sure I couldn't go much further and how their encouragement helped me.

The music tape, although scratchy and distorted, was a huge help on the interstate. My whole attitude changed when the sound track went musical. Ragtime was especially lovely. And honky tonk waltzes. James Taylor got me through central Massachusetts. Music was a drug, no doubt about it.

Seno and I were making good time on the Mohawk Trail when I needed a rest stop. This was Johnny Appleseed country, there really was such a person and here, at this rest stop was a statue of Little Johnny holding a bunch of bronze apples. I pulled a fresh, very yellow banana out of my front seat pack, laid it across the apples and was focusing the camera when an excited man came up to me. I was desperately hoping that this was not a relative of John Chapman, the hero known as Johnny Appleseed. He pointed at my roadster.

"I have one of those!" he said.

Now I've owned my 1940 Ford coupe for over 20 years and during that time I've had dozens of people tell me that they used to own one *just* like it, only it was a Plymouth, it was a 1941, it was green and it was a sedan. So when this guy said that he had "one of these" I thought, great, he's probably got a 1962 Jeep or something.

Well, no. From the pictures, he really did have a white Seno, a cute little reproduction of a 1927 Bugatti complete with leather strap across the hood and very authentic old tyme wheels. Ed's car had nice little foot step pads, very civilized. Not like Seno with his if-you-can't-climb-in-here-you-can't-drive-either design.

Unbeknownst to me Ed Dionne and his wife Nancy of Lunenburg, Massachusetts had been chasing me for miles hoping to have the chance to chat. Ed, a happy 60-ish looking fellow, was hopping all around my car noticing all kinds of things and asking good questions. I told him about the upcoming event in Carlisle, Pennsylvania which was to be a special just for this breed of car. Nancy took down all the information I had. "I don't expect to make it myself," I said, still feeling crummy about how time was shortchanging my trip. The event was eleven days away. Ed climbed in my drivers seat. Nancy and I both took pictures. They were pretty dumbfounded to think that I had driven all the way from Oregon, but there were my license plates to prove it. They looked at each other. "You can do this too," I said. They still looked at each other but neither one said no.

I drove on, getting through a lot of Massachusetts faster than I figured. The weather was perfect, sunny sky, trees and flowers doing their best to catch up and not look so autumn-like. Curiosity was getting the best of me, I was wondering just how much time and distance I realistically had. I convinced myself to take an exit, any exit and I ended up in the parking lot of an industrial medical supply place, no other businesses or homes anywhere around. I unloaded my trucker's atlas, my calendar, my address book, my cell phone and my map of New England. I called my friend Marilu in Arkansas and was relieved that the balloons she had planned for me didn't start going up until May 27. I still needed to get to Irving's for the guest appearance at his writing class. Then there was the Carlisle car event. I realized by telling Ed and Nancy about it just how much I really wanted to go. It was a national meet! But would there be enough time to get through Virginia, Tennessee and over to Hot Springs? I played with bits of paper marked with mileage estimates.

I decided and redecided Irv's class. If I didn't try to kill myself getting to his writers' group, I didn't need to be blasting through Massachusetts. So at Greenfield I got off on a more civilized Highway 5 north to Vermont.

Now here was the highway of my fantasies. Green hills, tree shadows falling across the pavement, cute little cows and farms, a Norman Rockwell version of what "See the USA" campaigns are all about. I pulled the plug on the "Get There" mode. This was motoring. I got stuck behind a caution yellow school bus and didn't mind a bit. The road was doing a waltzing sort of thing with curves and I was totally enchanted. I was also getting thirsty so when the bus pulled over at a General Store I did too. My neighborhood has Safeway, Albertson's, Nature's or Zupan's but not a general store. I also wanted to change from my hard shell helmet to the leather one because the speed was so much slower here.

A bevy of softball girls poured into the General Store and I waited in line with them to pay for my bottle of cold pop. Pretty soon they were all over me about Seno and I started to hand a couple of them cards. They all wanted one. I complied. There was a little discussion about how "girls can do stuff too" and as liberated as they all seemed to be, they were amazed that a woman was piloting this vehicle. I told them to do whatever they put their little female minds to and not to get saddled with gender pigeon-holing. One of them asked for my autograph. They'll do fine.

The road continued its happy wandering northward and once in awhile I could see I-91. This was one of those terrific stretches where you had your choice of blasting through to where you wanted to go or twirling around next to it, breathing pollen instead of diesel.

Overcome with a jolly bravado I saw the western-style log entry way and the lettering GETAWAY MOUNTAIN CAMPGROUND. Then I found myself going in the drive and next thing you know signing up for a spot. Had I *officially* lost my mind? I was spending the night in the car?

Well, I'd done it twice before, testing the possibility in my own driveway. So why not?

Roadster Lesson #11: Either develop a reputation for being unreliable or learn to live with the stress of your promises. You can't have both.

33

Stan Fraczek called my roadster "The World's Smallest RV." And he says he wouldn't have believed it if he hadn't seen it.

It really wasn't difficult and it really did work and I really did sleep in until seven a.m.! I am sure that one of the reasons that I got such a good night's sleep was because I wasn't worrying about the safety of the car. I was *in* it!

My rented spot consisted of a patch of grass near a field of wildflowers and a wooden picnic table. That was it, totally it. I draped my lovely soft efficient red sleeping bag across the bench seat of the roadster and unzipped it halfway. The small travel pillow went right where a passenger's right arm would rest. Anything I may have needed (flashlight, a power bar, water, keys, shoes) during the night went on the floor of the car. I pulled the waterproof car cover over the front fenders, unrolled it the full length and secured it over the boat tail. Then I stood next to the left rear fender, crawled in under the cover, into the sleeping bag, curled up, zipped up and went to sleep.

I had not camped in 26 years. My hip bones have never forgiven or forgotten those miserable and sleepless nights of attempting to be an outdoors person. There was no part of pleasant in that experience although stories about it provided me and my Spousal Unit of The Moment with great comedy. When our neurotic city dog landed in the middle of our rain tent, splattering muddy paw prints like a Rorshak test, the hiking packs and the thin mattress pads were put away for good.

For me to have done this and actually enjoyed the experience was right up there with campaign finance reform and lower taxes. Desirable but improbable.

Ellen had signed me in the evening before and the hills had cast too great a shadow already for her to get the pictures she wanted of the roadster with her campground. She promised me coffee in the morning if I'd stay until light. Done deal! More than fair exchange! As pretty as she was thorough, Ellen showed her father-in-law Stan Fraczek how to make coffee and how to use the camera just to make sure she'd get her photograph. Stan and I got to talking...

"I read the information about your trip," he said, "and I'm living my dream too. It's this place. Used to be a cornfield and now it's a campground complete with wood heated swimming pool. I wanted something that I could do with my family."

Stan, his son Dave, sweetheart of a lady Ellen and their son Jason developed this convenient campgroup right off of Highway 5 near Ascutney, Vermont. It was pure whim that I pulled in there and walked into their lodge building. The brand new bath facilities were sparkling clean with the heady aroma of pine. Not Pine-Sol cleaner. The walls were made of freshly cut pine. It was a totally impulsive act to pull in there and say sure! I'd like a spot of earth for the night. But a lot of people who actually know what they're doing, do exactly that. Some folks park their RV's and just plain live there! Others leave one rig and drive back and forth between Vermont and some place warm, like the Snow Birds that live in both Arizona and Oregon.

"But this is the first time," Stan said, "that I've *ever* seen a four cylinder RV!" I just couldn't leave until I had parked Seno under their arch and got a shot of Ellen with the car.

I climbed into my seat and for *once* I was ready to go, not whimpering about traffic or wanting to stay put. I was looking forward to whatever amazing adventure would present itself next. It took this long but I was finally in the mental state that I wanted to be. Now if I could just live the rest of my life like that!

Seno and I crossed the Connecticut River into Claremont, New Hampshire and I hunted down the location of a Wal-Mart. There were conservationists in my home state who regarded this chain of discount stores as the work of the Devil himself. K-Mart might agree. I was not so persnickety, but I was fairly unfamiliar with what Wal-Mart had to offer because my house was not conveniently located near one of these Warehouses of Conspicuous Consumption and I was not your usual Wal-Mart shopper anyway.

I was just a lady who needed to have her glasses fixed. One of the itty bitty screws had worked its way out of the hinge and then disappeared between the cracks of the picnic table. Once I got past the the senior greeters, the dragonfly lawn flags and the nauseating yellow Kodak display (everything was far too jolly here for a Tuesday morning!) I found the optical department. The plump manager fixed my eyeglasses for free and once I understood how cheap the frames were I ordered another pair as a much needed spare. To be ready in 24 hours, she said. I said, "That's too fast. I can't handle that kind of service. Make it 36 hours and we have a deal." I didn't want to be hemmed in by still another scheduled time and date.

I went through Sunapee to get to New London and mailed more photographs home to David, the Mother Hen of My Web Site. More and more people were following my escapades around the country by going to www.GoingTopless.info and clicking onto Update. The web site address was printed on the boat tail of the car so that people seeing it could check in. David was posting my email on the site in the form of a journal. I encouraged anyone who took photographs of the traveling roadster to send them to "Topless Web Guy" in Portland. Al and Geraldine Layton, for instance, were at the Red Caboose in Pennsylvania and sent photographs of the rain clouds and wrote, "We were quite inspired. It had rained on her earlier that day and she was not completely dry yet." Peter and Marie Haake of Vassar, Michigan sent photographs taken as I'd entered Perkins Cove in Maine. And when I photographed people I'd met, they could go to the web site and see themselves there.

At the New London post office I asked about where WNTK Radio might be and the postal clerk of the small town looked a little surprised, as if a person could see all of New London if I just looked outside. I continued on Highway 114 and off to my right I could see a woman sitting on the hood of a car talking on a telephone. That's not too odd but it wasn't a cell phone. The phone cord, coming out of a window, was pulled tight and the phone console, one of those multi-button things, was on the car. The receiver appeared to be surgically attached to the head of Arnie Arneson, a woman who had interviewed me long distance for her radio show several months ago.

I had no prearranged meeting scheduled with Arnie of WNTK but I made a point of stopping by to see her. She had a fat datebook opened on her car hood desk, stabbing the air with a pen, putting someone on hold while jamming the buttons on the phone console. This was the switch-to-decafe-for-gawd's-sake radio tycoon Arnie at work lining up guests for her show and shouting orders to a fuzzy guy inside the radio station. I parked next to her outdoor desk and waited. Arnie didn't raise an eyebrow. She worked me in for a 20 second conversation, said to contact the *Concord Monitor*, tell them she sent me, gee, it was nice to see you, I'm on the air in 45 seconds, bye. I asked why she was doing business on a car hood and she looked at me like I was a loon. "Too nice to be indoors!" She spoke as if she were writing a telegram and was being charged $100 per word. And that's probably not too far off in the nature of her line of work.

I agreed to meet the *Monitor*'s staff photographer in a place we could both find. We picked the library in Franklin, New Hampshire, north of Concord. Seno and I got there first and wandered around this town named after Benjamin Franklin and located at the confluence of the Winnepsaukee and Pemigewasset rivers. New Hampshire was so much older than other states, it was more like a well loved wooden bowl, it had a patina to it. The town of Franklin, population 8,300, had a dip in it and the upward hill was lined with interesting buildings, shops and I wanted to just stay and look and look and look at everything. The architecture was so old a person would just have to feel comfortable here.

Sometimes I used Seno almost like a wheelchair. The car was so small I could wander up to garbage cans or sidewalks as if I were on foot. We crept down a side street and rolled along next to two boys with skateboards. The roadster invited conversation, I was a motorized Alyce because of no top. The two teenagers wondered about the car and I was wondering what that large stone arch up ahead was. "Entrance to a city park," they said. The bottoms of their skateboards were gashed from use. "So how about a demonstration?" I requested. Mark and Ronnie obliged with a performance, careening off the sidewalk and doing flip maneuvers. I had to hold my grandmother tongue to keep from telling these two that they really should be in school.

I positioned Seno under the arch for a photo op and a herd of people from inside the Proulx Community Center building came out to watch. I posed this jolly crew for a web site picture and met Tom Carbono, director of the Franklin Parks and Rec. They directed me to the library, so close I probably could have crawled to it. Franklin's motto: "A Friendly City on the Move." I could certainly vouch for the friendly part.

Back in 1828 the town wanted to be named Webster, after their favorite son whose birthplace was three miles away. Some other town already had that name so they selected Franklin. But the Official Seal of the City of Franklin pictures an image of Daniel Webster seated under a tree, not Benjamin Franklin.

I parked in front of City Hall within easy sight of the library and was impressed to be greeted by Donna Nashawaty, City Manager. I hadn't expected such royal treatment but the staff peering out the windows had alerted her. She was a car buff and had her own purple, homemade car, a Bradley. She came by the "car obsession" genetically...her maiden name was Studebaker, yes, *that Studebaker!* From Independence Day to Labor Day Donna helped organize Thursday evening car cruises in Franklin. My little gear heart ached to come back and have a burger with this spunky lady who was immediately a street rod sister, understanding what it was like to be female and have a genuine interest in cars and believing that every woman should have a purple car at least once in her life.

Ben Garvin listened to this squealing girl exchange for awhile before he introduced himself as a staff photographer for the *Concord Monitor*. Oops! back to work for both of us once I got a snapshot of Donna holding a photo of her purple baby.

Ben did not want a lady with a car, standard issue photograph. I suspect that his whole life was anything but standard issue. He asked where I was headed next and I said northbound on I-93 toward the mountains. He wanted a shot of Seno doing 60 miles per hour on the highway. That seemed reasonable until I noticed that there was no driver in his car, he was alone. How was this supposed to work?

He drove four miles to the interstate and I dutifully followed his blue-grey modern car. We easily merged onto the roadway and gradually increased speed to over 55 miles per hour. When traffic cleared a bit, Ben pulled into the left lane and I stayed in the right. I saw him lean over and I saw the passenger window go down. No power windows evidently. Then a black camera appeared in the window, its lens pointed at me. Was I supposed to smile and wave?

Passenger cars appeared behind us and Ben pulled over into my lane. When they passed he jockeyed over to the left lane and the camera appeared again. He had arms like Michael Jordan to be able to do this. I needed to keep my eye on my lane but I noticed that the camera strap was blowing in front of the lens. Trucks doing 70 miles per hour overtook us quickly and once again we lined up, Ben in the lead. We kept this up for miles on I-93 until, at one point, Ben was in the passenger seat instead of the drivers seat and must have had his left foot on his accelerator and steering with his left hand, firing his camera with his right. Since there was no way he could focus or compose a shot, I imagined he was getting a lot of sky, many shots of his camera strap and not much else. My job was to try to live through this dangerous mission, drive my course and watch my rear view mirror for fellow travelers who hadn't received notice that we were filming here. I had no way of letting him know there were speed freaks behind us wanting by. My horn hadn't worked since Illinois. He never signaled for me to pull over so that he could get a still shot, a sure shot, a more sedate shot.

I'm not sure the general public realizes what the media does to bring dramatic photography to their coffee and newspaper enjoyment.

Finally he waved and disappeared off my screen around Plymouth, New Hampshire to my eternal relief. Now I could settle in for a nice ride to Lincoln where I'd take the eastbound route. The expanse between exits was widening and hills had grown to mountains. I was comfortable with bottled water at the ready and no pressure to be anywhere or meet anybody. I had no reservations anywhere or fears about finding a place to stay in this off season. Playing with the press was fun but it was my trip after all and I figured that was the last story I'd be doing for awhile. The road was all mine.

Seno was running beautifully. We passed a few cars and a few cars passed us. I was never really sure about the speedometer but we seemed to be cruising at 65 miles per hour most of the time. Everything seemed right with the world. I reviewed the camping scene in my mind and applauded myself for being so prepared and now for being such a hardy soul. I was getting a different picture of myself. Wind was buffeting the car but now I was an old hand at working with it. The sun was beginning to cast some shadow and the further north I went the fewer vehicles there were on the road. I didn't want to have my music on, I wanted to relish the sights, the sounds, the smells, the whole wonderful sensuous experience of life on the road in a topless car.

Suddenly I noticed the stabbing flash of headlights coming from my rearview mirror. I glanced at it and saw the face of a big rig with his brights on headed right toward me. The word Freightliner looked so much bigger in the rearview mirror of a tiny roadster. Had he just chosen this moment to turn on his lights? I drove on. Then another flash and I moved my head, making it obvious that I was checking my rearview mirror. The truck's right signal began blinking. So he was turning off, big deal.

Only there wasn't an exit and wasn't going to be one for many miles.

Again the driver flashed his lights at me then signaled to the right. Oh, my Lord, I thought, there's something wrong with my car! I strained to hear anything different and there was nothing. There was no worse vibration than usual. I couldn't smell a problem. I could feel my face flush with panic, however, something must be falling off or unraveling, perhaps leaking from my roadster. Again the headlights blinked right into my mirror, the truck staying with me in my lane. And again the turn signals as if motioning me to pull over.

I believe the phrase is, "What fresh hell is this?"

After a series or four or five flashes I slowed and pulled over to the shoulder of the interstate. There was no gas station visible in either direction, no highway signs, no exits and no other traffic either. There was only beautiful empty New Hampshire. I had planned to get out and examine the car for flaws but I noticed that the truck had pulled over as well and came to a stop behind me. I stayed seated and the driver walked up and stopped, hands on his hips, standing on the passenger's side of the car. He wore a T-shirt with a wolf graphic on it.

Seated in my car, my eye level was about par with a 5-year old so everybody looked big to me. This guy looked especially big and judging from his arm muscles, he didn't spend all his time behind the wheel. He looked my car over from boat tail to nose.

"Is there something wrong with my car?" I asked.

His chin had been down as he had eyed the car and now he looked up a bit and smiled. I wish he hadn't. I'd seen better teeth on a jack o' lantern. He began asking questions in broken English. "Whot esh thees?"

What we had here was the French Canadian version of Billy Bob.

" '27 Bugatti," I answered tersely. "Is there anything wrong with it?"

More language I could not understand. He was nodding his head approvingly and admiring the car.

"Is there something wrong with my car?" I asked again.

Again more looks of admiration. I had kept Seno's engine running and my feet poised on the pedals, my shift positioned in first gear. One more time, you French weirdo, I thought.

"Your lights," I said, "Was there something wrong with my car?"

He was shaking his head as if he were trying to say, "How about this car. This is really something!"

I checked my lane for oncoming cars and hit the gas. And I didn't stop until I rolled into Lincoln.

Roadster Lesson #12: Leave, free or die.

34

I drove The Kanc.

Stan, the campground guy in Vermont, told me that people came from all over the world to drive New Hampshire's Kancamagus Highway, SR 112. I didn't doubt it. The Kanc was the southern most of three highways that ran east and west through the White Mountains, said to be the most heavily used forest areas in the United States. The Appalachian Trail runs through here although only experienced back country travelers "thoroughly familiar with the terrain should attempt the higher elevations." Many believe The Kanc to be one of the top fall foliage trips possible on the Planet.

The White Mountains were such a jumbled confusion of peaks that I don't know how anyone could get completely familiar with them. It was as if someone took Oregon's Cascades and said, "We have to pack these into a tighter area." If you think the cities are overpopulated back east, you should see how many mountains they managed to squeeze together in one state.

The first week in May, the White Mountains were not heavily used. Except for the construction crews, I had the 36 miles of The Kanc pretty much to myself from Lincoln all the way to Conway. The roadster had no trouble with the climb, the altitude or any more truckers. We hit the Kancamagus Pass, elevation 2,890 feet, at the maximum speed allowed and then followed the Swift River which cuts an interesting rocky gouge through the hills. The fir and pine were mixed with the deciduous trees that promised to light fire to a spectacular autumn. I tried to imagine what that must look like on a bright fall day, all those intense reds and yellows. What also came to mind was taking this road in a line up of other cars, like a funeral procession. The trade off for color was the peace and ease of driving this mountain range in May.

I wondered sometimes, especially when the signs read DANGER HIGH WINDS 25 MILES if I could blow over and tumble like a purple leaf down the mountain side. Trucks were known to blow over. Would I? Should I gain weight to hold the car down? Then I thought, come on, we gotta weigh 2,500 to 3,000 pounds and there's nothing but the boat tail that is aerodynamic. I'd have to be going backwards at 60 miles per hour to begin to lift off. Still, the wind moved the car sideways in an unnerving way.

Memorial Day was nearly three weeks away and most of Conway was like a hibernating bear that didn't want to be disturbed. My Internal Financial Director was relieved that all the cutesy businesses were still locked up for the winter but so was the youth hostel. By the time I found Rite Aid's one hour photo department to have my film processed, I was at the end of my limit. I had once more hit the wall of my energy. Without retail therapy soon I was going to drop in my tracks.

When I wore my helmet into a store and they hadn't see the car, they must have thought I had to wear it so that I didn't hurt myself while I was out with a hall pass from the loony bin. My film was processed in a record 35 minutes.

Before I left Conway I met Bob Pletschke while I was dropping my photographs into the mail box without getting out of my roadster. He pulled up in a funky foreign car and spelled his name for me. "Couldn't get any more consonants in there, could ya?" He said he was in third grade before he could spell it. He also told me about his son Kris who crossed the United States in a Dodge van, did 9,000 miles and never ate in a restaurant or slept in a motel. I could actually grasp that but I wouldn't want to travel with this kid, who, we figured, lives within two miles of my house in Oregon.

Only men complain about the loneliness of motel rooms. Women love motels and hotels. There was nothing to clean, decorate or organize. For me, a motel room was the ultimate focusing environment...if I could keep my hands off the TV remote.

I was surprised that I was not homesick and didn't seem to miss much about my home or life in Portland. When I saw little kids, my heart would momentarily ache for Gracie. Then they'd do something obnoxious and I'd snap out of it. I felt like I had no strings. This was supposed to unnerve a person. I rather liked it.

Highway 302 didn't have a cool, macho name, it was just a number on my paper map. So I figured that the next day, driving the middle of the three White Mountain highways, would be a Grade B experience compared to the spectacular views I'd been blessed with on The Kanc. Well, how *wrong* could I be?

The next morning it was just above freezing when I flipped the frost off Seno's cover and packed up for the day's drive. The air snapped with cold, there were no clouds and the sky was a pale, prom dress blue. Giant puffs of my breath preceded me going back and forth from my car to my room. I wore everything I could put on. I even put the Harley Davidson glove warmers on under my Antarctic mittens. I was as ready as I was ever going to get for the coldest road of my entire trek.

There was much more of mountain this day, mountains that meant business, mountains that weren't there for the tourists. Mountains that growled instead of purred. I was taking it methodically wanting to put the scenes into my mind with a laser because I knew this was going to be a drive I didn't want to ever forget. I passed the Cranmore Ski Area, Cathedral Ledge and Bear Peak. The car showed no signs of weakness, downshifting when I needed to for the pull over the Whites. We slipped between 3,000 foot North Moat Mountain on the left and 3,000 foot Mt. Parker on my right. The road was a light ash color and smooth. I saw three cars in 20 miles. Where was everyone? Perhaps the travel industry really was suffering from lack of participation. If this was all the traffic this beautifully built highway ever got, then we've overdone it.

Two layers of socks and my boots did not deter the cold.

The curves through the mountains were wide and graceful and fortunately did not require a great grip on the steering wheel because I didn't have it. The muscles in my hands strained through their protection to handle that wooden wheel.

The grandeur of these lofty mountains was split by the rushing, frothy Saco River. It was so angry and churned up that it ran a tawny brown color. The scars of many landslides marked the Presidential Range, mountains named after Washington, Jefferson, Madison and Adams. We have those in Oregon too, I thought. Once you named something, that was it, no duplicates, right? Another myth brought down. Surely New Hampshire didn't have a volcanic Mt. St. Helens...

My friend Dayton Hyde had told me that hypothermia was an excellent way to die. The cold eventually addled the brain and a person relaxed into a kind of euphoria. I seemed to be in Stage 1. My blue jeans were becoming stiff in the freezing cold. They were losing the battle between my 98.6 on one side of the fabric and the wind-chilled alpine air on the other.

When my discomfort overwhelmed my ability to admire the extraordinary scenic views the next stage was the vibration in my solar plexus. I hoped that I was shivering because I was excited to be seeing these majestic peaks up close and personal. Seno rolled on and on in this denial.

There were no gas stations, no motels, no ranger stations and no rest stops, nothing. The shoulder of the road was wide enough but what good to stop? Without some form of heat, there was nothing to do but press on. The skin on my face tightened, I was wincing isometrically. I was so cold that if I'd had a penis, it would have been sucked up into my pancreas.

I passed the stop for Arethusa Falls. With a drop of 200 feet it was the highest waterfall in New Hampshire. And five miles to my right was the site of the highest wind ever observed by man, 231 miles per hour recorded at Mt. Washington in 1934.

Doing about 65 miles per hour I noticed the Crawford Notch General Store just in time to spray gravel and turn into the parking lot. There was one lone red pick-up truck parked outside of this large, dark wood oasis. I pulled myself from the cockpit of the car with all the grace that you'd use to lift a 100 pound sack of flour. I staggered through the unlocked front door and came to rest upright on a wall. When I opened my eyes I saw Tom, the proprietor, who said, "So it's cold enough for you then?" I exhaled warmth and discovered I was still alive.

New Hampshire was the first state to declare their independence (from England) and adopt a provisional constitution and government. If Tom had his way, they'd do it again.

He was the only other living thing there amidst lots of dead things mounted or skinned on the walls. A row of skunk skin caps hung over his head. He told me that Crawford Notch had forty citizens and was probably the smallest burg in New England. I saw no burg there...just a few scattered businesses near the highway separated by lots of space. He was angry about another New Hampshire town. I had driven through there the previous day. When I heard his story, I could understand his frustration. His property tax had doubled in two years because of a new budgeting and allocation method. Essentially little Crawford Notch was, according to Tom, having to buy cop cars for other communities that couldn't support themselves.

"We don't have a police department," he emphasized. "Don't want one, anything happens we can handle it on our own. No fire department either. They want that stuff they can tighten their belts and get it. Not my fault they've overextended themselves down there."

I thought that Tom would make a good Oregonian. We took turns complaining about how small business gets hammered, we were singing to each other's choirs. He said that he was Concord's (state capitol) worst nightmare because he wouldn't stop expressing his opinions and fighting for his little community.

Crawford Notch General Store had only just opened for the season. I might not have made it if Tom hadn't chosen May 8 to open. His business card read: "Crawford Notch, WHERE NATURE IS STILL

BOSS." In this rugged country, there was no question of that. The Appalachian Trail probably passed within feet of his store but the only one out on the trail that day would have to be Big Foot, Sasquatch, the Abominable Snowman.

"How fast your car go?" he asked. When I told him he punched some adding machine keys and looked up. "It's 17 degrees in your car."

35

I met New Hampshire's other Old Man of the Mountain, the 40-foot-high profile that appeared on the commemorative quarter. I learned that a grinder was a sandwich and I met a dad who named his teething daughter Porsche, after the car (not Portia after the Shakespearean character). Morrie was the same guy who got his first speeding ticket at the age of 12, even before he had a drivers license. I also met the Department of Transportation crew Gary, Scott, Fuzzy and Ray who thought that my roadster was the funniest thing they'd seen in a long time. I read an interesting ad on my paper place mat: "Insure with Burns Before it Burns" by the Burns Insurance Agency. There was also an ad for Stumpage Contractor. Not sure I wanted to know what that was. A little blond waitress said, "I want a ride!" I said, "Bring hot coffee. We'll talk." Real maple syrup cost 75 cents extra on my pecan pancake.

Famous Clark's Trading Post was still closed for the season but a black bear performed his pole-sitting routine for me while I watched from my roadster outside the locked gate. I crossed the Connecticut River at Woodinville, connected with I-91 and arrived in White River Junction, Vermont just as they were taking the bagels out of the oven at The Bakers' Studio on Main Street. Melissa, no stranger to road travel herself, served up an Everything Bagel with veggie cream cheese. I think it must have been the best tasting bagel in the known world.

I checked back in at the Claremont Wal-Mart and sure enough they were willing to sell my prescription glasses to me for less than $40 and fit them to my face as well. My glasses weren't this cheap when I was twelve years old and that has been a few decades ago.

I was perfectly willing to try my hand at camping again but I had that Vermont lady's card (from the Red Hat Society convention in

Chicago) in my journal and thought I might just call her up for coffee and a chat anyway. She said she was serious when she made the offer to come stay with her, despite my Capote quote about making friends with people from Vermont. I hung up the pay phone in White River Junction and I was on my way across Vermont to Rutland.

On my way there I succumbed to the wanton charm of this state. Every little town brought audible "oh's!" out of me, each one outdoing the other for title of Most Quaint Place You've Ever Seen. No wonder every New Yorkers' dream was to own a Vermont B&B. Whitesville, Ludlow, Mount Holly nestle between the two large sections of Green Mountain National Forest. From a distance, peaks appeared painted in deep blue-green. Fields of kelly green stretched like flat carpet on either side of the road. Those famous Vermont black and white cows were more than just ice cream carton decorations. There was obviously a reason Champlain named this area *les verts mont*, the green mountains. Even their coffee bears the name.

It was completely unlike me to accept an offer from a stranger like this. But the whole trip was to find out what I might be like if I didn't have to be like *me* all the time. And she had such a nice face. Although they said that about Ted Bundy too.

I was supposed to drive through Rutland to get to Janet's house but I almost didn't make it. My head kept snapping around looking at the variety of architectural touches. Circular white gingerbread on one wraparound porch. Frilly iron fencing. A widow's walk. Oval beveled glass doors. It was as if an 1880 copy of *Architectural Digest* had exploded and come to life. Of course, the Norman Rockwell Museum is here! Where else would it be? Norman may have used some of Janet's neighbors and relatives for models in his paintings.

Just when the town began to be country, literally at the bend in the road, I found the lane to Janet's place and turned at her mailbox and into her driveway. Then like a shaken picnic blanket laid before me was a green lawn, looked like a city block that ran downward and then dipped gracefully up again. I just turned off the engine and sat and stared. There were some trees but mostly it was just the richest looking pasture you could ever imagine. And *this* was her backyard!

I spent two days with Janet and King. Partly because the rains came and shut down roadster travel and partly because I very much needed the rest and partly because Janet was such a convincing person, I believed that I wasn't imposing. "Never mistake endurance for hospitality," my dad cautioned. Seno and I were both handsomely garaged--me under an heirloom bedspread and the roadster in a real garage.

I've always counted it a good week when I could get my hands in dog fur and King had plenty to spare. He was a very classy, noble looking German Shepherd. He had fierce Mr. T looks with a Mr. Rogers heart. And certainly for me one of the best things to come out of the Red Hat Society convention was Janet. In Chicago she had her hair done up in a glamorous 40's style rolled up off her face with her red hat worn back on her head. At the same time she was everything a Vermont woman was advertised to be: level-headed, practical, lover of plants and animals and definitely not confused about life. One thing Janet would not know how to do and that was be pretentious. We took walks, split a pizza, had breakfast in a local ice cream place and girl-talked for hours. Janet worked different hours and I envied the way she could just sleep whenever she wanted. I mean, she slept like everybody else but she could pick and chose her times like turning a light switch on and off.

On one of my lone outings into Rutland I took Seno to the post office. Again David was getting a stack of photographs for the Going Topless web site. The federal building housed the post office on the main floor and I suppose courts and other things as well. Just to do postal purchasing, I had to go through a metal detector manned by two funny security guys. One of them was a Gold Wing enthusiast. To you civilians, that's a person who likes to ride a chunky highway Honda motorcycle and sometimes very long distances. So we had lots to talk about, mainly how to handle life in the rain on the road. He loved my roadster, insisted that the other guard go out and have a look, then gave me the web site for some lightweight rain gear. A person picks up tips like this and pretty soon life, even life on the road in an open car, gets worth living.

Then I stepped up to the counter to mail the next installment to David and the dark-haired postal clerk asked, "Why do you have a house full of eclectic stuff?"

I wasn't sure I'd heard right since my mind was attempting to remember the web site for Frogg Toggs.

"Are you psychic or have you been to my web site?" I asked.

Neither. He was taking courses in criminal psychology and profiling. He was "reading" me from how I looked. With his Brooklyn accent he rattled off a list of his family's educational accomplishments which I couldn't follow completely. First generation, he said, family from Sicily. He had movie star hair and if there had been no one behind me in line, I would have stayed and listened to more. It seemed the whole place was full of interesting people with interesting information. The image of the taciturn Vermonter went right out the window.

According to *U.S. News & World Report* you could expect a typical Vermonter to cherish autonomy, restraint, civility, tolerance and compromise, were suspicious of anyone's claim of possessing absolute truth and maintained an automatic, almost instinctive, hostility to enthusiasm. Zeal, for instance, would be regarded as the enemy of liberty and pleasure-seeking outsiders were known as "flatlanders." Based on this, I expected a state full of people who looked the part of the wife and farmer in "American Gothic." What I actually experienced was more like the colorful characters in a Peter Max painting.

When I pulled up outside the Salvation Army store (I couldn't stand it anymore, I had to go thrifting or die!) two great guys, Norm and Dennis, started it by asking if I was donating my roadster. By the time I left the store we were all friends, they gave me a name badge and made me honorary staff. It didn't hurt that I also found a perfectly lovely purple chiffon dress too. This dress was amazing. I could wad it up and it wouldn't wrinkle. I want a closet full of dresses like this. And all $14 each too.

If not for a few modern cars, my videotape of Rutland, Vermont would look like historical film footage. Every time I put the camera away I'd see something else and have to get it back out again. Old mansions were now photo studios, law offices and boarding houses and hadn't lost any of their architectural charm.

My second and last evening at Janet's house she got out her bag of runes and I reached in, shuffled the stones and pulled out the Death Rune.

Journal Entry: May 9

Unless I want my mail forwarded to Rutland, Vermont I'm going to have to get out there tomorrow and drive that little car. I can't just stay here and make a pest of myself. Although it is damned tempting...

36

Getting out of Rutland, Vermont was harder than getting in. There was a nasty traffic snarl and a big fat orange DETOUR sign in the middle of town. I followed in line with the other creeping vehicles. There were no further directional signs so I got royally off track. Hailed a fellow entering an industrial building. I knew I was in trouble when he began his directions with, "Go back the way you came..."

I was never completely lost but there were times when I had to wander around a bit. Highway 4 eventually gave me Highway 30 and I had to go north to get south. Lake Bomoseen was on my left and so blue that I stopped and parked under an unusual tree just to enjoy the cloudless morning.

At the Made in Vermont coffee place in Orwell, the sign on the door read: CREAM PUFFS TODAY. When you think about it, Mattie said, they have all the same ingredients as a bowl of cereal, so they must be breakfast. She was intrigued with the roadster and fortunately was one of those people who couldn't contain her enthusiasm. I answered questions although my attention was definitely more on my plate full of cream puffs. Mattie had moved her business to this new location, didn't know if it was going to work but people kept coming in. Two men, obviously regulars, arrived in head-to-toe brown camouflage, a great red beard on one of them. They were out to snag wild turkeys and claimed that the birds tasted just like regular Butter Balls. I had seen one of the big birds in a field, the first wild turkeys I could ever remember seeing. They said that was more than they had seen. Before I left I had learned whose babies were sleeping through the night, who owned a white Corvette and which gas station was going to be renovated. Had I ever had trouble talking to strangers? Only my whole life.

Walking into a roomful of strangers and attempting small talk was for me on the same pleasure level as root canal. Nobody really believed this because I speak to groups for a living. A possible explanation for this dichotomy was explained by the greatest speaker I've ever had the privilege to hear, Wally Minto. He asked, "Who do you think I'm talking to when I'm up in front of an audience? I'm talking to myself. The rest of you are just eavesdropping." Wally, a profound public speaker and the most effective teacher ever, was an introvert. That wasn't my assessment, that was Wally's self description during a week long training in Lake Tahoe. A keynote speaker was not engaging in a dialogue, he said, it was a one-way communication for the most part. This accounted for why many speakers had the I.Q. of a Valley Girl after a program. They're set on output, not input and they can't hear you. Like Wally, I too could move a group of 3,000 people to tears or laughter but when it came to cocktail parties, receptions and little social affairs, I'd rather clean an oven.

There was the story of a famous opera tenor who was asked how much it would cost to have him perform at a wealthy socialite's dinner party, he responded, "Five hundred dollars." The hostess was surprised with delight and invited him to stay for dinner. "That will be $5,000 extra," he replied.

So the fact that I could so easily slip into conversations with people on this trip was all new to me. I credited Seno with opening doors of communication with people the same way Charlie the dog did for Steinbeck. I hoped that this new facet of myself, this new comfort would last after the trip ended.

I photographed Mattie with her store sign and she insisted on giving me a gift, a small America flag on a stick. She pointed me toward the ferry and I left thinking cream puffs were certainly desirable over wild game birds. With all the gear they had, you know those turkeys were going to cost about $300 a pound.

And seven dollars would buy a one way passage on a cable ferry that had been crossing Lake Champlain since 1759. It connected Central Vermont with the Adirondacks. (www.middlebury.net/tiferry)

The fifth and sixth grade classes from Stockbridge, Vermont were all over that little ferry, a flat platform that made the crossing on used ski lift cables. I had rolled the roadster on board with only two other vehicles and the kids were drawn to it like ladies to chocolate. I lifted three of them into the drivers seat and the rest were sprinkled all around the car for their pictures. Larry, perfectly cast as the ferryboat operator with his Santa beard and great smile, must have hauled a stadium full of youngsters across Lake Champlain and appeared to have the patience required of such a job.

A finer day for a crossing could not be imagined. Both water and sky were intense clean peacock blue. The trip was far too short for me and the kids, probably too long for the teachers trying to keep them from rolling overboard like marbles. They were on their way to Fort Ticonderoga on the other side of the lake and when they exited, I thought, I could use a history lesson too. Memories of the significance of this fort were very hazy so I made an unexpected detour to this battlefield museum.

The impressive iron gate and stone entryway made me feel like I was entering the grounds of a millionaire's estate. A magnificent tree-lined drive added to the drama of the place. How nice it would have been to have seen my car doing this historic drive, cannons and markers all along the route.

This day, May 10th, was not only Opening Day for the Fort but also a particularly historic day for America. Two hundred twenty seven years ago on that date, Ethan Allen and his rascally Green Mountain Boys successfully captured Fort Ticonderoga from His Majesty's 26th Regiment. They stole the cannons for George Washington to use--a decisive action for the rebelling colonists. It was America's First Victory of the American Revolution. And here I was for this momentous occasion, what a lucky surprise!

The star-shaped fortification looked French because it was. The wilderness fort, looking more like a European castle, was the scene of skirmishes between the British and the Marquis de Lotbiniere. Located at a critical point of control, Fort Ti (as the locals call it) would always be a focal point of fighting.

"The strength of the Fort exceeds ye most sanguine imagination. Nature and Art are joined to render it impregnable." (Eli Forbush, 1759) Attacked six times in two wars, the fort never suffered a direct assault on its walls.

I walked the battlements, ramparts, barracks, parade grounds and peered over the cannons at the lake. Fort Ti with its complicated history and complicated defensive structure took awhile to see. There were so many cannons, I lost count. The displays of personal items brought home what it must have been like to be one of the hundreds of men who served there. I met Lisa, Jackie and Bill all staff who serve there now. (www.fort-ticonderoga.org)

Highway 9 droops and wiggles like warm taffy from Canada all the way to New York City. Seno and I enjoyed its curves for the length of Gorgeous George (Lake George). All the clouds were gone from the sky and from my worried mind. At one tiny pull out I had to stop, spread a beach towel and just sit and let the water diamonds stab my eyes. Surely Life would always be this perfect. The lake lapped near my head sounding like 50 thirsty St. Bernard puppies.

I found the world's largest Uncle Sam at the south end of the lake at a miniature Disneyland sort of attraction. His hands were posed in a grabby sort of gesture that reminded me of the IRS. He was 38 feet high and weighed over 4,500 pounds. At that size, just how big would his...well... This was just a fiberglass effigy. Unlike Elvis, Uncle Sam was dead and his grave was up ahead in Troy, New York, 50 miles to the south. Heck, I didn't even know he was sick.

At Glens Falls I got tangled up in gas stations, McDonald's, Dexter Shoes and a thing called Price Choppers, Ames and it had to happen: Adirondack Outlet Mall. The day was heating up and all the stopping and shifting was wearing me out. I tried escaping the wall-to-wall effort to get between me and my money by trying I-87 but the wind was violent. I had to opt for slower Highway 9 all the way to Albany. As usual Seno found the rougher section of town--like a dog to carrion. What was it about this car that drew him to high crime neighborhoods?

I consulted five maps and couldn't really decide which side of the Hudson River Saugerties, New York was on! I was having a devil of time trying to locate the KOA Campground so when I passed a group of firemen standing outside a fire station, all waving, I stopped for directions, remembering that these people have to know where everything was, in case whatever it was catches fire. Five of them surrounded the car and one had a T-shirt that read GIRLS ARE EVIL. I thought it was a fire station, not Fire Island, I could have been mistaken. When I asked for directions to the camp, the tallest one just pointed. Just past his finger and in the direction I was headed was the huge yellow and black KOA sign.

I was very busy with domestic chores that night. This time my camp site included a an electrical stump, a metal post with two electrical outlets. I set my egg cooker on top of the stump, plugged it in while I went about my other homey duties like operating the coin laundry machines. If I didn't get my clothes washed soon Seno wouldn't be the only one going topless. I made my bed for the night just as I had taught myself in Vermont. I arranged everything I needed and left only stealable items on my picnic table. I folded warm, dry clothes and peeled hard boiled eggs feeling very accomplished in my new simplified and efficient life. I crawled under the cover and into my bag, a tired but happy camper.

Roadster Lesson #13: It's OK to talk to people and it's OK to owe them a favor.

37

Getting Seno ready for the day's travel was more like packing a purse than a campsite. The simplicity was a delight. And once again, I had slept well.

She was into basket weaving and quilts, he was into sailing and fly fishing. They said they were "just trying it out for ten years," which I assumed meant the relationship...or perhaps they meant their RV. Jane and Larry from Staten Island were on their way to Stowe, Vermont. I met her while I was cooking a fresh batch of eggs on my makeshift stove, the pipe with outlets. She was beside herself; she couldn't believe I was from Oregon and had driven this little car all the way across the country. She was bundled in her Irish sweater, had the red hair of someone who'd spent the night outdoors. "Larry! You won't believe this! Come on over here!"

Larry looked me over like he thought I was going to ask them for money.

I toured the Catskills expecting to see lounge singers on every corner, like the movies suggested. The closest thing to that was a life-sized plaster Elvis Presley, complete with microphone at a tag sale near Ashokan. (Goodness, I could have sold it in Memphis later for a terrific profit if I could have gotten it in the car!) The sale was a rummage collective fund-raising event with a half dozen little areas set up along the roadway. I got to go shopping still in the car, slowly rolling by all the worn bicycles, ugly lamps, broken lawn furniture, old pots and pans, questionable appliances and card tables full of clothes without getting out of the car. I bought a purple bowling ball bag from Carol for a dollar but left her the purple bowling ball. Seno was probably relieved that he didn't have to haul it.

I stopped for coffee at Christy's and a fierce woman next to me repeated the word "moron" to her breakfast partner so vehemently that I couldn't help but overhear. It appeared to be her favorite word. "Social movements all go bad," he said to her. "Idiots" was her next favorite word and eventually all was taken over by the word "assholes." I had to leave to keep from doing something she and I would both regret later.

On and on I wandered in the chartreuse Catskill Mountains. I found a cold stream, a bridge, fresh pine furniture, garden shops, a zen monastery, a Mobil gas station with eatery called "Fillin' Station," a seven foot long Yellow Submarine and a guy who chased me down wanting to know if I'd like to buy his 1951 Bentley. Did I look like I could drive two cars at the same time?

I finally found the elusive and mysterious Highway 9W. I was beginning to think it was a cruel joke like a snipe hunt. But it did show itself and I was over the Hudson River bridge, graceful silver thing with arches and spires. I arrived at Vassar College as if I was used to driving there every day.

I had my Topless Web Guy David to thank for this next amazing piece of my adventure. I'd been picking up my emails from him at various libraries along the route and when I hit New England he wrote that his daughter attended Vassar, was I going to be near Poughkeepsie?

I found the college, found the dorm and eventually buffaloed my way through the locked doors. Kelley was on a rescue mission and when she returned to her lodgings with brother Robby in tow, they were gracious enough to take me to dinner and with the help of another Kelly, Vassar-ite, filled me in on the rather different environment of higher education in the lofty, thin air of this elite school.

Founded in 1861, Vassar had been consistently ranked one of the top liberal arts colleges anywhere. And it looked every inch of its reputation, its architecture alone was enough to strike fear into the wallet of even a well-heeled parent. Just over 2,000 students were privileged enough to call this home at any given semester. According to *Parade*, August 2002, Vassar students are reportedly the happiest.

Vassar shows up in films from time to time--everything from *Some Like It Hot* to *The Simpsons.* On one episode Lisa Simpson, who repeatedly referenced Vassar, said to Homer, "I won't be able to get into an Ivy League school and at this rate, I probably won't even get into Vassar." Homer responded with, "I've had just about enough of your Vassar-bashing young lady."

David's daughter Kelley and my own daughter Kelly were both blond, both brainy and had birthdays one day apart. They both came equipped with a social conscience. Kelley and her brother Robby had smiles that would blind a Crest executive. It being the eve of Mother's Day I couldn't help but think that any mom would be awfully proud to have dinner with these two.

The more I got to know Vassar the more I realized that it seemed to be more than just a college education. You graduate from anywhere, you have a degree. But you graduate from Vassar and you have an obligation to make something of yourself because so many of their graduates have. To make an outstanding contribution, no matter what, appeared to be implied. It seemed a given that you would cure cancer or win a Pulitzer. Over 75% of Vassar graduates went on to higher degrees.

I got to go higher at Vassar too, all the way up to the third floor of the Alumnae House with a grand view of the circular drive and my roadster parked as if he belonged there. The English Tudor manse reminded me of Oxford with its dark wood, doorways with points on top, and the cut glass. It all said, "I've been here for a *long* time." A bowl of fresh flowers pumped scent into the living room lobby. How was it possible that I was going to get to actually stay here? Surely, at any moment someone was going to catch on and throw me out. Kelley assured me that yes, I really was spending the night there and no, I didn't have to take an SAT test to do it. David had covered everything. David had done so many great things for me that I could spend the next 20 years just paying off that karmic debt. He worried about his two kids. I tried to console him with things like, "Being a parent is like being pecked to death by a duck." It was another one of those Belushi-with-the-beer-cans times. The only way to make his heart lighter was to surgically remove it from his chest. I had no idea when I started my trek that I would have the great good fortune to spend the night at Vassar.

And the AAVC (Alumnae and Alumni of Vassar College) should know that their contribution dollars are not being spent frivolously on things like Sealy Posturpedics for the Alumnae House. The beds have been around since Mary McCarthy.

I felt very grateful the next morning, leisurely having quiche and melon for breakfast in the historic Alumnae dining hall...until I noticed the sprinkling dots on the asphalt in the circular drive. It held off while I carted my things downstairs and out to the car. It stayed dry until I hit the Hudson River bridge.

That was the last moment of no-car-trouble I would have.

The metal grating on the bridge was the last straw for the welds on my left rear fender. I heard it crack loose and felt the fender flopping willy nilly next to my left elbow. I made it to the other side, stopped, called AAA who basically came, saw, shrugged and wished me "good luck." The clouds were descending. I got out my red duct tape and started in. Pretty soon I had what looked vaguely like a Union Jack of red tape securing the spastic fender. I looked hard at the little car.

"Is this as far as we go?" I asked. I didn't know if the tape would hold for one block, one mile or one hour.

38

I still wasn't able to accurately read the sky and predict the weather. The rain started and I had to pull into an abandoned restaurant and found their outer door open. I put on my yellow rain pants in the glassed in lobby area. Then I piled on all my jackets and topped the whole mess with the red poncho. I did my best to memorize the complicated path from Poughkeepsie to Irving's house in Chestnut Ridge, New York. I didn't want to consult a map in the rain. I had something called Bear Mountain to go over and West Point, the military academy. Surely if I got into any real trouble those nice Army guys would save me.

If I expected "windshield time" (that meditative state induced by long drives) today I wasn't going to get it. When the brakes got wet they started grabbing and the tires skidded. I had to take it slow even though that prolonged the agony. I could only hold the wheel and pray I'd make the next turn. I took solace in small things: I wasn't hungry, I had plenty of gas, the engine was running well, I didn't need a bathroom.

There was nothing to do but keep on keepin' on. It rained like the sky was crying its heart out. My heavy gloves soaked up water like kitchen sponges. It was easier to drive bare knuckled, gripping the cold, wet wooden steering wheel. When the winding road came out toward the river away from the cliffs, the wind gusts would move the car sideways.

There were two welds that held the fender to the car. What would happen if the other weld broke? Another reason to go slow and cautious. I'd have to react quickly but not panic. Keep control of the car despite the fact that the fender may fall forward and the tire run over it, or fall backward and land in the street, a hazard for some other car. Or if the duct tape held like I was hoping it would, the fender might flop up and attempt to land in my lap. What would this unlucky problem do to the rest of my trip? Was there to be a "rest of my trip"? What was I supposed to do with this fender? If it came off the car where could I stow it?

I needed more space in the car, just in case I'd have to carry the fender. In Oregon they would frown on such nonsense. It was illegal to drive a car without fenders in the rain. Fenderless cars only came out when the sun did. What were the laws in other states? What would they do to me if I had only 75 per cent of my fenders instead of 100 per cent? If I was stopped by a cop could I say, "Well, it just now fell off and I'm on the way to have it fixed? Don't know of any good welding shops do you?"

I mentally started taking inventory of everything I had packed under the bonnet and in the front seat with me. If nothing else it gave my mind something to do besides get hysterical as I drove on for miles and miles and miles in the pouring rain. I vowed to get a cardboard carton and fill it will everything I absolutely, positively might be able to do without and mail it home. A small fender was a very large item to shove into this car that barely had room for me. I was constantly shoving the pile of maps and cameras and food that would slide over from the passenger area. Then it dawned on me that I could strap the broken fender to the spare tire!

Why do cars have fenders? What purpose to they serve on a car like this? Can I get by without one? Could I still keep going? Mud and rain water splash around a bit but other than that, was it possible to run with just three fenders? The damned thing would be less of a hazard off than duct taped to the car.

More curves, more steep hills, more downshifting. I took a cloth and wiped the windshield. Both sides. The slower speeds meant more raindrops to contend with on the helmet. On and on. Now it was getting dark and headlights were being switched on. "This is a hell of a way to spend Mother's Day!" I thought. And then, "You must admit, Al, this is no ordinary Mother's Day..."

Travel has creative and unimaginable risks. Movie cowboy Tom Mix was crossing Arizona in his 1937 Cord when a suitcase flew off the rear shelf, hit him in the head and killed him. He was buried in Forest Lawn, California, the car was taken to Vegas and the suitcase ended up in Dewey, Oklahoma. Now tell me the airlines didn't have something to do with *that!*

The arches in my feet began to cramp. They were probably oxygen-starved, I thought, because I'm not breathing. Hare Krishna, Hare Krishna, Krishna, Krishna, Hare, Hare. Big breath. Hare Rama, Hare Rama...

The words of Elisabeth Bishop came to mind. She said, "Should we have stayed at home and thought of here?"

Journal Entry: May 12

I have never in my life been happier to see the inside of a garage than today. I drove 70 miles in pouring rain basically held together with band aids. Irving helped me with the route selection when I called on my cell phone somewhere on the west side of the Hudson River. Once I was dry and warm I collapsed into a pile of Christina's fresh scones. Between bites I looked up welding shops and auto fabricators in their local Yellow Pages. There were two. Were they any good? Could they be trusted? Could I feel any more vulnerable?

I needed Matthews and Howard and John and Phil and Laurie and Paul, all my car people back home. I needed a reference! Where was that Early Ford V-8 Roster? I didn't know the names of the towns so it didn't do me any good to look! Irving poured through the list of New York addresses in the roster. Seno, soaked with rain, dripped sadly in Irv's garage. It seemed as though the roadster was crying. The red duct tape was doing a championship job of holding the left fender. Then I discovered that the right rear fender had also broken a weld but was still held in place. My car is falling apart!

It some point a person has to ask themselves: is it time to abandon this project?

Irving found the name of someone near us!

39

I've done presentations for police departments in Washington State, New Hampshire (that was how I got those police patches to give to the coffee place in Laramie) and the FBI has hired me to do my full range of programs. After a few short years cops may take on a jaded persona. They weren't being know-it-alls, they had just seen humanity in a way that most people cannot imagine. They saw people get themselves into both humorous and horrible situations. If cops scratched their heads in disbelief every time they saw someone do something totally stupid, they'd have no hair left at all. And some of them don't.

I would think a DEA (Drug Enforcement Agency) law enforcement officer serving in New York City must be pretty much at the crossroads of bizarre human behavior, the intersection of evil and more evil, midtown between dumb and dumber. What most police departments see in a year, an NYPD cop probably sees in an afternoon. But DEA Special Agent (Ret.) Ross Kindestin was not expecting my call on Mother's Day evening and when I told him a) what I was doing, b) what I was driving and c) what had happened, he said, "*What?* No way!" as if it were a crank call.

OK, we both owned old Fords but beyond that had no blood kin and no introduction by friends. Strangers don't get any more total. I said, "Ross, I need a reference. There are two welding outfits in the phone book..." He immediately said, no, no, no and then he said, "I'll call you back, what's your number?"

The next morning Irving and I got up at 5:30 a.m. to meet Ross at a prearranged spot by 7:30. I followed Irv's silver Audi in pouring rain though city streets and part of a freeway that was a frightening nightmare of traffic and speed. I experienced the one moment on the trip where I was absolutely certain that I was going to die.

I would not be able to find this place again if offered a Packard speedster for the location. There was a little landscaping and what looked like new industrial storage buildings. Warm light was coming from an open bay, a huge garage door. Seno and I popped in there dripping wet. I pulled myself out of the cockpit. I wasn't sure I wanted to take my helmet off and reveal what kind of a blockhead would try crossing the country in this tiny, now wounded topless car.

I pulled my gloves off and shook hands with Ross who immediately gave me the impression that if you were adrift in the Atlantic, you'd want him on your lifeboat. As Paul Duchene would say, he was a guy "who knows stuff." And for this morning's task, he knew John Magee who owned the place and Joe Welfel who knew how to do stuff. Everybody was bent over the fenders, pulling yards of duct tape to get a better look.

"Well, they're welded to the brake drums!" they exclaimed as if I was trying to use mascara for nail polish.

My big question was: Is it terminal?

Mechanics learn not to promise *anything.* They have a persona all their own too. They seem to enjoy the drama of watching me sweat.

"Just leave it here," Ross said. Then they showed me the shop.

Oh, me. There was an elegant 1933 Lincoln sedan. And over there was a very rare 1953 woody. The whole place was as clean as my kitchen, but then I don't use my kitchen much. This was not a cramped, oily, shade tree operation. There were hoists and light and a sense of order. This was the Park Avenue of shops and when I saw the kind of classic iron they were restoring I was in awe. Bringing my little Brand X go-kart in here was like asking Dr. Christiaan Barnard to perform a tonsillectomy.

John, full of energy like a guy who has a pot of regular coffee flowing through his veins, was the czar of this kingdom and reportedly had dozens and dozens of done classic and vintage vehicles. Sedans, roadsters, lead sleds, street rod coupes, stockers with Detroit air still in the tires, cabriolets, convertibles. Joe, looking more like a long-haired rock star, was the welding wizard who just shrugged when I asked what he thought about my roadster's prospects. That shrug either meant, "Lady, we'll give you your car back in a body bag" or "This is so simple for me, I can't even act disturbed about it."

Mechanic must have the same root word as "panic."

I felt like I was leaving my dog at the vets. Seno and I had bonded. We'd escaped Canadian truckers, drag raced with a bus in Atlantic City, watched the ocean at sunrise and even slept together. Leaving was difficult. Ross walked around my roadster. "I'm not sure this thing is really built for cross country driving," he said diplomatically, creating the understatement of the season.

But Irving had the perfect distraction. We warmed up with a bagel first and then arrived on time at his writers' group. Seven people read seven autobiographical stories aloud and I was caught up in each one of them. I really was enthralled by the writing of this powerful little group. I felt I should have been charged admission for such entertainment.

Irv was entering his fifth month of retirement. When he woke up in January 2002 and fired himself from his own business, he spent about 15 minutes being depressed. Now he was taking classes in philosophy, the cosmos and writing. He had written a piece about our rather confusing first meeting in Oxford (I thought he was occupying my room, he thought I was trying to break into his room) and so that was why he wanted his group to meet me. I didn't want to spend too many minutes on what had brought me to New York because the whole idea of crossing the country seemed like an idiotic thing to be doing. Irv and I had imagined Seno actually making an appearance at this class, but that idea didn't make it over the Hudson River bridge.

That night I played with Mao-Me and Mr. Beasley, the cats that let Chris and Irv live with them and I slept in the guest bedroom, apart from Seno for the first time in 33 days.

It was a completely different mood the next day in the shop. When Irving and I arrived, I almost leaped out of his car before it came to a complete stop. "He brought his car!" I hollered as I grabbed both still and video cameras. There in glorious black and white was a 1939 Ford highway patrol car, totally tricked out with lights, siren, funky old radio microphone, handcuffs and a machine gun in the back seat for good measure. Wow! what a car! Ross posed with it, I posed with it, Ross and Joe posed together, I posed with them. I was so taken with the idea that an ex-trooper and DEA agent would actually have an old cop car, I was like heated popcorn. Ross showed me pictures of a younger Ross in his trooper uniform. How utterly perfect for him to have this car!

I pulled out the baby pictures of my cars and we all sat down over pizza and had a howling good time. Turns out that John and Irving both came from The Bronx and they were shouting street names at each other bringing back old memories. Joe and Ross and I swapped details about various cars we own and owned. Our little party must have sounded like an Italian wedding. We discussed Carlisle, Pennsylvania a car capital of sorts, many different car events scheduled there throughout the year. I had hoped to get to Carlisle for the upcoming national replicar event (the one I had told Ed and Nancy about in Massachusetts). John had been there many times and offered the best route. Look at this, gotta tell you about this, have you heard about that, did you know, I know this guy who, did you see...and on and on. We shifted partners in conversation every few minutes and continued yelling. It was more like being with a roomful of brothers. New Yorkers really can yell and listen at the same time. Oh, yes, and by the way, Seno was fixed.

With most things mechanical I just do my best to listen, nod and hope a trickle of information may make sense to me some day. But today I could see the welded brackets and even more importantly the braces Joe had added to secure the mess. The fenders were still welded to the brake drums which Joe said was a bad design and even I could comprehend that. Although they were plenty rugged now, the flawed design would eventually overcome the superb patch job. "They need to be stainless steel and bolted to the frame of the car, not the drums or the body," Joe said.

He had also fixed the brakes and changed the oil.

As near as I could tell, because there wasn't much hierarchy or formality, John would be the one to approach about the cost of this part of my adventure. I had personal checks, travelers checks, VISA, Master Card, just wondering which he'd like for the work.

None of it.

Oh, my God.

I looked like I was going to cry and John gave me a look of disgust like "don't do that" so I didn't. I have never identified with Blanche in *Streetcar Named Desire* and I did not know how to "depend on the kindness of strangers." It was a role totally foreign to me. He left. The rest of us piled into Ross's cop car and siren screaming, lights flashing tore around through the industrial park with Irving hollering from the back seat, "I want my lawyer!" We got to see a section of John's car collection in another warehouse. A Corvette engine stuffed in a woody, a hi-tech black street rod roughly valued at the cost of my house, a baby Lincoln convertible.

I had a great time with these people. They never once said, "Look, lady, call this number, it's a car transporting outfit, get on a plane and go home to Oregon." Not for an instant did they try to convince me to give up on the idea of driving my dumb little car any further. I'm not sure it ever occurred to any of them that I should quit. They all just jumped on board my dream and made it possible for me to continue even when I was wondering if I could go on.

There were hugs all around. "Be careful. Drive safe."

I backed out of the shop.

"And don't call if you get past Carlisle!" Ross added.

They were my angels: TEAM NEW YORK, I called them. Joe, Irving, Christina, Ross, John, Kelley, Robby.

I couldn't spend a dime in New York State. With everything New Yorkers had been through that year they still had some compassion and energy left over for my little problems. I was grateful beyond expression and overwhelmed.

40

I was reluctant to leave the security and care of TEAM NEW YORK. Part of me really, really didn't want to get in the car. But thanks to Joe, it was probably in better shape than when I left home over 4,000 miles ago. I was also loathe to face I-287, my least favorite highway so far, and I could have dragged my feet for a few more hours. Chris had already gone to work and unless I wanted to tag along with Irv to his doctor's appointment, I really needed to leave.

I followed his Audi to the on ramp and he waved. Poof! like that my Cary Grant friend was gone like turning off a television screen. My map did not illustrate I-287 well and I saw signs for Albany and New York City but nothing for where I wanted to go. Finally! A New Jersey sign and the road dipped south. Trucks and speed. But not as bad as the day I came up from Somerville--that was hell on wheels--big truck wheels. I was doing the speed limit that day and being passed by objects that could be rented out as tenement housing.

Passed Boonton and came to the exit for Highway 46, a "proper road" that connected towns with real businesses and real people and maybe even a pet or two. A brilliant sun was out between a very few puffy clouds as if it were Oz and would never rain again. A lovely Highway 57 took me through a New Jersey that appeared reasonably sane with trees and schools and mail boxes and driveways.

I crossed the Delaware River praying the fenders would stay on. They did and I exited for downtown Easton, a place I'd been looking forward to visiting for several months. I was here to learn how Crayola crayons were made. Most grandmothers are very familiar with Crayola's products; I'm a particular fan of their clay. Downtown Easton really was the traditional town square complete with military statue but with water element, jumping fountains added. There was a sweet shop on one corner, angled parking all around. I expected Shirley Temple to come tapping down the street at any moment. Easton gave me the impression that nothing bad has ever happened here and nothing bad ever could. Sure, it was an illusion...and I liked it.

The very bright, very decorated Crayola Factory exhibit and gift emporium anchor one side of the town square. There were two story high crayons, embroidered shirts, back packs that looked like Crayola boxes, play stations with plastic buckets full of crayons and tubs full of white clay. I wanted all of it. I found little wooden boxes with type on the lid that read: TRUE BLUE HERO. Inside was a single big blue Crayola. Ross needed one of these I thought. And there was a very funny embroidered T-shirt with the Cheshire cat and its smile was a set of crayons. Christina should have that I thought.

Finally did learn how crayons were made. They started life as a liquid, not even a thick liquid. This stuff, about like milk, was poured, sloshed over rows of empty cylinders. When they cooled, they were popped out by the hundreds in one stroke. I watched the machine wrap them and then the craziness required to get 48 different colors in one box. Admission to the factory included three tokens that you could exchange for product. I had to keep all my tokens as souvenirs; they have a cartoon character Crayola embossed on a metal coin. It wasn't actually *the* factory, it was more a 20,000 square foot "unique family discovery center." (www.crayola.com/factory)

I was enjoying Easton so much that I wandered on foot for awhile and found a muralized alley that insisted on be investigated. If townspeople only knew how sweet and intriguing these little touches can be to a visitor, well, there'd be more of it. The mural had pieces of silver mirror and some of it was mosaic-like. Painted metal chairs and tables were encouragement to investigate further. The Purple Cow Ice Cream Parlor beckoned. City planners, this was what people wanted, human-sized streets that seduce a traveler with interesting things to see, water features, flags and banners, pots and posts with flowers, arches and open gates, environments that make a person want to sit and read in the sun.

When I walked back to Seno he was surrounded by his fans again, ages ranging from seven to about eighty seven, I think. One old lady said, "Nice buggy."

Young guys asked: "How fast will it go?"
Old guys asked: "What kind of gas mileage does it get?"
Women asked: "Is this your only car?"
Someone will always ask: "What do you do when it rains?"

A person revealed their value system by the questions they asked. Their fears and desires were handed to me in easy-to-read parcels.

I barely managed to get me and my gifts stuffed into the cockpit. There wasn't room for anything any more. I drove directly to the post office just three blocks away. Fortunately everything needed to package or box stuff was all right there in the post office. I mailed the gifts and once again had queries to answer when I returned to Seno. One Baby Huey looking guy, probably 30 or so asked about a top. I said, "There is no top. It is a topless car." Then he looked right at the web site address on the boat tail and asked, "What is the 'Going Topless' about?"

So my response may have sounded like I was addressing someone who had an I.Q. of toast. I couldn't help it. I again said, "It's a topless car. I am driving it top-less--the car is topless."

Argh. I vowed not to stop again for a long time.

I drove through Hershey, Pennsylvania every woman's favorite town, hoping I wouldn't be dragged off the road by the tempting smells. Hershey hosted the biggest car swap meet in the known world and all old car buffs know it. "Ya goin' to Hershey this year?" was typical car club conversation even on the west coast. So I'd *done* Hershey complete with the little Disneyesque ride through chocolate land that shows how the addictive stuff was made. But they don't sell it for one cent cheaper than can be bought anywhere else, so I hadn't planned a stop. I didn't know until I drove down into the dip with the green park that the street would be lined with people. No, they were not the advance team for our arrival. They were Hershey workers on strike. Sitting in lawn chairs and waving printed signs on wooden sticks, the afternoon protesters were relieved to have something interesting to look at. Me and Seno. We became an instant parade with strikers hollering and cheering us on as if we were arriving at the finish line. A very fit old bicyclist with muscular legs and a baseball cap came up on my left. "Trade you titles straight across," he suggested. "Some days it would be tempting," I answered, knowing full well that this pleasant sunny afternoon drive with all parts of my car in tact made the adventure look easy.

When I tired of staring into the western sun I searched for a motel and found one perfectly tucked away and secure. I didn't see a vacancy sign so I parked, went in and stood at the check-in counter. I could hear a television and I could see into what looked like the manager's living room. I waited and waited. No one came. I pinged the bell. Still no one. I was thinking about leaving but my body was too tired to move. The motel's business cards were stacked there so I got out my cell phone, called the number and could hear it ringing. Suddenly a man appeared to answer the phone and I discreetly pushed the "end call" button. "Uh, wrong number, I guess," he said. I smiled. And checked in.

41

When I emailed Paul in Oregon that I had made it to the Carlisle, Pennsylvania national replicar meet, his email response was, "I hope they have enough tow trucks." I believe my response back was something like, "I have five fingers and one of them is for you." I didn't feel like communicating with him for the rest of the trip.

In any special interest group there are purists and there are enthusiasts and they get together on only one issue--who the bastards are. I'm sure the national kennel club has their elite breeds and their not-completely-sanctioned breeds but they all agree on what a mutt is. I suppose if you're into knitting there are those who probably look down their noses at acrylic yarn. Sometimes I think people get involved in their avocations just so they can divide and judge other people. It's all part of the human condition evidently.

In the vintage and classic car world there are "genie" people, short for "genuine" and they strive (some of them fanatically) to have their cars look just like they came off the show room floor. Pop a Chev engine in that Ford or change the original paint color and the car was now a "street rod." Before I got into this car craziness, I thought that a street rod was some sort of mean vehicle that drag raced on city streets. Well, some do but the term street rod has come to mean any deviation from the original. There are street rods out there in the six figures with tilt-air-cruise, exquisite craftsmanship and safer than any original car. Depending on the condition (and the brand) street rods frequently go for higher prices.

But genie people or street rodders, they all knew who the mutts were. Replicars. Kit cars. "Smells-like-a-boat-on-a-hot-day" cars. "It's-not-real" cars. Plastic cars. Homebuilt cars. Impostors.

Get around anybody with an old car and say the word "kit" and watch the body response. The neck stiffens slightly pulling the nose into an upward position. The eyes may glaze over as if profoundly bored.

Now here at the Carlisle, Pennsylvania fairgrounds was a national meet of these cars. I thought it was pretty amazing that Seno and I should actually be able to be at this place and at this time. It would be like accidentally being in Liverpool on the day the Beatles stopped off to dedicate their hometown plaque or something.

Who knows what Seno was exactly. He was built in somebody's garage more than 35 years ago and with no manufacturers' identification anywhere, his heritage was only a guess. Now I've got "real steel" at home. To the purists, I can show them the pictures of my 1937 Packard sedan. That's Eleanor and she is painfully stock which means she'll go from zero to 50 in 15 minutes (downhill). To the street rodders, I can show them pictures of Franklin, my 1940 Ford with the 283 small block and the heart-melting dusk pearl paint job. To either of these groups I don't even mention that I *have* Seno. It was too embarrassing. Brand X doesn't even begin to describe it.

So I was looking forward to a car event where Seno could park on the grass with the others (instead of off site) and be among his kin, sort of. I fully expected to see other 1927 Bugatti replicars and hoped to get some ideas from them.

Kit cars had their slick magazines, their cruises and their clubs, now here was their national meet. I was looking forward to being around car nuts that didn't get their knickers in a twist over the word "fiberglass." What I saw were imitation Cobras that knocked my socks off. And sports cars that sparkled with deep, rich paint jobs. Over 1,000 cars were due at this event and over 20,000 people. A whole fairground full of "mutts."

I shopped the swap meet section, always enjoying the odds and ends (mostly odd) that coagulate at these events. In-your-face statements on license plate frames, antique chauffeurs badges, Dremel heads by the thousands, flags, car wax, peddle cars, juke boxes and enamel hat pins. Some purists feel that wearing an MG pin when your car was actually a kit car of an MG was like wearing a military medal when you never went to war. (I really tried to avoid all this. Over my lifetime I've watched myself join groups, not just car groups! and as soon as I get a whiff of politics and elitism, I slip out the back, Jack. I like looking at *all* the cars, probably because I'm looking at shape and color.)

I photographed some great dogs sleeping under swap meet tables and avoiding the sun. I had the best hot pretzel that I'd ever had in my whole life. I was having a good time.

Ah, now, what's this? Looks like a baby '59 Cadillac. The fins so big they had to have two tail lights. The ultimate fins. But they weren't on a Caddy. The were on a Miata, a little silver 90s sports car. What a hoot! It was highly unlikely that Mazda would have created this. I met Peter Ronco Jr., 74, who thought of this whacko idea and then executed it beautifully. He said the Miata enthusiasts hated it and the Cadillac people were livid that he "ruined" a '59 to create this. He'd had the junked, wrecked Cadillac sitting around for 40 years and it was out past redemption when he took what he could from it and transplanted the distinctive fins to the modern convertible. His Ronco "Miatillac" had won awards at various car shows and been photographed in newspapers and magazines. One person's abomination was obviously another person's heart throb.

I couldn't be a purist. It took too much energy.

I wandered across the fairgrounds to check on Seno. An intense blue car was parked behind him, a swoopy thing with gull-winged doors that were wide open showing off an even more intense yellow interior. The owner matched his car, a Bradley. No, he didn't have wings but I'm sure if he could, Steve would have grown a pair. He was wearing a blue tank top that matched the blue-blue of his car and his hair was dyed neon yellow. Permanently dyed.

"Everything on the car I done," he said (direct quote). He built the car, painted the car and then taught himself to sew so he could do the upholstery too. Not shy and not boring, Steve Striharsky of Milford, Pennsylvania added, "I'm an attention junky." I suggested that his car should have its own web site.

If I wanted colorful characters on my journey I certainly found them. From the Russian who teased and toyed with visitors at the Hindu temple to the sunny-topped car nut in Carlisle, there was something for everybody on this trip!

But no other Bugatti showed up, real or fake.

I didn't like the term "kit." It made it sound like the car came out of a cereal box. So I would say "home built." That was a little bit like saying "single" instead of "divorced." Both are true but one had less stigma than the other. Alyce, I thought, what would happen if you called a spade, a spade instead of an "instrument"? Try it. Let's see if you can actually say it and see if the sky still stays up. Call it a lesson in ego adjustment.

So I did. The next 12 people on the trip who asked "What is it?" I replied, "Nothing special. Just a kit car." And the sky did not fall. And it did not seem to deter Seno's admirers either. While *even the guy who sold me the car* had a descriptive and derogatory name for it that I cannot print, the purple roadster had its fans.

I had a little meeting downtown with David Blymire of the Carlisle *Sentinel.* With historic markers on nearly every corner, David told me that Carlisle was the origin of "Molly Pitcher" who was probably a real person and evolved into a concept--sort of like Rosie the Riveter. A Molly hauled pitchers of water to soldiers during the Civil War, legend goes, and then took over firing cannons when soldiers fell. There were probably many Mollies but the original came from Carlisle.

I loved driving around Carlisle in my roadster because there were spires, turrets, slate, even round porches way aloft with wicker chairs under weather vanes. Such an interesting town required a topless car to take advantage of the sights.

Now I was again on my way to the Ironmaster's Mansion at Pine Grove Furnace state park just south of Carlisle. I was looking forward to seeing a familiar place, a rare thing on this trip of every day something new. The temperature had dropped from the summery heat to a chilling find-the-gloves late afternoon. A few sprinkles dotted the roadway. I raced through the Pennsylvania countryside, made my correct right angle turns, up and into the forest and barely made it to the hostel.

I checked in with Shawn the piano playing caretaker again. In the kitchen I met Karl, a Philadelphia lawyer just in off the Appalachian Trail. Some mishap had caused him to "miss his drop" of supplies so he had no food. Hey, not a problem, I said and the two of us got in Seno and with what was left of the day, ran between the raindrops into the Mt. Holly Food Market. Karl suggested spaghetti and I said, sure. This hostel and spaghetti, just seemed to go together. Diane the sweet checker at the market wrote down Seno's web address and said she couldn't wait to get home and look us up on the internet. There was barely room for me, tall Karl and the sacks of groceries and it didn't help that the two of us got to talking and therefore, momentarily got lost in the confusing countryside north of the hostel.

That's the second time I'd been tangled up in the same area!

Karl and I both wanted to take Shawn up on his offer to show us how the old mansion had been used during the Underground Railroad days. I asked him if the place had any spirits. "I'm not exactly sure, but..." he began. The young caretaker had lived as the hostel keeper for a few weeks before he decided to explore the underside of the house. Why he had elected to do this alone and while the big, old house was empty was beyond me but he did. He said he took a fully charged flashlight with him. Once down there, looking over the stone walls of the cellar and finding the pathway used by slaves to escape to the next safe point, the flashlight dimmed and the light nearly went out. He exited in a hurry. "There was nothing wrong with the flashlight," Shawn said.

Under the stairs was a little, odd-shaped closet and set into the floor was a wooden square with an iron ring in it. Shawn pulled it up and we could barely make out a ladder going straight down into the darkness. Karl had a small spelunker's headlight strapped to his head, a simple portable thing for us to use as light. He went down the ladder first descending into the dark. I climbed in right after him. The phone rang and Shawn left to answer it. The cellar reminded me of the one in my country grandma's farm house so I wasn't too creeped out...at first...by this one. Karl and I located two holes that would have been difficult escapes for a full sized adult. He shined his light into the adjacent chamber and we could see the place where Shawn said most likely was the tunnel to the forest. Slaves had to travel at night to insure their safety even in Union territory. If the family who lived here had been caught helping this human property escape the South, they would have forfeited everything, including the house. What a sobering thought that was. It reminded me of the house in Amsterdam where Anne Frank and her family hid for two years.

"Some of my relatives," Karl said, "were passengers on the Underground Railroad and may well have crossed through the Ironmaster's Mansion." About that time the light strapped to his head began to dim. We beat a hasty retreat to the small square hole at the top of the ladder.

Karl's cooking brought out another hostel visitor, Lori from Boston. It was easy to strike up a conversation in a hostel because travel was always the common denominator. Karl had 13 more days on his Appalachian Trail trip. He seemed quite serious and very physically fit. Lori had been to a Beltane festival in Florida and sounded like the ceremonies included the Great Rite. One more round of "It's May, it's May, the month of yes, you may!" Lori and I squealed with laughter when we both remembered the monster exhibit on the shores Loch Ness. She had been to Intercourse, Pennsylvania and Blue Balls. Nothing there, she said. I wasn't that interested in place names to consider going there. I drew her a map of how to get to the Purple Cow in Easton. The most accurate travel information available seemed to come from youth hostels. And as for youth, none of us were teenagers.

Later, snuggled into sleeping bags, Diana, a military vet, joined the slumber party in the women's dorm. Unlike most slumber parties, however, we were all beat from our various adventures. Tired pups ready to call it a day.

It poured rain all that night. In the morning the drizzling continued and I took my own sweet time in the shower and having breakfast. The longer I waited, the better my chances for the weather clearing. Everyone left on their personal quests. I knew I was supposed to be off the grounds by 9:30. I stayed and helped Shawn with chores until ten o'clock, sweeping the women's dorm area.

There was nothing to do but get in the car and drive it. It was very dark and closed in even at mid-morning. Wet roads, trees still dripping out of the woods to Highway 30. After only 20 miles I had to stop at the first available cafe to thaw out. Warm oatmeal helped. Back in the car I draped a large beach towel across my legs to help stay warm. The rain had let up but it was one of those days when I had to wear everything I owned.

Made short work of Maryland, the twenty first state for Seno, which consisted primarily of Hagerstown. Crossed the Potomac, then into a small piece of West Virginia where I had to stop to thaw again. I viewed buying something to eat as payment for getting heat and bathroom privileges and I desperately needed both. This time I had corn chowder and a biscuit. More carbs.

There seemed to be an abundance of trailers, mobile homes, double wides and modular homes for sale. And businesses with FOR SALE signs. In Martinsburg a grey wood one story building without windows had a pink sign: SHOW GIRLS. What, I wondered, would a West Virginia show girl look like?

Arrived in Winchester, Virginia and my signal to myself to look for Highway 7 eastbound. But I got hooked on the historic burg with its large, stately mansions and instead followed signs to the Chamber of Commerce tourist information place. On the way there I saw an old Model A. In the distance I spotted a turquoise '55 Chev. Two old cars headed in the same direction meant that there was a car event going on somewhere. Maps from the patient and thorough information lady and with 20 pounds of paper propaganda I was out the door and to the park.

Seno created quite a stir even though this was a "legit" car event with dozens of marvelous classics and high dollar vintage iron. I barely got the roadster stopped near the vendor stands when we were surrounded with curious people, definitely not shy about asking questions. My 1927 Oregon license plate really threw everybody for a loop. Yes, I had indeed driven the thing over 4,000 miles now. I handed out my little information sheet with Seno's web address. A large fellow named Ron said he had something I should see and he held up a sample graphic that read: CRUISIN' TOPLESS. I thought that was a fun item to have so I unbuttoned the red shirt I'd been using as a jacket and tossed it to him. This little family's business has the motto "You Pick It, We Stick It." His wife Dawn melted the image onto the back of my shirt, I popped Amber and Bryce, their kids, in my car and pretty soon the roadster and I were like one of the regulars there in the park having a good old time.

I saw a 1917 electric Detroit, a 1932 Lincoln KB, a very trick 1953 Ford fire truck and a still-driven 1911 Model T, its tires were muddy! Sometimes I think that owning an old car was just an excuse for grown ups to go play the park.

Winchester, at the top of the Shenandoah Valley, was once Shawnee Indian camping grounds that attracted Pennsylvania Quakers in 1732. The owner of the royal land grant that included Winchester hired George Washington (yes, *the* George Washington) to survey the area. Washington had his office there for three years and right in downtown Winchester, I visited the place, still standing. During the Civil War poor little Winchester changed flags seventy times during the four year conflict. Thirteen times in one day. Stonewall Jackson knew the area well because he lived there with his wife and his headquarters were on North Braddock Street. In fact, our forefathers' names were all over Winchester! There were houses from the Revolutionary period, plantation period, antebellum mansions and more recently, of course, the birthplace of Patsy Kline who was probably "Crazy" about the place. Patsy died in a plane crash in Tennessee in 1963 but in 1995 her "Greatest Hits" album sold *six million copies!*

"The Apple Capital." Well, they would have to duke it out with a few towns in Washington State. Winchester was 72 miles from Washington, D.C. but it really was a world away. I had my hands full trying to drive and take in all the fine old estates. I finally gave up and parked near George's survey office. There was a street fair going on and I was delighted to run into lemon poppy seed muffins and the Queen of Hearts (Angela Woods) and Alice (Leslie Bowery) and a huge papier mache tea pot, courtesy of the Winchester Parks & Rec. Of course, Alyce had to have her picture taken with Alice.

The architectural sonata in the middle of Winchester was the library with just about every major geegaw ever put on a public building. I loved it! Inside on a bench was a realistic bronze of a little girl reading a book. Just made me want to sit down next to her and spend the afternoon reading. I sort of hoped that it was one of my books she was reading. Across the street really was the Big Apple, no relation to NYC. I have no idea what that thing was made of but a human being standing there would have been about the size of a worm.

The clouds drifted higher, the sun came out and Seno and I crossed the Shenandoah River with an easy drive to Bear's Den, the hostel in Bluemont, Virginia. Nestled high in the picturesque Blue Ridge Mountains, I think this used to be the stone home of a wealthy doctor. Now it was a 26-bed hostel and so much a part of the forest that I had to actually be at the house to see it.

An older fellow with an Amish-style beard used my arrival to teach a younger man named Mike how to check someone into the hostel. Mike had three sons orbiting him like little moons: Ryan, and twins Justin and Nicholas. I had my pick of bunks in the ladies dorm room but the hostel was going to fill up that night. I stowed my things on a bottom bed as far from the bath facilities as possible. I was a veteran. I knew that if I had my sleeping set up by that bathroom door, I'd be disturbed during the night.

This hostel was not only located on the Appalachian Trail, it was owned and operated by the AT Conference. Third grader Ryan volunteered to show me where the Trail was and where "The Rocks" were. We walked down, down, down a narrow path through very dense woods and came to an outcropping of cement-colored rock. The lack of vegetation on these rocks allowed me to see all across the Shenandoah Valley. I could see the highway, a divided four-lane ribbon far, far below. Rain clouds had turned pink and there was a hint that possibly a sun was up there. The expansive view was like an aerial view from an airplane. Only no sound. Not a rustle. Way off to the west, lights that looked like tiny Christmas lights were beginning to come on. Probably the town of Berryville, Virginia. I got my first taste of why they call these mountains blue. They were.

I watched until the light shifted and gave me a whole new scene.

When Ryan (such a gentleman!) and I arrived back at the hostel a familiar dark Jeep-style sort of ride came wheeling through the stone gates. Whoa! It was Diana the Navy lady I'd met at the Pennsylvania hostel the night before!

"Did you know you made the front page of the Carlisle newspaper?" she asked and, of course, I had no idea. She gave me her copy, I read the article and by golly, David the reporter needed an "A" from Alyce for getting the information right! Of all the high dollar cars pampered and displayed at the fairgrounds, my little Seno was right there in all his purple majesty as the lead story on the front page.

The group at the Bear's Den that night was even more eclectic than ever even for a hostel that close to the nation's capitol. Diana was traveling across the United States by herself, off to see relatives in Texas and eventually get to California. A couple arrived, she an exotic woman from Nepal (unexpectedly extroverted) and he, Swedish looking and named Hans. Everybody was invited to walk down to a cabin that the AT group had restored. The scrapbook of pictures showed the terrific work it took to get this thing back up to living standards. The couple had rented it for the night. It was spartan, I suppose but so surrounded by trees that a person would have to know exactly where it was to find it again. Later a gab fest took hold around the big stone fireplace in the large living room. I located my brochures about the Palace of Gold and everyone was as amazed as I was about it. Didn't anyone in the world know about that place except me and the Russian?

Journal Entry: May 18

For the first time on this trip I went back to being Alyce Cornyn-Selby instead of Seno's mom.

Hans asked me about my work and seemed to hang on the answers. A sucker for a good question, I rattled on until it is now approaching midnight, teaching most of my course and answering questions about self sabotage and my system. This has been the only time on the trip I have been asked about my work instead of the car. Hans thinks that he has found his passion and this time, he vows he isn't going to sabotage his efforts. He has good ideals, lofty plans and knowledge and drive. How many of us have had the same, me included? "We shanghai our own ships," he said. Man, has he got that right! As usual when I get into my subject, I get excited and now it is getting difficult to shut it off inside my head and get to sleep. A group of youngsters traveling together has filled the dorm room and I need to find my ear plugs. If they can block out the sound of Harleys at that hostel in San Diego, they'll handle anything these teen angels can dish out.

42

My internal Commandant Ruff Rider was in great form at 5:40 a.m. the next morning. He wanted to see plenty of miles today. There was no getting back to sleep once he had his heels dug into my psyche. All the other characters in my head could only groan and go along with his program.

Someone had beat me to the bathroom! "New policy!" shouted the Commandant. "When you wake up, *get up!*" Yes, sir.

I don't think the rest of me really woke up much before Front Royal, Virginia. The Kid in me had to stop the car for some goofy dinosaurs at an attraction that wasn't open yet. Shoot, nothing was open yet. There was no traffic going to the north entrance of Shenandoah National Park because *nobody* was up yet.

Skyline Drive was the first 105 miles of the Blue Ridge Parkway. It started, if coming from the north, at Front Royal and laid down neatly along the backbone of the Appalachian mountain range. It was a gorgeous piece of asphalt, smooth and perfectly maintained.

The park ranger taking the money was such a jolly lady I thought for a moment there that she was a mechanized Disney character. She was all atwitch over the roadster and said she was going to phone ahead to her husband, also a park ranger and he was at the Dickey Ridge Visitor Center, would I please stop by there? I did that and was "rewarded" with the "it's only a kit car, huh?"

"Yeah," I said. "It's only a kit car and I drove it all the way from Oregon."

Where was a Starbucks, anyway? I needed something more than mountain air and fabulous views that morning.

Seno and I did much sashaying. A waltz should have been playing as we took left curves, then right curves, then left curves, then right curves. My butt slid back and forth and back and forth across the seat of the car. I'm surprised I didn't start a fire. The views were great but not different enough to continue the entire length of Skyline Drive. Besides, I had just done this route three years previously and I'm sorry but it just wasn't as interesting (to me) as Glacier National Park or the Lincoln Highway. I exited at Highway 211 and headed west to Luray.

Going through town I was pleasantly surprised to find us driving by a 200-year old brick building painted purple with red windows. Now there was a photo just waiting to happen. I positioned my purple and red roadster just to the right of the red door and walked across the street, the early morning light just perfect. A creepy, grizzled old wino staggered toward me and I knew what was coming. Seno attracted all kinds but I didn't have to stay and answer all questions.

Caves were not high on my list of natural wonders but after seven million years in the making, I thought Luray Caverns might be worth a stop. I was way out in front of everyone that day so I made the first tour there. People get married in caves, I've always thought that a tad odd but then they've got no where to go but up after that. As usual, when I parked Seno in a large parking lot I secured everything and snapped the tonneau cover knowing that I may come back to nothing under that cover. Getting my hard shell helmet finally adjusted to my head meant that I probably couldn't replace it easily. I had to carry the thing with me like a purse.

Some of the chambers in this cave were 140 feet high. I liked that because I get a little nervous and wonder about earthquakes usually about the time I've paid my admission and gotten well into the tour. With this spacious cave, I didn't get that attack of claustrophobia that sometimes hits me. And the Luray Caverns had one terribly unique thing that was worth seeing. The Stalacpipe Organ was the world's largest natural musical instrument. If a frozen, dripping chunk was struck, it would emit a tone. Well, some music nut attached bongers to different chunks and connected everything so that it "played" sort of like an organ. They played "Oh, Shenandoah" when I was there. It really was angelic music.

Gluttony may describe my willingness to see still more old cars displayed there at the Luray Car and Carriage Caravan. It was all part of the caverns so I strolled through. This exhibit started with a stone wheel, for heaven's sake and went up from there. I was very impressed with the Conestoga wagon. I didn't know they were as big as ships. For most normal people this would have been one old car too many for the miles I had traveled so I won't even go into what was there.

I settled in for a good long haul on the interstate and hours of wind buffeting me relentlessly. At least it wasn't raining. And while the sun was shining I needed to make as many miles as I could. Just one good rainstorm and I'd be in bad shape for Memorial Day holiday in Tennessee.

I-81 didn't exactly parallel the Blue Ridge Parkway but it kind of did. I had wondered when I was plotting routes just what the Blue Ridge Parkway was. It didn't have a designated number like all roads do. I had romantic visions of driving the entire length of it, all 469 miles from Shenandoah National Park to the Great Smoky Mountain National Park. It was an Appalachian Trail for wheels. But at 45 miles per hour, that was eleven hours of driving without stopping. I calculated that would be about 24 hours of roadster driving, which would mean I'd be in Virginia for three days. The Commandant would never stand for that. I began to think of the Blue Ridge Parkway as a driveway, an elevated bike path.

So I hauled ass with the trucks all day long on I-81. I managed to convince myself that I was once again in danger of becoming my father if I didn't stop to see Natural Bridge. I had never heard of this wonder and wouldn't have if I hadn't picked up a Natural Bridge brochure at Luray Caverns. It was less than five minutes from the interstate, the brochure claimed. I could invest that amount of time.

Sure glad I did. The only reason I was able to see it was because a Forest Service guy named Ben York watched Seno for me. There must have been 200 or 300 cars parked outside the big exhibit hall entrance to the path to see the Bridge. An enormous hotel, the size of the Supreme Court, was across the highway. But off to the left was a little parking lot and the little Forest Service office. This was where I met Ben and he volunteered to guard my roadster with his life. If it hadn't been for him I would have had to just go back to I-81 and keep driving.

Thomas Jefferson paid two shillings (about $2.40) for Natural Bridge in 1774! Route 11 crossed the top of this natural limestone arch. The thing was 215 feet up if it was an inch and spanned about 90 feet. It was listed as one of the Seven Natural Wonders of The World, right up there with Niagara Falls and The Blue Grotto of the Island of Capri, Italy. In fact, of the Seven Wonders, five on the list were in America. One wonders who made up the list...

It was a cloudless warm day and the walk along the cold stream was just what I needed. For all my hiking to prepare for the trip, I really hadn't kept up my walking routine. Legend has it that during the Revolutionary War, men would pour drops of molten lead from the top of the Bridge and then when they picked them up out of the river they were metal spheres and they could be used as bullets. And I really did love it when I discovered that George Washington had left his G.W. carved into the cliff, the left hand span of Natural Bridge. Oh, George, you graffiti artist you, we'd have you arrested if you did that in Portland.

As near as I can tell, Natural Bridge was privately owned and that accounts for the intense tourista atmosphere. Do we really need another Frisbee with a bad drawing of Natural Bridge on it? On the other hand, this was America, after all and profit was not a dirty word.

I couldn't afford to take too much advantage of Ben's time so I walked down the path, saw the Bridge, walked under it, admired the clear water, tried to comprehend the incredible distance to the top and then hiked back to my car. It was Sunday and every grandma in Virginia was being hauled to Natural Bridge that day. Seno and I drove over Natural Bridge so we could say we had done it and then went back to the interstate.

I-81 was not without its pretty spots. Someone had planted mass quantities of wild poppies in the grassy strip between north and south lanes. These plantings had grown into entire carpets of poppies. They were fabulous! Most were multi-colored pink, red and white and looked like a living Monet painting. Some were all one color and just really did a lot to ease the long ride. Beautiful. This kept up for miles and miles. Every time I looked at the map of Virginia, however, the state seemed to get bigger.

Seno and I turned south after Pulaski on I-77 that went to Charlotte. When I stopped to get gasoline I consulted my ever present American Youth Hostel book and found there was another hostel near Galax,

Virginia so I called. "I hope you don't get lonely," friendly Alex said who answered the phone and took my reservation, "because there probably won't be anyone else staying tonight." If I got lonely, I told him, I wasn't aware of it and the way I was traveling (which he would soon see) loneliness was the least of my problems.

I turned onto the Blue Ridge Parkway at Fancy Gap. Seeing only one store and not thinking it at all fancy I began the monotonous task of counting the little wooden peg mile markers looking for the hidden turn off to the Blue Ridge hostel. The road was all graceful curves that could make a person seasick after awhile and I was so paranoid about missing the entrance, I began making myself crazy. The sun was getting low in the sky but now in the thick trees it was getting downright dark. Even though I was going slow, I whizzed right by the grey gate and had to back up. There were probably three cars on the Parkway for all the time I had been on it. An amazing contrast to the weekend traffic on the interstates.

There was a narrow winding path, not a road really, through the trees. The sun winked and blinked like a beacon as I drove and I could feel myself begin to relax. The forest was carpeted with leaves as if it were autumn. Such a sweet drive and a path just barely big enough for Seno to slip through. When it finally ended at a grey and white house, two dogs did their best to bark and warn anyone who would listen. What sillies! I knew they were good old dogs. I let them come up to the car and sniff my hand. They both instantly got wiggly and welcomed me.

Not so the strange lady who scowled very intensely at me. She had a cordless phone in her hand and was beating it on a picnic table. I pulled myself out of the car and I wasn't sure I should try to walk past her. She stood up and marched away not speaking. I could leave, I thought, but I'm at the end of my energy rope and there was nothing in the way of lodging within miles. I knocked on the front door and was warmly greeted by cordial and funny Alex, a cool grandpa kind of guy. He showed me up a flight of outdoor wooden stairs to the airy second floor that was a large kitchen and a larger dorm room.

Journal Entry: May 19

Very cold. Very tired. Could barely get stuff out of Seno and answer questions. Warmed up with oatmeal and hot chocolate. It's only 8 p.m. but I am overcome with exhaustion. Getting down to freezing tonight. I've got a month to go. The North Carolina state line is probably only three miles from here. I need clean hair and clean clothes and warmth for a few days SOON. Thank God I have this place to myself. I'm so tired I can't speak.

43

Prior to this trip I only experienced true comfort in a temperature range of about three degrees, somewhere between 72 and 75. Now I had been experiencing dry, blowing heat for hours at a time and stretches of cold that I could not have imagined.

The upstairs of the Blue Ridge hostel was aptly named; I was certainly blue. I had slept in my clothes, including my parka and piled blankets from empty beds onto my bed. I had so much heft to my sleeping covers that I couldn't easily roll over. When I did extricate myself from the bedding and immediately put on my boots, I was so cold I didn't want to take a very needed shower. At this point I had been inside my clothes for three days. I wanted to start clean even if my clothes weren't. I didn't dare wash my hair--it would have frozen to my head.

I looked around the room. There were 19 beds and just me. I felt my resolve cracking like a bridge made of match sticks. Today was Day 24 of my lone trekking and I had been away from home for 39 days. My perspective about loneliness was that it didn't really exist. My rap on that went something like this: "If you're alone and engaged in something interesting--your hobby, a sport, a good book--then we call that *being alone.* If you're alone and bored, we call that loneliness. It's an unnecessary word. It is really just boredom." A solution to boredom seemed easier to fix than a solution to loneliness. I hadn't been bored since 1969 when I my main purpose in life was to sit and wait until my Spousal Unit of the Moment returned from Viet Nam. What a freakin' drag that was. Thank God I wasn't back in those times.

I held a cup of hot coffee, instant but who cares, the cup was warm. One end of the second floor was glass windows that faced east and looked over the acres of forest. A sunny, happy morning, a scene from a color calendar. It was beautiful, the vistas of fluffy trees. But redundant. Like seeing a thousand posters of Mt. Hood lined up in a subway tunnel. My favorite mountain, yes, and in breathtaking color, yes. Overkill, certainly.

I wasn't sure I felt rested even though I knew I had slept. From exhaustion.

The backs of my hands were unfamiliar to me. Brown and cracked and dry, they had aged 15 years gripping that steering wheel. My cuticles were in shreds.

From the look of my face, my sunscreen wasn't working. The stuff was in the form of a glue stick and I could just rub this white goop quickly over my skin. Efficient, yes. Effective? Evidently not. Normally I had the familiar Oregonian pallor of the Pillsbury Doughboy and looked probably a few years younger than my actual age. Not any more. The only make up I had worn for weeks was lipstick. Some people try to turn back their odometers but I looked the way I did because I was getting to be a high miler and some of my roads had been rough. Case in point, that Viet Nam thing. My approach to the aging process, especially the face was: I'm going to look like my mother soon enough, it's inevitable, why try to hold it back? Let it go. Now, looking in the mirror, it was my *grandmother's* face. I wasn't quite prepared for that.

My eyes appeared to be permanently bloodshot. As much as I tried protecting them, the long hours of straight-on wind stretched their ability to recover. My Southern California Jan's eye drops were soothing but not enough.

My long hair, hopelessly and terminally dry, was not even a concern. There was only one way to wear my hair for roadster travel and I couldn't deviate from that: the standard, at-the-nape ponytail, knotted just right so as to not interfere with the helmet. And the helmet, damned thing! The constant jarring was still breaking the hair on my forehead at the hairline and rubbing it down to the scalp.

Is it any wonder that I didn't recognize the Road Warrior in the mirror?

My back, addicted to the curative powers of Dr. Don Walker in Portland, was in surprisingly good shape. Remember this was a 55-year old vertebrae taking this trip. Despite the unusual sleeping surfaces I'd encountered and the hours spent driving, that part of me seemed to be thriving. Perhaps the constant vibration of the road was like a day-long massage.

"Come on, let's get with the program," I encouraged myself to snap out of it.

Where was Commandant Ruff Rider this morning? Was he still asleep? I hadn't felt his compulsive yammering inside my head yet. That was the problem with those voices, they wouldn't stay center stage. That's why people appear to be so inconsistent. It's because different parts take over at different times. Just talk to a person trying to make up their minds about a relationship. One minute it was all guts and I'm leaving and the next minute it was all fear and I'm staying.

There was plenty to read in the hostel. Notes were everywhere. "Use water one minute, shut off, soap up, then rinse two minutes." "Clean up drips." "Put shower curtain inside." "Use hot pads under hot stuff." "Let dishes air dry." "No food or drink in dorm room." "No smoking." "Napkins in bag." There were photographs of Reagan and the American Constitution appeared in several places. A calendar by something called Heritage Foundation read in part, "exposed the worst of Clinton's executive orders and identified ways to repeal them."

There are usually only two options in Life: stay or go. I was beginning to almost look forward to the jolt of that cold shower.

When I finally descended the wooden stairs with my arms loaded with my gear, I was once again ready to hit the road. The fluffier of the two yard dogs was curled up next to Seno's rear tire. I gave her grateful pets for guarding my little car. A coating of frost cracked when I began to roll the car cover.

"Got down to 29," Alex said happily. He and his bathrobed wife were up, out and jolly. When I had stowed my stuff in the car and appeared ready to go, she gave me a gift, a folded paper star, a complicated origami kind of thing. "Do this to pass the time," she said. There was no sign of the odd person who had been smashing the phone on the picnic table the evening before. But then, as James Coburn said in *Dead Heat on a Merry-Go-Round*, everybody hates the phone company.

If it was 29 degrees out, doing 45 miles per hour for wind chill, the temperature inside the car would be somewhere around the same number as my number of husbands. Chilling.

I turned the ignition key and the cold little engine fired right up. Oh, the blessings for small wonders! I let it warm a bit, put the folded towel across my legs for some extra warmth and with the face shield up on the helmet, I waved three layers of gloves to my hosts. They said what everybody said, "Good luck! You're gonna need it!"

I enjoyed the drive back up the lane. What a fabulous piece of property, I thought. I settled into the Blue Ridge Parkway and began to feel my optimism return.

Half of America's population lives within a day's drive of the Blue Ridge Parkway. Where was everybody? Here in the crisp, clear air, surrounded by sparkling streams and stone bridges a person really could renew themselves. Something healing about this amazing road. Several motorcyclists passed headed northbound. Because of our mutual exposure to the elements I felt a kinship with them. And they frequently waved or gave a "thumbs up" which I always returned if I wasn't dealing with a curve. I thought, this must be one of the ultimate bike rides anywhere in the world. The surface of the two lane road was absolutely flawless.

There were hundreds of business along the 469-mile Parkway but they were tucked in so deftly that I wasn't accosted by them. Here were gristmills, weathered cabins, split-rail fences, wildlife and very small mountain towns. If I wanted, I could rock climb, visit Indian villages, tour gardens, see folk art centers, hike, fish or go broke taking pictures. All toll free. It was fabulous now, I'm not sure my heart could take it in the fall when something other than green took over. It might be painfully beautiful.

Every year when I paid my taxes I told myself that my dollars were going to the national parks. I didn't pay for senators' lunches or $300 military hammers, all my donated bucks went to the upkeep of our fabulous park system. So the Blue Ridge Parkway was mine. This piece of rationalization brought to you by The Fleecing of America. I couldn't write my tax check any other way.

Seno was in fine form. Everything on the car was working except the horn. We drove to Statesville, North Carolina where I spent nearly two hours thawing in the library updating my progress to David and weeding through over 80 email messages. For some reason, the Universe had chosen this particular moment in my life to assault me with junk e-commerce. While I might get three or four marketing messages in a week, I was now getting scores of offers for viagra, mortgages, credit cards, weight loss cures, pornography, investments and things to increase my penis size. Obviously there was no attempt on anyone's part to prequalify the recipient.

There were other interesting messages though. One from Texas: "Had never heard of you before and I have been inspired just from your website. I am a 53-year old Registered Nurse and recently applied to a local university. I received a letter of denial for acceptance. Ordinarily I would have said, 'Forget it.' Just reading and learning about you and your trip sparked that go-after-it-babe! thing in me. I sent a letter of appeal. I received a second letter of denial and decided to contact the University and speak to a real person. My good gravy! If you can instill that motivation and encouragement without even knowing...just think if I get the opportunity to hear you speak in person!! Thanks for the inspiration that you didn't even know you were a part of until now!!!!! Have a super trip and I wish you were coming to Euless, Texas!!! Susan Rogers"

Hmmmmm. If she only knew how cold and broken I had felt just that morning. But I *was* still rolling. I took inspiration from her emailed note.

And from my motorcycle mama-friend Carolyn who had crossed the country on a Harley: "Traveling alone is the best. I found that people would tell me the most amazing things. I carried a full map of the United States and as I traveled along, I marked my trip in red. Soon the line took on a life of its own and was very impressive. Press forward! You can do this!! Carolyn."

I wasn't exactly at the end of my rope, but I could *see* it...

The planted fields of poppies continued to carpet the edges of the interstates even through North Carolina. Unobstructed sun caused the color to appear to radiate. I could imagine filming commercials for fabric softener or facial tissues with children running through these huge fields of flowers. They were the best part of the day. Wouldn't my purple car look glorious in an acre of this wonderful color? I wondered about trying for a photo. Such a stunt would have invited an arrest and I had no desire to run into any Bufford T. Pusser wannabes.

Something clogged the interstate causing everything to stop just east of Asheville so I gave myself the gift of quitting early that Monday. Motel 6 was conveniently located right off of I-40 so I opted for that. I parked, registered, then hopped back in Seno to move him closer to my room's door. He wouldn't start.

"What fresh hell is this?"

Seno was completely and totally dead. I unzipped a bag, pulled my cell phone and dialed AAA. While I waited I sorted laundry, an easy task since everything I owned except the purple chiffon dress, needed washing. A tow truck arrived and I described my situation. A dead battery didn't make any sense because I'd been driving all day with no problems. Seno had never misbehaved like this before.

"Well, get in and try it," the guy said. So I did. I turned the key and the engine fired right up. I collapsed over the steering wheel in embarrassment.

"Ignition just probably got overheated," he said. "They do that. Happens again, just let it cool off." And he left.

I ran errands around Asheville getting film processed, mailing postcards, getting a sandwich. More and more I was confronted with men who had neglected all dental hygiene. Southern accents had been showing up since Virginia. I had seen *Deliverance* and now, decades later it was affecting me. I was unnerved by anything involving broken teeth, a Southern drawl, baseball caps, beard stubble and Firebirds. The clerk in the drugstore, the gas station attendant, even the guy fixing my sandwich all appeared to be men who would make a pig very nervous. Every time I stepped up to have an exchange with someone I could hear the banjos tuning up in the background. It was getting very unnerving.

I spent the rest of the day washing everything I could get my hands on--me, my clothes, my supplies. I even wiped Seno down as if he were a horse. From the 29 degrees that morning up in the mountains, it was still cool down here in the sunny flatlands. The TV news announced, "The cold today in North Carolina has broken all records."

Yes, and it was record *heat* in Iowa. And record high *wind* in Massachusetts. I tried not to take the weather personally but that was getting difficult.

I crawled into a fresh clean extra large Wright Brothers T-shirt, slipped between crispy sheets and fell fast asleep in a nice warm North Carolina room.

If you have to have a map of your house in order to find your way around, then your house is too big. When the number of rooms of your home exceeds your I.Q., then it's time to stop building. If the grounds of your estate is bigger than some Hawaiian islands, you've got far too much money.

The "Guest Guide" for the Biltmore Estate was 16 pages long. America's largest home, this French chateau built in 1895 was a country retreat for George Vanderbilt. Retreating from what? Slaving over a hot art gallery or commiserating with carpenters? I went nuts with my contractor having my attic finished, I can't imagine the horror of trying to build a house with four acres of floor space!

If you're a Vanderbilt then you can hire Frederick Law Olmstead, designer of New York's Central Park just to create a backdrop for your tidy little mansion in Asheville, North Carolina. This place really was over the top. I've toured the "cottages" in Newport, Rhode Island but, by comparison, they are just that. George Vanderbilt wanted a European style, self-supporting *village* complete with horse trails, creeks, a lake, hay fields, vineyard, pastures and gardens. A single room in the house was larger than the square footage of some entire homes. In the banquet hall there was room for several double wides and a duck pond. One hall was ninety feet long. And some people thought *my* house was big!

Unlike Hearst and his castle on the west coast (toured that just one year previous to this), the Vanderbilts were sure of themselves and their taste. They didn't opt out for collecting and displaying religious images because they were "safe." They honored champions of power like Napoleon. They even had his chess set. There was little religion here at all. One ceiling, actually 17 canvases, had been in a palace in Venice. Instead of painting the ceiling, they just applied the canvas. The basement had its own bowling alley (set up your own pins). Open for occupancy 50 years before Hearst's San Simeon, the Vanderbilts hadn't grasped the concept of the ostentatious possibilities of a swimming pool.

Most of the portraits were of glorious Vanderbilts, not old European aristocracy. The rooms were loaded with tapestries, parkay floors, wrought iron, carved fireplaces, elaborate and vast bedrooms--the usual stuff. Allow hours.

Admission $34. Cappuccino and a pastry $11.80. Don't go near the Vanderbilts unless you have money. And they made it easy to spend it. Bistro, Deerpark restaurant, Stable cafe, dining room, Biltmore Inn, Bake Shop, Ice Cream Parlor, Conservatory Cafe, Toymaker's, Wine Shop, Confectionery, Bookbinder's, Christmas shop and Gardener's Place. Most mid-sized American cities don't have a Calendar of Events the length of the Biltmore's. December holidays here must boggle the mind.

Even though Seno and I were some of the first ones there that morning, there was a slow moving line. We were singled out by a guard and told to park near some trees where he could keep an eye on the car. I didn't even have to ask for this extra service. The guard, Don Jolly, told me that the Biltmore Estate was frequently used as a backdrop for advertising photography of automobiles. They had a policy for dealing with expensive cars on the grounds. Mine was misjudged but I'll take the pampering any day. If I hadn't had the extended help, my visit would have been cut cruelly short. And with the Biltmore, a person really shouldn't rush it.

On the map Asheville wasn't that far from the Great Smoky Mountain National Park. Out of several possibilities I seemed to make all the wrong choices for the rest of the day. DETOUR in the South, I was learning, meant STOP, not "we're sending you down a different road, probably less convenient but you'll get there just the same." At another point an accident occurred on a bridge about three minutes before I arrived. So we sat, engine off, along with several hundred other motorists and trucks. I read my Biltmore Estate book, had lunch and filed my nails with Cummins diesels for a soundtrack. I called Howard in Portland and chatted, cleaned up the inside of the car and struck up a conversation with a couple of truckers. The afternoon wore on. Clouds started rolling in.

When Seno and I did finally get our shot at the bridge, we took off. Map versus reality was difficult to match. There was the option of getting back on the Blue Ridge Parkway, the slowest going but well maintained road that couldn't go 30 feet without a curve. The sky was getting seriously grey. I got into my wet gear just in case. I decided that if the rain got going I would pull over, get the car cover out and on the car and climb inside. I had food, water and a way of staying dry.

The sky worsened. After a dozen plus miles there was an exit and I took it. A different road would have motels and shelter options. Now add traffic. North Carolina, too, seemed to get bigger instead of smaller. I kept at it and kept at it until I finally arrived in Cherokee, sort of an Indian version of Atlantic City with casinos, ruby mine, Santa Village, fake teepees, moccasin shops and spears for sign posts. Made it through this corruption but needed to stop and tank up sometime just in case there might be a national park in my future. I didn't think I was ever going to find it.

There were 238 miles of paved roads in Smoky Mountain National Park and, by the time I got there, I was only interested in the ones that would get me over the mountains and into Tennessee. That was a horrible way to feel about a park but my patience had been sorely tested.

The blue haze on the hillsides had been there longer than environmentalists have been screaming about pollution. I didn't know the source of this blue but I got my question answered about the park's name. Things really do look smoky, evidently always have.

When the sign read, SCENIC VIEW POINT, they weren't kidding. It felt like looking out from the top of the world. I noticed a lone motorcyclist at the first view point. And from then on, through the entire park, we seemed to stop at all the same things, each time giving a wave. He, or I suppose it could have been a she, had about the same schedule we needed to meet, I guess.

Some vistas were parking lots of campers and grandpas and dogs. At others I was left alone to gaze, except for the motorcyclist. We leap frogged through the winding park highway toward Gatlinburg. Views had names like Charlie's Bunion, Newfound Gap, Gregory Bald and Cades Cove. A person could fish, camp, hike, ride horses or throw someone easily to their deaths. Some of the squabbling families seemed to be in conflict about which in that list of activities they wanted to do first. Families. The "f" word.

Here was more than 520,000 acres of prime mountain country and 120,000 acres was old growth. There was a wider variety of trees here than perhaps in the west because it didn't appear to have a timberline where things stopped growing and because they got what they thought was "copious rainfall." I'd be happy if I didn't have to experience any of that.

There was every possible shade of green. Miles of it. Pretty soon my vision just seemed to swim in green. That's all there was. It was a totally green world.

And then I hit Gatlinburg. Garish Gatlinburg. It was almost as if the people there were sick of a monochromatic green world and wanted to pack every color into their town environment. So much green for so long. Uninterrupted *leaves*. Now there was Ripley's Believe or Not, Hard Rock Cafe, an aerial tram, Guinness World Record Museum, Virgil's Motel, Pizza Jerks, an alpine slide, Kiddieland and the only car museum that I passed up. The World of Illusions was not far from the Chapel of Love. Too, too appropriate. Then there was a thing called Christus Gardens, sort of a combination of Forest Lawn, Opryland and a Baptist Church. If a person missed that during the day, I heard that a 30 foot cross lit up at night. There was more Precious Moments, mountain baskets and country crafts than should be in the entire world. Gatlinburg was Country Western meets Lucerne, Switzerland.

The road thinned of businesses eventually and got quite rural and still no sign of the address I was trying to locate. From the internet (look out for *anything* that begins "from the internet" I've discovered) I had the name and location of a hostel. It was not a sanctioned American Youth Hostel (AYH) but the price was appealing enough that I wanted to pursue its location. When I found what appeared to be a vacant motel there was a sign: RING BELL. No one responded. Then I saw a map of the little area there and the map instructed, go here and "Ask for Mrs. B."

Seno and I continued up the path through a grassy area. I saw a cross. Then some Biblical verse. More grass. Low buildings. Seemed to be a retreat center for some Christian-type group. I thought of the wonderful temple in West Virginia. "Equal time," I said aloud. Be fair.

Peacocks. A stream. More wooden buildings. A tiny handmade bridge. Finally what looked like a home and I parked in the driveway, pulled myself out of the car and a friendly woman with a thick southern accent said she couldn't help me but that I needed to talk to Mrs. B. This caregiver type of person led me into a living room and Mrs. B was the frail queen of this country universe. I had my print out from the internet listing but the price she wanted was four times what was advertised.

There was a very old dog with tangled fur at my feet. I petted him. Said what a nice dog it was. The words came out of my mouth with a slight southern accent. When I showed them the price the old lady said, "Can't even wash the bedding for that!" I told them I had my hostel sleep sack and didn't need bedding. I was prepared to go elsewhere, they obviously weren't used to renting space to visitors, despite what the internet had claimed. The only advantage I could see for staying there was that Seno would be secure. We got through a few more "Where you from, chile?" and with each answer my speech got further and further below the Mason-Dixon line. I said "Ma'm" a lot and then I played the trump card and said I was homesick. I paid for the room, all right but not with money. Good thing we came to some sort of agreement because I didn't want to listen to myself start quoting Bible verses.

Probably one of the more bizarre places I have ever stayed, the room wasn't the least bit hostel like, more hostile like. Think very, very, very cheap motel room. It had a list of no's: no phone, no bedding, no cups, no clock, no TV, no amenities of any kind, no security. There was the standard issue naked light bulb that hung down in the middle of the room. It was more like a tent I could stand up in that had its own toilet. There was a small space heater that stunk like burning dust when I turned it on. It looked like a fire just waiting to happen. I opted for cold rather than risk an electric short.

Oddly enough there was no Bible in the room but an *American People's Encyclopedia Yearbook*, events of 1958. Castro, for instance, was a rebel rattling around in Cuba. Who would have thought 34 years later he'd still be in the news. In Oregon Mark Hatfield defeated then governor Robert Homes. (Whew! Now there's a huge federal building in downtown Portland with Hatfield's name on it.) Construction of Lloyd Center Mall was beginning and newsworthy because it was inside a city instead of in the 'burbs. (Run down and then royally renovated, Lloyd Center was two miles from my home.) John Day dam, the last of the dams on the Columbia River was being constructed at a cost of $350 million. Oregon was getting ready for seven million visitors for its centennial. The University of Oregon football team met Ohio State at the Rose Bowl and lost 10 - 7. Well, some things never change.

I'm not sure the strange room had been used since 1958.

I fell asleep that night with the unnerving hollers of peacocks outside my window. They sounded like humans calling for "help!"

The next morning I decided that I was *not* going to have a can of pop top tuna fish for breakfast. I'd saved money by putting up with the ghastly hostel that wasn't a hostel, I wanted a "proper breakfast." Had eggs and coffee with the construction crew of Highway 321 outside of Gatlinburg and then headed north to Pigeon Forge.

It was sort of interesting that after miles and acres and days of seeing a billion trees that when "civilization" appeared here in Tennessee, there were *no trees*. There was either one or the other but not both. Pigeon Forge looked like Vegas of the 1950's. Flat and stripped of all trees. There was a wide two lane asphalt road for the northbound, a median, then a wide two lane road for the southbound. It was a shock to come out of Virginia, the Blue Ridge Parkway and the Smokys and get hit with miniature golf castles, Santa on a pole, the Three Bear gift emporium, pawn shops, Laser Tag, fudge factories, NASCAR-land, water worlds and country crafts.

This was also the home of Dollywood and I thought it might be fun to get a picture of Seno with the entrance sign just to prove we'd been to Tennessee. Once I arrived at the gate sign I could see that it wasn't going to work. The sign was too close to the road, there were too many cars and I didn't want to risk anyone's wrath by driving up on the grass. Next thing I knew we were headed down a long driveway and chatting with the guard. I was still looking around for something I could park Seno next to that would I.D. Dollywood. Before I could say "corn pone" my Master Card was being racked up for $34 and I was on my way into the park.

I did not expect to like Dollywood but it won me over and so did she. If anybody deserved success it was Dolly Parton. One of ten kids in a two room house no bigger than my living room, her upbringing was *not* glamorous. Dolly was big haired and gorgeous even as a teenager and she got her taste for rhinestones and glitz from Porter Wagoner, the skinny guy who hired her and was eventually eclipsed by her. Even during the ugly 60's Dolly was beautiful. Yes, she had talent. A lot of kids did. Yes, she was beautiful but a lot of girls were. She had a great voice but she wasn't shy about using it. In fact, this lack of shyness has got to be one of the reasons for her tremendous success. And she developed a great sense of humor that most pretty girls never get around to developing. Dolly Parton, a one off.

I went through the "new" display (it was all new to me) where I went into Dolly's "attic" and eventually saw her dresses, shoes, hats, awards, recordings of her with every famous person worth singing with, then saw her grizzly childhood. No apologies. No whining. Some of how she was treated bordered on child abuse--she tried to give herself a bloody nose so she'd be allowed to sleep in the house where it was warm. She never presents this information for sympathy.

The theme park was squeaky clean, ala Disney. But things were piled up closer together. Everything was on a more human scale. I liked it more than Opryland or Disney World or Six Flags. I didn't feel like I had to walk too far to see something either fun or silly or beautiful. Water features were everywhere, dribbling, splashing, pouring over water wheels. The activities were spaced right with the eateries, junk to buy and bathrooms.

Dolly seemed to be a cross between Patsy Kline and Liberace. She was a whole lot more though, employing or honoring everyone she has ever known or who has ever helped her. How tall is she? "Five feet one," she answers on tape, "but six foot two in heels." In one of the clothing stores I got to talking with a clerk and asked if she had ever seen Dolly. "Seen her? I grew up with Dolly. And she hasn't changed a bit, has she, Ethyl?" "Nope," the other woman replied. Dolly Parton appeared to be the genuine article, as they say in the south.

My granddaughter Gracie would have loved this place.

There were seven stages nestled in amongst all the shops and craft demonstrations and rides and every 15 minutes there was some show beginning. The one that I saw was called "Let the Good Times Roll," a musical celebration of the fifties. Where they found so many talented kids to put on one stage was a miracle to me. There wasn't a loser in the bunch! And these people couldn't get by with just singing well, they had to do everything else well including athletic dancing. Pro's all.

And if I got tired of all that I could step up to Dolly's wig computer and try blond "big hair" on my own face.

I was there on a Wednesday and by noon the place was filling up. A weekend in June would be--well, I didn't even want to think about it. Who knows if Dolly Parton actually gets a dime of the hefty entrance admission fee but she just makes you feel good about giving up your money. A person could get howdy'd to death here. (www.Dollywood.com)

Pigeon Forge was warming up that day and I hadn't made it very far before I felt the pull of a car museum there. It was a small one and concentrated on having cars that were there because they had been owned by someone famous, not because they were classic, or indicative of some style or even all that old. Buford Pusser's Toronado, Elvis' Mercedes and James Bond's Aston Martin. Three other cars were worthy of note because of the stories than came with them. Stringbean's lime green Cadillac was featured. I was unfamiliar with this banjo picker popular with the Grand Ole Opry crowd. An interesting newspaper story told the grim details. Evidently after a performance, Stringbean (David Akeman) and his wife, Estelle, were murdered in 1973 for their money but the bad guys never found it. The police didn't find it either. She had $2,200 hidden in a tobacco sack in her bra and Stringbean had $3500 so well hidden in his bib overalls that it took the undertaker to finally find it. Now there's an odd story.

Over in the corner was Al Capone's 1928 Cadillac which had some interesting features. Al had it painted the same green and black as Chicago's squad cars were back then, reinforced the sides with one quarter inch boilerplate and put in one inch thick glass. The back window was hinged so it could be dropped down during shoot outs. That Al, what a practical guy. Because the car was confiscated by federal agents, FDR ended up using it for a year!

If bad taste were water, Hank Williams Jr. would be a flash flood. His white convertible had six shooters (pistols) for door handles and the shifter! Hopefully the firing pins had been removed but hearing of Hank Jr.'s reputation, probably not. Hundreds of silver dollars (547 dollars!) were glued all over the interior of the car and there was a saddle across the hump in the front seat area. Little chrome horses leaped out of the continental kit.

Legend has it that moonshiners and their wild driving were the origins of what has become one of the most popular sports in the South today, stock car racing. Testosterone was thick in the air on the strip in Pigeon Forge, the town literally named after dead birds.

"Enough lollygaggin', let's git," I said to myself, getting into the spirit of Tennessee.

Rolled through the correct amount of Highway 441 and turned left at 411 past Happy Hollow and Smoky Mountain Knife Works. I could have gone on to Knoxville but I had plenty of energy in me and the temperature was just right for rolling down a really wonderful wide highway in a roadster. At last! Good weather. And if I got tired of this blue highway the interstate was running parallel about 17 miles away.

Every now and then I would get a big whiff of intoxicating floral perfume. It was familiar but it took awhile for me to identify it.

Every time it happened my memory would go further and further back. Odors are like that, they can trigger things long passed. Supposedly olfactory abilities are the last physical senses to leave us when we humans are dying. How somebody figured that out, I have no idea.

Honeysuckle! That's what it was! I remembered the honeysuckle that wrapped half way around the corner bedroom there in Stillwater, Oklahoma. That was over 30 years ago! Yes, what a lovely scent! I loved Seno for all the senses that he allowed me to have on that great drive across Tennessee.

Music and Tennessee. They weren't spelled the same but they were just about synonymous. It appeared that everybody was in a band or sang gospel or had a recording contract or was just about to get one or knew somebody who was fixin' to get one. In Tennessee, they've got a thing about tunes like New Yorkers have a thing about routes.

Just getting gas I could see things were slightly different. This was the land of Moon Pies and eight flavors of jerky at the gas station check out line. These may be two of the four major food groups, the other two were possibly grits and fried cheesecake. If it would sit still for even a moment a Southerner would fry it. I thought I was seeing things when I saw fried *cheesecake.* And I learned on this trip that the plural for "y'all" is "all y'all." In some Tennessee towns you can get a DVD movie and bait at the same store.

As much as I was enjoying my drive across America's 16th state (Seno's 24th state), I was going to have to get into the tangle of interstates just north of Chattanooga. So I made the right hand turn at Ocoee and pulled over in the far end of a fast food parking lot. I needed my better map and a power bar so I popped the clasps on the bonnet and lifted the hood. I was shuffling things around in there when a guy walked up behind me and asked, "Having trouble, sir?" I figured right then that I may have been on the road too long. I really wish I was making this up. I'm not.

Poor guy had his reality totally disturbed. Engine wasn't where it was supposed to be and there was no telling what I was...really.

Every day I studied my maps and tried to memorize all the route numbers before starting the day's trek. And every night I sat in bed and read maps like most people read novels. I was making such good time that I was about to arrive in Chattanooga. If I didn't have a clear idea of how things were supposed to go in this city, I was going

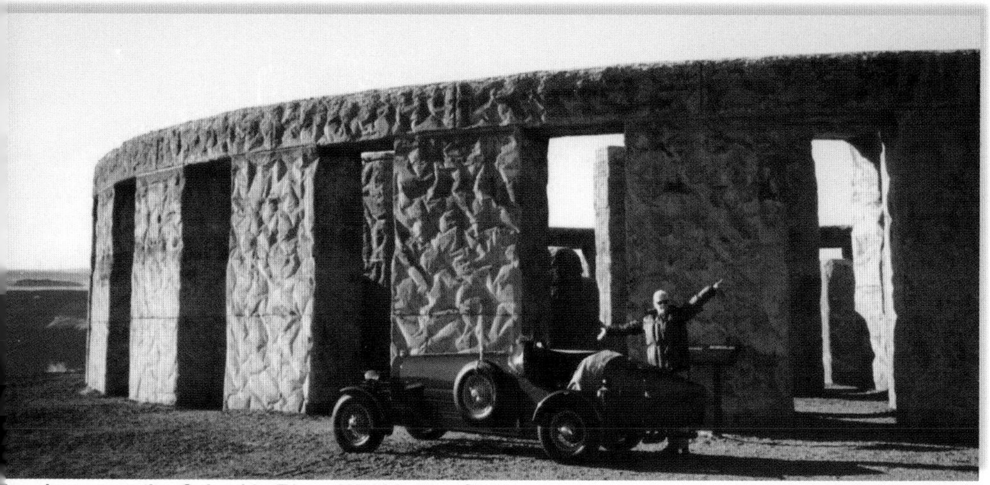

tonehenge on the Columbia River, Washington State

Carhenge outside of Alliance, Nebraska

ergeant Barry Portman in Princeton, Illinois

Howard & Bud (Roger) Clark

Christina Holmes &
Irving Greenwald, New York

Where was this photo taken?
Ask Terry Dickman, he won the contest!

The Ironmaster's Mansion,
Pine Grove Furnace, Pennsylvania

The Peter Shields, Cape May,
New Jersey

Crawford Notch, White Mountains of
New Hampshire--17 Degrees cold!

How slaves were hidden for th
Underground Railroa

Jeffrey Leestma, President of th
Automotive Hall of Fan

Historic Publick Hous
Sturbridge, Massachuset

Photo: Stuart Nudeleman

gunquit, Maine's distinctive lighthouse

›nna Nashawaty, Franklin, NH with her purple car

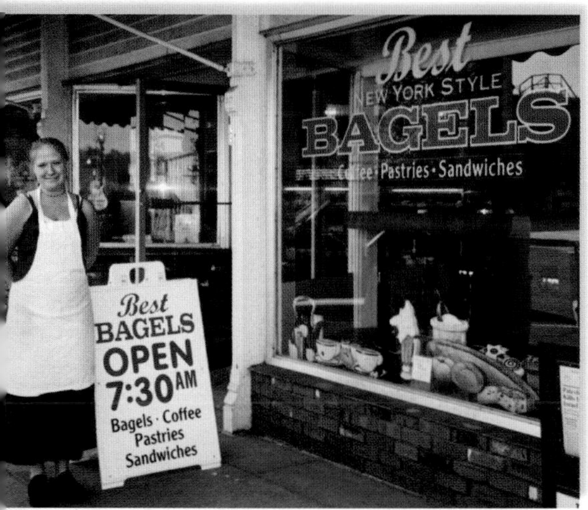

elissa & Best Bagel, White River Junction, Vermont

Daredevil photographer Ben Garvin
of the *Concord Monitor*

Janet Swan, Rutland, Vermont

Ellen and Vermont Campground

Stockbridge, Vermont 5th and 6th graders on ferry to Fort Ticonderoga

Robby and Kelley, part of Tea
New York at Vass

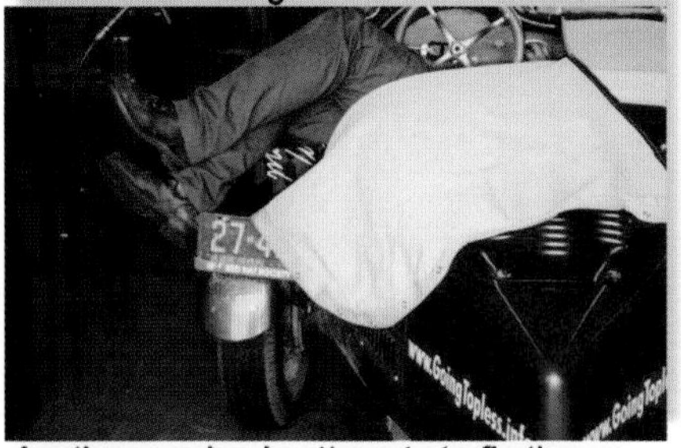

Another mechanic attempts to fix the roadster; this one is Jerry in Montana

Seno goes to Vassa

Found out how Crayola crayons are made in Easton, Pennsylvania.

Team New York: Ross Kindestin and Joe Welfel with a sincere desire to see me Hit the Roa

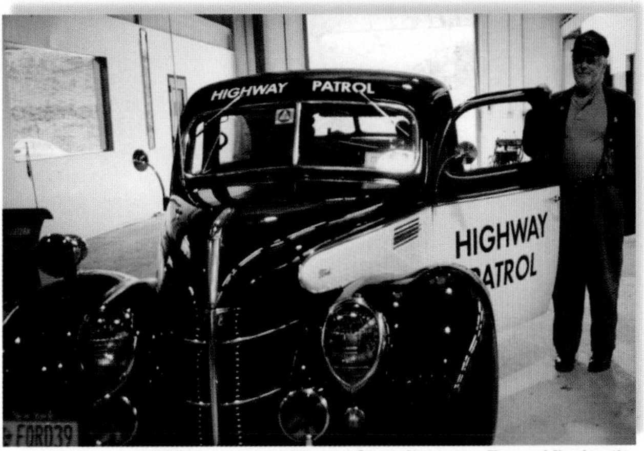

1939 cop car with my favorite cop: Ross Kindestin

World's Largest Uncle Sam,
Lake George, New York

THAT NIGHT at the Chattanooga Choo Choo, Tennessee

The Miatillac, '59 Cadillac fins on a Miata
in Carlisle, Pennsylvania

Steve Striharsky with his Bradley in Carlisle

Large turtle on open stretch of road in Arkansas

The Memphis Belle's face,
Memphis, Tennessee

Flo Hawley and the Steamboat Arabia, Kansas City

Red Hat Society in Hot Springs Village, Arkansas

Marilu Grose, Vera Liermann and
Sara Willis, Hot Springs Village

Robin Gabe at the Indian
Mounds, Arkansas

Tinker, Lynette's bird and
my only hitchhiker, St. Paul, MN

Alyce, Michael and Lynette join the
Grand Old Days, St. Paul

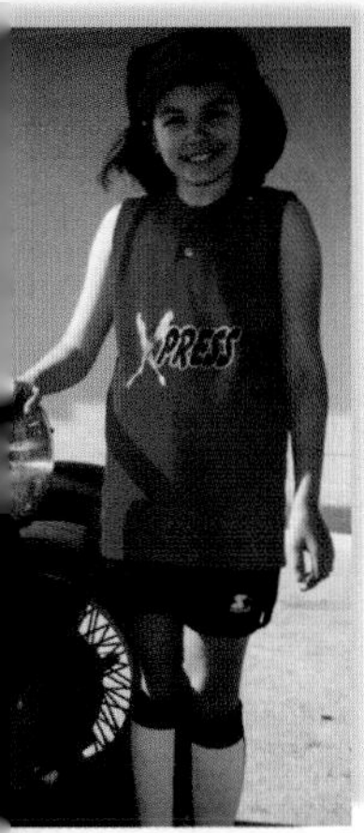

he next Dolly Parton?
shlyn Staggs in TN

John Hollansworth & the 1917
Peerless in Hot Springs Village, AK

lot a very enchanted day when this shot
vas taken in Mitchell, South Dakota

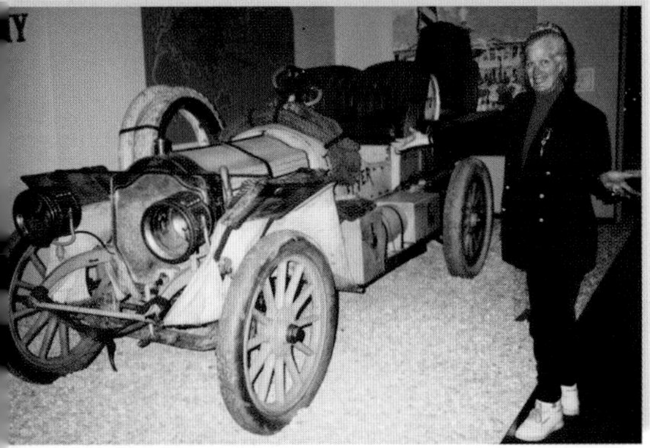

he Thomas Flyer, topless car drove around the world
1909, Reno, Nevada

an Barry, Sparkle Lady of Billings, Montana
nd her "trike"

Horses sniff Seno at the Wild Horse
Sanctuary, Hot Springs, South Dakota

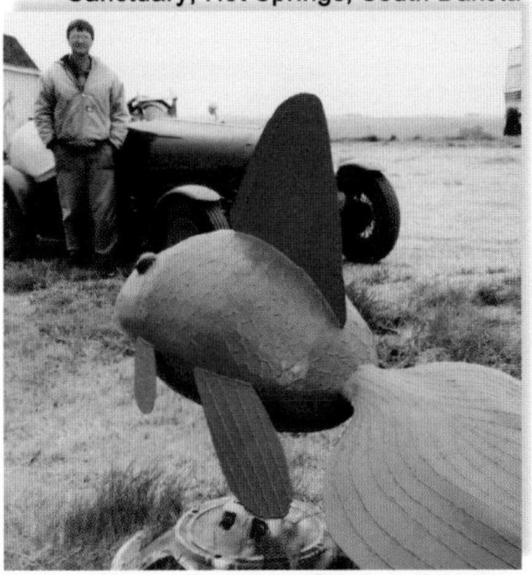

Wayne Porter, sculpture artist near
Sioux Falls, South Dakota

The very glamorous, charismatic
Poison Waters at coronation, Reno, Nevada

Last picture of Seno, shown here entering the North Gate, before he was nearly destroyed by Yellowstone

Ellen de Lathouder up for a morning ride in Des Moines, Iowa

Nancy Boldt, Sally & Elizabeth Flesch from Fort Madison Iowa touring Yellowstone

My old faithful mad
it to Old Faithfu

Some of the Red Hatters in Rapid City, South Dakot

Nelda & Joe Collins (Anderson, MO) and Tina & Bradley Lowe (Gore, OK) saved the day in a remote area of Idaho

The Finish Line! Presenting the commemorative sign to Pacific City, Oregon

None the worse for the we

to end up in Georgia. I needed to get on I-75 southbound but then switch over to I-24, come out the west side and then exit at Highway 64. I-24 dipped down into Georgia, gyrated and crossed over a lake or river. When I was the one doing all the driving and all the navigating and all the reading of signs, I had to know what I was doing and not second guess the Highway Department.

So I was unfolding the map of Chattanooga and getting a serious look when I saw the two words CHOO CHOO on the map in the downtown area. I sort of snorted to myself. I wondered what that was. Maybe a children's park or something. Well, it wasn't very far off the freeway. I could probably afford the time. Coming west out of Chattanooga I could easily find a campground or a motel. I felt that I had enough energy to handle it.

Seno and I climbed on to I-75 and joined the crowd headed into the city. I made the important switch to I-24 without any trouble and I waited for the 180A Exit. I found Market Street, made the left and all I could see were the backs of industrial buildings. I had the street names memorized so I wouldn't overshoot or get lost. I thought, "I've got one more block. This isn't looking good." I arrived at the intersection of where something called Choo Choo was supposed to be and I didn't see much. Then I turned my head to the right, looked up and saw a huge sign on top of a building. The flat sign was in the shape of a train. It was outlined in neon and spelled out the words Choo Choo. "Oh," I thought, "it's the sign. They've put up this big sign because of the famous song."

Then I looked down a bit and I thought, that looks dangerously like a train station.

I decided to investigate further. There was a line up of vintage train cars. I parked and ambled into one of the greatest nights of the trip.

Holiday Inn, those kitschy green and yellow guys with creamed corn and Rotary meetings, these unlikely folk had purchased the old Chattanooga train station and made it into a fabulous resort complex that could even accommodate conventions. It took awhile for me to grasp all this. After I parked, checked out the little shops and wandered through the lighted lattice and trellis dining room, I was pretty much gobsmacked in the lobby. Built in 1909, it was the old train lobby with a free-standing 85-foot dome and a spacious area big enough to play NBA basketball. The only thing that told me that this was no longer a real train lobby was a) it was a bit too elegant and b) there were no loud speaker announcements. I was truly stunned. An immense floral arrangement in the center of the carpeted area could have been rented out to a family. I must have acted like I had just wandered in off the farm. I casually picked up a brochure and tried to understand this amazing place.

"Ever slept in a sleeper? Four dozen restored passenger cars are now decorated Victorian style..." the brochure read.

Oh, I thought, this is going to hurt. I turned to the desk clerk behind the registration desk. "You have train cars? To stay in?" He looked at me, like, well, duh, of course. And then, "How much?"

OK, so it did hurt. So it cost 9.4 times more than last night's lodging. Slack-jawed and agape I walked back through the white garden dining area and back to the "platform." To the right was the Chattanooga Choo Choo, the actual engine parked there on Track 29. It was painted up like a kid's storybook train and then just around the corner was a blue neon sign: DINNER IN THE DINER. The large old-fashioned train clock above my head, right across the face, said: CHOO CHOO TIME in a lovely script.

I think I may have been in actual pain at that moment. I was as close to being in love as I had been for ten years. It was like when I saw my 1940 Ford for the first time. I felt like I hadn't breathed for several minutes.

I walked back into the stunning lobby, looked at the desk clerk who eyed my travel ensemble wryly and I said, "Vacancy?"

I got the key to train car No. 732 and raced out to the car to get more than my usual assortment of gear. Where was that purple chiffon dress? A tall fellow dressed in a train conductor's uniform told me to move my roadster next to the little guard building so that it could be watched over all night. Ironically, his name was Ernest Porter and in a delicate southern accent he told me how his mama had brought him to the train station when he was a "chile" so that he could visit relatives in Alabama in the summer.

I struggled getting three bags from the car to my train car but I couldn't wait for hotel help. I was far too excited. It was quite a step up to board the train and I sort of threw the bags up there, hobo-style. I even tripped and fell getting me on. Reminding myself to calm down and breathe, I finally got the metal door open. Wow! Unlike the caboose in Pennsylvania, I had an entire train car to myself. The curved ceiling came down and met the painted metal luggage racks. A queen bed was at one end, a mirrored bureau at the other, a desk handsomely appointed with all the upscale hotel goodies, a settee sort of couch, a curvy chair. It looked like my house in Oregon! The bathroom was a brilliant success especially given what they had to work with. The architect must have retired after working on these train rooms. What a challenge! It was a spacious area with a full-sized tub and the little toilet was right where the toilet had been 100 years ago. Everything, and I do mean *everything*, was painted a warm cream color.

I pulled the tie out of my hair, flipped open my make up tray that hadn't seen the daylight for nearly two weeks, put some eyebrows on, some blush, real lipstick (not Chapstick), a dab of Passion and powder to fill in my gaping pores. I found my grey locker bag and shook out the dress. Yes! no wrinkles! It felt like I was late for prom night. I stepped back from the mirror surrounded in all that white light. "Hey, it's a girl!" Even my hair was cooperating, enjoying its release finally to my shoulders.

Humming the tune, I took my barest essentials. I mean, how could I go to dinner carrying a fanny pack? Argh! My prep time: about 13 minutes.

"Pardon me, boys," I sang out loud the words to the famous song, stretching my sun burnt hand out in the most feminine gesture I'd seen me do in weeks. I hopped down off my train car and checked my stride as I crossed the tracks to the dining car. I swear my hips felt different. I ran into Ernest and he accommodated the photograph of me with the Chattanooga Choo Choo.

"That guy over there..." Ernest said, "axe me, 'That's not the same lady drivin' that car, is it?'"

Thanks, Ernest, you just made up for that sumbitch that asked me if he could help me with my car, "sir."

Every table was a window seat when you had "Dinner in the Diner," which I later found out was the Number One Best Place to have dinner in Chattanooga. "This is big," I thought. "This is wonderful." I looked out the train window, past the fresh pink carnations on my white linen tablecloth and I saw the fountain splashing merrily in the white wrought iron gazebo, all surrounded by early blooming pink roses. Of course I ordered champagne. And shrimp scampi with a Caesar salad. I savored every bite and every sip. And I smiled a great little smile to myself when I had the delicious thought that I didn't have to act interested in someone's boring conversation because they were picking up the tab and best of all, I could do anything else I wanted with the rest of the evening, like go peacefully to sleep without any traditional fooling around either. "You nasty little bitch," I said to myself. Power! Good grief, I felt so powerful. And after 42 days of praying my across America, it was like getting back in touch with a part of me that had been shelved due to prolonged fear. This was one of the most romantic evenings in the history of the world. And that sort of mystified me because I was perfectly alone. I'd have to redefine *romantic* for myself.

(I liked men. I loved men. I wanted the same thing they did, time alone with Alyce.)

After dinner I had to stroll back over to that historic lobby and sit in a pillow-soft chair and gaze all 85 feet into the mandala that was the train station dome. I wondered about the people and circumstances that the building's memory held. Soldiers leaving and those left behind, standing in this station. The soldiers arriving and the country parents greeting them, their only trip to the "city." Couples leaving on honeymoons and daughters returning from husbands. Kids, like Ernest, going off to grandma's home to spend the summer. People fed up or pissed off or just leaving for anywhere--taking the geographic cure. Some old folks getting on a train for a medical appointment or get a treatment somewhere. Exhausted mothers with several squirrelly kids not looking forward to a long ride.

The origin of the Choo Choo was the Cincinnati to Chattanooga, first north-south connection in 1880. The song says "leave the Pennsylvania Station at a quarter to four, read a magazine and then you're in Baltimore." I couldn't make sense of that route and still wind up in Tennessee. (www.choochoo.com)

That night I woke up twice just to sit up in bed and look around and relish where I was and then slip back into a blissful sleep under those *ironed* white sheets. I enjoyed myself so much that my Internal Financial Director forgot to whimper.

Alyce's Top Ten fabulous places to stay in America/Canada:
The Old England Inn, Victoria, B.C.
Kona Resort, Big Island, Hawaii
The Crescent in Dallas
Opryland Hotel, Nashville
Authors in Key West
Lover's Leap, FantasySuites in Shakopee, Minnesota
The Empress, Victoria, B.C.
Chattanooga Choo Choo
The Peter Shields, Cape May, New Jersey
Hotel del Coronado, San Diego

Tie: Loews in Denver, Four Seasons in Seattle, Stein Erikson Lodge in Park City (Utah), FantasySuites in Edmonton, Canada, The Royal Hawaiian in Waikiki, The Venetian in Las Vegas.

I couldn't possible rank them. Experiences depend on traveling companion (how good the sex was) or weather or music playing or number of authentic antiques or enormity of the floral arrangements or a waitress that calls you "Sugar" in the morning. Seven of my top nine, I've stayed there alone at least once. To put it mildly, your experiences may vary.

Roadster Lesson #14: A girl is not a woman until she *pays*.

45

Somebody stole the I-24 West sign. Or somebody forgot to put it up. That required some backtracking to get the purple roadster on the right road and headed in the right direction.

To say I had "separation anxiety" from No. 732 and those crispy clean sheets was a royal understatement. But I was two days away from the start of Memorial Day weekend and still more than 500 miles from Marilu's safe haven in Arkansas.

I was going to have to pass up Queen Mother Linda Shultz's offer to meet the Red Hat Jezebels in Brentwood, Tennessee and Louise Munier's Red Hat offer to tour Atlanta. I had also received an email from Leigh Hendry of the Tennessee State Museum in Nashville. She had heard about me (and read the exploits) from her friend Lisa who was the PR lady I met at Fort Ticonderoga! Leigh wanted to plant an idea for a "Cool Women's Tour" and suggested that I come to her piece of the Planet and that we "smaller, less visible Mother Teresa's" of inspiration get together. I hardly fit the Mother Teresa M.O. but any excuse to go to Nashville would be totally entertained, you betcha!

To reward myself for not whining too much getting away from Chattanooga, I stopped at the first good rest stop on I-24 and browsed the travel brochures. Tennessee had lots to offer but I had to pass on most of the music stuff. When I hopped back into the roadster a man appeared in a pale blue business shirt who hadn't been my age for a few years. Of course he asked about the car but I didn't realize until he gave me his card that he was a hi-miler celebrity himself. I'd been talking to David M. Swisher of Bowling Green, Virginia who was the original Million Mile Man, the first to reach 1,000,000 miles on a BMW motorcycle. I had my hands full getting back and forth across America! This guy had been topless all the way to the moon and back! We completely agreed on preferring cold over heat when doing distances, my car being more like a motorcycle than your average roadster. Said he'd ridden in 5 degree cold and did all right. He was of fair complexion too and gave me advice about what to do to make life even more comfortable on the road. Once I realized how much time he'd spent on two wheels I thought maybe he was really 24 years old and just looked my age because of his travels! Every little bit of information I garnered, I valued.

I also made easy work of getting onto Highway 64 and I stared at that number for the rest of the day. It was one of the best roads yet. I made it to Fayetteville for lunch which had been my goal since reading about it in a brochure at the rest stop. It appeared that a person could dine in an 1860 prison there. I had film to process and messages to check. Fayetteville seemed like a good choice.

It was. The town had a town square like *Back to the Future* ringed with businesses and people going about their small town routines, going in and out of hardware, jewelry and antique stores. It seemed that people have been coming to the Fayetteville area since 1540 when Spanish explorer DeSoto camped here. Now there were Civil War reenactments followed by holiday high tea and house tours. I was on a little bit of a side street, taking my film in when I met two fellows in suits, one with a baby. Business suits were not something I saw much of the entire trip. "Going to a funeral?"

Well, actually they were. They were in the business of going to funerals. They owned the Higgins Funeral Home across the street. Charles and Clay were interested in finding out who on earth was driving that purple roadster. "You like purple cars," said the grandfather of this three generation welcome wagon, "you should see our purple hearse."

I saw it, I photographed it, I loved it. How could I not? The exact same car (the black version) was parked in my driveway at home and my name was on the pink slip! Of course I loved the car! Now I could see what my 1973 Cadillac hearse would look like if I ever painted it purple.

Clay Higgins had biked the Oregon coast. Finally! Someone who could pronounce "Oregon" correctly! And knew where it was! They had business to attend to and I had work to do too but what a nice family. If I dropped dead in Fayetteville, I knew I'd be in good hands. (www.higginsfh.com)

I was interviewed by Jeff Neal, staff writer/photographer of the *Elk Valley Times.* He wrote one of the better articles about the car and the trip.

It was warming up quite nicely. For the first time in weeks I was down to one jacket. I parked Seno on Fire Hall Hill, went into Cahoots, sat down and ordered an enchilada. I learned that the iron bars weren't there for show, they'd been holding prisoners since the 1860's in this limestone rock jail. Instead of transferring all the historic information from the menu to my notebook, I asked the waitress if I could keep the simple, one page, quick printed menu. She turned instantly suspicious and said no, that wasn't allowed and what for anyway? That kind of took me by surprise and then I realized that Seno was not visible from inside the restaurant. I didn't have my sweet baby to open the doors of communication and credibility for me. I had forgotten that I was just a woman in a restaurant, a stranger and certainly nothing special. I explained what I was doing and gave her my card, told her where the car was parked, ate my lunch and wanted to split. If I wasn't careful, I really would be having lunch in a jail as the waitress was grumbling about "getting the manager."

Time to "get out of Dodge," as they say...

The afternoon was warming up but the sky wasn't that crisp blue that I loved. It was a dull, let's-sit-out-here-on-the-porch-and-just-think-about-work kind of sky. I could not keep a thick enough layer of sun screen between my lips and the Tennessee air. I crossed over the Natchez Trace Parkway and whined a bit that I was so close to Nashville and was having to pass it up. In the heat and dust of the roadster I could only keep driving and fantasize about sitting in the arbor of the Opryland Hotel sipping iced tea. Been there, done it, want to do it again.

Ah, Tennessee. Towns were spaced correctly on Highway 64 and provided some entertainment at proper intervals. Went through McBurg and wondered if that name might be a good one to designate a town full of franchize-style businesses. Southern California, where orchards become housing developments in the blink of an eye and have all the charm of a dried school cafeteria sponge, could use a term like McBurg. A sign in Lawrenceburg tweaked my funny bone: DAVY CROCKETT MOTEL AND BODY BOUTIQUE TANNING SALON. If you've got a hometown hero, work it.

Somewhere around Waynesboro, Tennessee there was a gas station and I was gittin' plain out o' gas and so was Seno. I met pretty Ashlyn Staggs wearing her softball uniform. Her team was the Piggly Wiggly Express and Ashlyn said she could belt out a tune and although she was only ten, it wouldn't surprise me if she had her own theme park in Tennessee in a few years. I remembered the advice I gave to myself while reflecting on Dolly Parton's Life: you got a voice, honey, use it. It was the difference between the shower-singers and Music Hall of Famers.

I drove west into the sun for miles and miles and I liked Highway 64 but I really was getting my fill of asphalt that day. I cut a piece of duct tape from my roll and stuck it on the face cover of my helmet to block the blinding sun. Windshields are also useful, I discovered, for holding a visor up over your head. I was passed by convertibles with their tops up and their visors down. No, for heaven's sake, let's not get mussed up. If they were waiting for a better day for a topless drive, it wasn't going to happen. Having a convertible and never taking the top down was like buying a box of Whitman Sampler chocolates and never opening it.

With every mile Highway 64 was climbing the charts on Alyce's favorite road list. It had just about everything I needed for a long stretch of just motoring. Running almost the length of Tennessee, it was divided, finished and smooth. The drive was getting long, however. I so wanted to get within striking distance of Memphis and give myself a short morning drive into the city of Kings. I made it to Bolivar, totally spent. I knew that if I was tired driving the car, I was going to be exhausted when I got out of it. I pulled in at the first motel sign I saw. MOTEL, that was all it said. I parked the roadster outside the office door and went in to register. The guy behind the counter was a relative of the manager in Princeton, Illinois. I asked him if my car was going to be safe here.

“Sure,” he said, “this is a small town. No problems.” That set the hair up on the back of my neck.

Yes, well, Princeton was 7,200 people too. I got a metal key, not one of those plastic security cards, I noted. I shooed men in jeans from around Seno (he attracted them like flies) and moved the car closer to the wooden stair that led to Room 210. The room was on the second floor and that distance from my roadster was the next thing that bothered me. An option I had considered once before: getting a room, using its facilities but sleeping in the car as if camping. I knew I would have to do that here. On closer examination, the whole place seemed a tad seedy and only pick-up trucks were parked in the motel's lot. I didn't see any grandmas. As I was moving and getting supplies, a swarm of boys on bicycles circled the car. “How much is it worth?” one asked. I looked at Seno's wheels and wondered how much they might bring at a Bolivar chop shop.

I climbed the stairs and tried to open the door with the key. I'm good with keys, at age nine could even pick a lock. The door wouldn't budge. That's it, I thought. The last sign. I am not supposed to stay here.

I marched off to the office, turned in my key, got back in my car and kept going until I found a name chain motel with out-of-the-line-of-fire parking. I paid the damage, settled in without losing any vigilance. Not the most relaxing of evenings. About ten p.m. three guys started pulling at Seno's cover to check him out. I flung open my motel room door. This was intended to be a piece of communication that was assertive but not confrontational. OK, so it was confrontational. It achieved the desired results, however. I wasn't gathering any happy memories of this part of Tennessee. I slept for only a few hours next to the window with the curtains open and all the lights off. By five a.m. the next morning I had Bolivar in my rearview mirror and was headed west to Memphis.

I know why Elvis was on drugs. It was the interior decorating at Graceland.

And trust me on this one, you don't need an Elvis Presley Cook Book. They're sold with a $10 coupon off your next EKG.

I couldn't really consider myself a connoisseur of kitsch if I hadn't made a pilgrimage to the place where American bad taste got its start and continues its tradition today. Graceland has been on my "must see" list for over a decade. It was unclear whether this rock 'n' roll holy site's location was chosen because of the intersecting of two major southern interstates or whether the interstates were put there because of the position of Graceland. I'm betting The King was there and the highway department grew around Him. I exited off of I-55 at the billboard that read: IT'S NOW OR NEVER, an Elvis song lyric. That humor was encouraging. I felt like maybe Graceland and I might have a good visit.

On Elvis Presley Boulevard I drove past the Heartbreak Hotel which has been sold out for several years in anticipation of the 25th anniversary of The King's "passing" (from a technical standpoint, of course). The Burning Love Suite, I'm assuming, now comes with an updated, politically correct hygiene vending machine or an address of a clinic if the love experienced there becomes a bit too burning. I may be a bit off base here, but I'm not sure I want anything associated with "love" to have a flammable component.

I arrived so early that the only businesses open on the boulevard were the Ultimate Tacky gift and souvenir shops. Just what I wanted to study. Definitely part of the experience, at least half my attraction to Memphis was to see what would be offered there. I felt that the epitome of unusual products had to be at the honored home of Elvis who was the first star to get by with just one name. This would be the Mt. Olympus of Campy Gifts, the Epicenter of "Made in China" Imports. Surely the lid would be off of any restraint to entice an Elvis fan to part with money. I wasn't wrong. I found Elvis guitar picks and that made perfect sense. Might serve as a good luck charm for aspiring rockabilly wannabes. And candles for the frequent candlelight vigils, they were certainly functional. But Elvis Presley sewing kits? And printed copies of his will seemed over the edge. There were Elvis shot glasses, soap and flat cardboard Elvis faces made into fans, as in now I'm an Elvis fan. The swinging Elvis legs brought a chuckle, however, motoring back and forth as the pendulum for the Elvis clock. Teddy bears nodded their mechanized heads and sang The King's *Teddy Bear*. But for $10.99 you could actually own an Elvis Presley cookie cutter. If Elvis were alive and looking in these stores he might wonder, "Where were ya'll when my career was on the skids, you jerks? I could have used some of this adulation back then!"

But nothing will turn a fan into a rabid fan faster than death. From Van Gogh to Elvis, today's fans can pick up the mantel of guilt from their parents who refused to part with cold, hard cash to support these famous people.

All the houses Elvis ever lived in, except his modest childhood home in Tupelo, were in Memphis. None was more famous or more visited than Graceland. Over 600,000 people a year, in a non-anniversary year, toured here and the White House was the only American home to get more visitors. Once again, it was only because of the generosity of the entry shack guards that I was able to leave Seno and see the attraction. The morning shadows were still long, the place just about to open and yet I was assigned Tour 4 of the day. This Friday the entry lobby to board the buses for Graceland looked like NYC's Grand Central Station.

Before boarding the bus for the little ride up to the mansion, my bag had to be opened for inspection and every visitor was photographed, supposedly for a souvenir available for purchase later but when I declined I was told I needed to be photographed anyway as part of their "head count." I would think that Graceland would appear on a terrorist's list about the same distance from the top as my house. Security seemed a bit out of whack but no one seemed to care. Would Elvis himself be allowed in if he were here, I wondered? Probably not. No firearms allowed.

Standing in line by myself with wiggling swarms of fans *of all ages*, I felt like a spy. I wanted to study the crowd--what kind of person goes to Graceland? Germans. Retired people. Teenagers. Asians. It was such a mix that there was no categorizing them.

I liked Elvis I guess but I was too young back then for his white hot sexy style. That curled sneer of his was kind of scary and his eyes were small like you'd never be able to guess what he was thinking. The rest of him said that what he was thinking probably was the worst a mama could imagine. He always looked like he was saying, "I'll make love to any woman in the room." I found that unnerving. Perhaps Priscilla did too.

There were videos of past Elvis performances playing in the gift shops, the waiting area, the boarding area and throughout the house tour. He was the most amazing performer with charisma pumping from every pore. Elvis's ability to seduce was working overtime and I was weakening to its pull, trying to resist and stay detached and objective but losing.

I think I remember a tour guide explaining that Graceland was named after the original owner's Aunt Grace. Elvis moved in when he was 22 years old and just kept the name. Graceland Mansion was 15,000 square feet of white Southern Colonial style built in 1939, the same year the movies *Gone With The Wind* and *The Wizard of Oz* were released. Keeping in mind that Elvis hasn't been here since 1977, it was pretty amazing that absolutely nothing had changed. I began my tour as if this were an ordinary old home tour looking over the architectural touches but eventually the Elvis heat took over and it was no longer about walls and flooring.

The living room was white. Coated with white carpet, painted white and had a mile long white couch. And they say he entertained here. I would have to be on Prozac to have a party in a white living room. The shocking peacock blue drapes and the stained glass peacock room dividers were jarring against all that white. Evidently Elvis and the Krishnas of West Virginia both held peacocks in high esteem.

According to the audio portion of the tour and courtesy of the voice of Lisa Marie, the kitchen was the hub of the complex and came with 24-hour-a-day cook who would make anything you wanted presumably if it involved nuts or cheese. Lisa Marie also explained that Elvis had such a presence about him that she could "feel him" in the house before she actually saw him. He didn't come downstairs until he was ready to be seen and that included gold chains so you could hear him coming, like Marley's ghost. Action around the Presley home went on all hours with no let up in the fun. That fun included golf cart races down the hill and out onto the public street. No cop ever ticketed Elvis for these little transgressions in safety. Thankfully the bathroom where he expired (technically) was off limits to devotees.

Visually the equivalent of fingernails scraping a blackboard, the so-called Jungle Room of the mansion was mind-bogglingly awful. A dripping orange water feature at one end and olive shag carpet set the tone. Heavy, Hawaiian idol wooden carved furniture was upholstered in faux zebra fur. A little piece of the islands interpreted by the boy from Tupelo. It was called "playful decor" in the brochure. I took enormous satisfaction in knowing that nobody was going to be allowed to call my old place tacky after this. I have *seen* tacky and Memphis was its headquarters. Winston Churchill wrote, "We shape our dwellings and afterwards our dwellings shape us."

Things I didn't know before taking the tour: Elvis had a black belt in karate and liked racquetball, Elvis had a twin, Elvis watched three televisions at once (inspired to do this by LBJ). None of the TV sets I saw had bullet holes in them but who among us hasn't felt like shooting a television? Elvis liked anything that kept his adrenaline and testosterone pumping. He really was all boy, a teenager who went to seed.

You'll never see that part in Memphis. In the clothing display section, I asked the guards about the size of Elvis' clothes. They all appeared to fit someone about five feet seven and weigh 115 pounds. "He must have been tiny," I queried. No, they explained, these really were The King's outfits but they were taken up in the back and pinned. Even his military uniform. And especially the famous eagle outfit. (Where did he get the idea to wear chains on his butt like a belly dancer?) Those fat icky years were relegated to invisible history right along with FDR's wheelchair and Thomas Jefferson's slaves.

Both Elvis and Dolly Parton were raised poor in the south and neither had anything bad to say about their upbringing. Both certainly loved glitz. Neither one of them was ever shy about flaunting it either and we Americans love that! While Dolly Parton's life was presented as upbeat, Elvis and his dreams appear tragic. Far more people see Graceland than Dollywood. Do people flock here to kind of *warn themselves?*

The tour ended with a walk past four graves. Grandmother, mom, dad and Elvis were entombed there (supposedly). What I found interesting was that each of the huge flat bronze slabs were of equal size. Elvis's grave was marked in no bigger fashion than his nana's.

When floor-to-ceiling award rooms and round furry beds threaten to overwhelm then taking a rest in the Elvis Auto Museum seemed an upper. Pink Caddie and luxury motorcycles, if it was a boys' toy, Elvis had it. Including two planes on the tour, the *Hound Dog II* and the *Lisa Marie* jet. Northwest Airlines was advertising that they were the "official airline of Graceland" and presumably they fly only jumbo jets but what's the drug policy for the pilots?

Elvis won't get any older. He died and gave us all the gift of not watching him deteriorate. He will be held in suspension forever like the beautiful Marilyn. Who knows how many performances they had left in them? Death was an idiotic freezer of a collective fantasy. Elvis Presley was a generous contributor to Memphis charities and paid more hospital bills for friends and strangers than anyone can account for. It appeared to me that he was still taking care of Memphis because he had become an industry that kept thousands of people employed on both sides of the Pacific. The King was still packin' 'em in at Graceland when I was there...and he'd been gone more years than his entire entertainment career. (www.elvis.com)

I escaped the last of the clutching gift shops with just the purchase of a pin in the shape of the word Graceland, a memento for my Gracie. My Internal Grandmother reminded me that my own personal idea of Graceland was Gracie's playroom at my house. When I felt complete with the whole Elvis experience, Seno and I popped out onto Elvis Presley Boulevard like a piece of corn ejected from a hot air popcorn popper--expanded and *done*. I wanted to drive the length of the Boulevard into downtown Memphis. Probably not a good choice. Until they start making politically incorrect maps that show you where the high crime areas are, all city travel should be suspended by drivers in topless cars. I felt like we were a fat, short-legged albino buck at the height of deer season. It was Trenton, New Jersey with heat.

The sky was a chalky bright white and the humidity was as high as it could possibly get without actually raining. I was drained from fighting off Elvis's sex appeal and being in the hot, sticky car and trying to navigate inside the tight confines of a major U.S. city under construction was not pleasant. I accidentally passed Sun Studios where I could have paid for a custom recording of my singing Alyce self and joined Johnny Cash and Jerry Lee Lewis and B.B. King who have all done that. I figured that this historical Memphis business probably had enough challenges without adding my singing career to the mix.

Downtown Memphis wasn't soothing. Noisy, dusty, with nothing to say "WOW" about.

I wanted to see the largest pyramid in the Americas. Dwarfing the one I climbed in Mexico, standing 321 feet tall, there was a stainless steel and glass pyramid in Memphis that went at least $200 million over budget. I could only view it from a parking lot which put me at the top of a maze overlooking Mud Island. In order to get down to the unusual city park I had to ride escalators and a monorail which made it one of the more inaccessible city parks on record. I could see what they had in mind but the architect should be fried in Southern fat. People were not drawn to this area (and I had left crowds at Graceland). There was far too much endless brick. It was not a cheery, human scale place. What I loved was the park's most prominent feature, a scale model of the Mississippi River complete with flowing water. This "fountain" was educating as it was psychically refreshing. About 1.5 million gallons of water circulated through the model that was about five blocks long.

But I went through the hoops and it was worth it to stand nose to nose with the famous film star, the *Memphis Belle*, the B-17 bomber that was the first plane to complete its prescribed number of missions in Europe in WWII.

Old war planes exude a kind of old terror that doesn't go away. They will squeeze the awe right out of me. The men who crawled inside and flew through the air in them had a different kind of courage...not the kind that was instinctive where a person just reacts instantly to something awful. No, these bombardiers and gunners and pilots had lots of information--downed buddies, flak, miles to go, all the facts about the 8,000 different ways for disaster to overtake them. And they got in the planes anyway.

All the old war birds continue to stun. How did men ever do it? Knowing what they knew, how could they board these things and go up mission after mission?

Ed Armstrong, now 80 and living in Portland, limped a shredded B26 Martin Marauder bomber back to base in 1944 that was more air than plane. Only metal skin held the front of the aircraft to the back. The tail assembly was attached to the plane only by the aluminum sheeting covering the fuselage. I've seen the photographs. Flying it, much less landing it, appeared completely out of the question. I asked Ed how a person could go fly the next mission and he said the Greatest Generation had four things:
1. A total commitment of 131 million Americans to win a world war.
2. It was what I was trained to do as my part of that commitment. If I didn't do it, who would?
3. A complete sense of fatalism. It wasn't my time so I wasn't going to worry about it.
4. A black sense of humor--the constant stress had to be relieved by humor no matter how horrific the moment.

I had been visually and emotionally drained by Graceland and I took in the *Belle* as objectively as possible reading about how the bombardier and his instruments took over the flying of the plane when the drop zone was reached. The pilot didn't touch the controls again until he heard "bombs away."

FLAK was short for a German word about six feet long made up primarily of consonants and meant anti-aircraft artillery. Nowadays part of our language was the phrase "to take flak from someone." The ultimate fear for bomber crews was when the flak stopped because it meant, after a short silence, that the German fighter planes were due to arrive. Burned alive or dropped at 20,000 feet, the crews knew all that and had watched it all and still they went. The more difficult heroism is when you *know* and go anyway. I was moved to tears by the military plane and now 60 years later, there was no one around to thank for the effort.

Well, just try to vote intelligently.

I had to pass on making a personal inspection of the Pyramid. I am insatiably curious about nearly everything when I am half way comfortable. Today was not that day.

I had my own cockpit to get into and I was very spent, praying I could find my way across the Mississippi without getting lost in Memphis construction. I made it, traveling on the bridge that was longer than some counties. The water was just as muddy as the songs claimed and it was definitely rolling right along that Friday. Thousands of trees were up to their leaf tops in thick water. Dump trucks and U-Hauls and delivery vans muscled past me. I wasn't going to press the strength of Seno's braces on the wide metal bridge. I didn't want to have the extra challenge of holding a fender up while steering to Arkansas.

When I reached the other side I treated myself to a shady picnic at the first available rest stop. I had crossed the mighty Mississippi and had both fenders still attached; it seemed like a reason to celebrate. Traffic had slowed to a crawl and I wanted an alternative to Interstate 40, a dead dinosaur of a highway.

Every high tech interstate highway should have what Arkansas has-- a sweet, simple slower but smooth highway running parallel to it so that I could see the little towns of 900 or less, past junkyards and Sally's gifts and Rant & Pant Tavern. Highway 70 Memphis to Little Rock was not all that traveled even when it was obvious that it was a superb alternative to the hell of the interstate. Past rice fields and miniature modern Taras, past shacks (some occupied), yard sales and an old man in overalls fishing and waving from a canal. This was more like it! In many spots I could look over and see the moving boxes, the big rigs on I-40. I would continue on the country highway for as long as it suited me. And it suited me the rest of the day.

Outside Forrest City and headed westbound, the sun was just beginning to make things difficult for me again. There was little on the road to beware of other than the usual road kill. I had a morbid curiosity about each flattened animal I saw and for some perverse reason I do not understand I seemed to need to identify what the mashed fur had once been. Perhaps because I had a better view or because there was nothing between me and whatever it had been or maybe to honor its life somehow...for whatever reason, I would notice and make my identification as if I was being paid to keep an inventory. Deer was obvious but I hadn't seen any of those since New England. Cats and dogs, were they someone's pet? Would a little girl cry herself to sleep because Fluffy hadn't made it back home? I worried. Would she think her pet had abandoned her, left because she hadn't fed it right? Surely it would be better to tell her that the thing was dead. But would her parents see it that way? Would they just let her think she was guilty of some grievous omission rather than tell her the truth. Did she face a life thinking that she caused her Fluffy to opt for better quarters elsewhere than spend another night at her house?

Right about then the tire on the left rear trailer in front of me burst into my consciousness and rubber shrapnel flew into the air. For no apparent reason, the trailer's tire had exploded. Seno was doing about 55 miles per hour when it rained Goodyear, an interesting event for a regular passenger car, an exciting event for an open car. The driver of the pick-up truck slowly pulled over to the right. I slowed too, taking a quick mental check of my own safety. I came along side to see if the driver wanted help and the guy looked bored, like this happens all the time at this spot and he shook his head.

Outside of Carlisle, Arkansas I found a real life drive in restaurant complete with car hops. A real throw back to the 50's I definitely thought Seno and I should partake of this car-friendly experience, even if we couldn't actually have the tray suspended on the window. No window. There were several Sonic drive ins in the Midwest and I remember one in Stillwater, Oklahoma. Always a source of greasy onion rings, as I recall. I met Josh from Hazen, Arkansas who was unabashedly in love with my roadster. He said the one thing I needed to know about his state was that "the weather is never the same...you don't like it, wait ten minutes and it'll change." Yes, I do remember that from my days in the Midwest. "You can be knee deep in a mud hole here and still die in a dust storm." I also found a food thing I hadn't seen before: PANCAKE ON A STICK, the sign read. On this hot May evening I was more inclined toward ice cream. After our little visit, I waved "so long" and Josh said, "Take care and God bless." That was a nice Southern thing to hear, I thought.

Back on my road I continued westbound, to where I wasn't exactly sure. I didn't want to go all the way into Little Rock. I was pondering my options, not many accommodations were available on Highway 70, they were all over at the interstate, still running parallel. The sun was lower but appeared to be behind a smoke screen, it was so hazy. There was nothing blue about the sky. A white pick-up truck appeared in my rearview mirror. I noticed it because it had raced up and then hung there. I could see a male driver and a male passenger. Pretty soon they passed, stayed along side as if looking Seno over thoroughly. The passenger, arm at the right window didn't look at me, only the car. Once by, they moved into my lane and we convoyed for a distance. Then they raced off. There were no other cars behind me. There were no other cars at all. I maintained my pleasant highway speed and started hoping that there were going to be nice clean sheets and in a nice motel in my future.

Things were quiet and normal. I passed more country fields, little canal bridges, clumps of trees. Then way up ahead I noticed a vehicle parked on a side dirt road, the front of it pointed toward my highway. As I drove closer I recognized the white pick-up. It appeared to be laying in wait. I just noticed it and flew right on by. It spun gravel exiting its lair and gave chase.

Then I *really* became aware of the traffic. There wasn't any. I knew Seno had more power to him than I was using and I also thought that I had the 1600 cubic centimeter engine installed for a reason. This was not a testosterone laced machine by any stretch and I was already in fourth gear. But it was a straight-away, Seno's preferred driving condition. Without knowing precisely where I was, how far the next town was or the next opportunity to find an interstate sign and make a right hand turn and head for it, I continued on just slightly upping the ante by gently increasing my speed. No point in trying to blast away from the pick up. That might have been taken as a challenge.

They stayed back there. No flashing of headlights. No waving. They just sort of hung there as if on a tow rope. I was careful not to move my head to look at the rearview mirror. There wasn't an impressive array of options for me here. I just wanted to be completely and totally alert in case I had to do something with the car that might be out of the ordinary. "Life is a daring adventure or it is nothing," wrote Helen Keller. I was thinking that *nothing* right then looked very appealing.

What if they were part of the personal development movement who believed in realizing their full potential and that included ownership of a purple roadster by whatever means and methods would serve them? What if they had read those books I recommended about how to get what you really want? Maybe they'd been visualizing having a purple Bugatti and now here it was and surely this was a sign that they should have it? What if they had listened to speakers like me explaining to them the common denominators that winners had and about how they too could be winners? I eased the speedometer up to 70 miles per hour. Why hadn't anybody thought to teach a course or write a book on morals too? What if their daily affirmations included "I am worthy of all things" and they included roadsters on their list?

Without any wind to buck, Seno was flying. The center line was solid now, not flickering dots. The white pick-up drove as if it were practiced at flying in formation. I couldn't stop suddenly now if I needed to, my brakes were not that good. Was Fluffy going to make it home tonight? Please don't send Fluffy to Highway 70 right now! There was no additional vibration, no strain as the roadster escalated the cruise and the little speedometer needle moved to the marks between 75 and 80. Damn, why hadn't I memorized the string of town names and distances along this road? Where was everybody? Weren't there farmers anywhere that needed to go to town for fertilizer right about now? And where were the cops? Weren't they supposed to show up and issue speeding tickets on this road?

The white pick-up seemed to lag a bit. Was that just wishful thinking on my part? Or was there a curve up ahead that they knew about that I didn't? The road had been straight as a nail and not a sign post anywhere to indicate an upcoming town or anything. Then suddenly the truck surged, started closing up the distance between us and my denial about the situation began to fall apart.

"Hare Krishna, Hare Krishna, Krishna, Krishna, Hare, Hare..."

Half my attention was on the road and half my attention was in my rearview mirror. Then I began to think, "That's not a new truck. It's a little foreign made truck of some kind and it has dull paint and probably a dull driver. I'll bet dollars to donuts it hasn't been well maintained. It's been running flat out for too long now. There's got to be a town up ahead and if there isn't, I'm not stopping until I get to Texas."

I thought I had my right foot all the way to the floor board but I had about a half an inch left and I stomped on the accelerator pedal. "Hare Rama, Hare Rama, Rama, Rama..." The speedometer read 82 miles per hour just as I thought I saw the familiar blue shield of an interstate sign. In ten more seconds I could make out the small right turn arrow. Now how to slow down enough to make the turn but not enough to be grille bait for his front bumper? There would be gravel around that sign post, brakes are soft, steering good though. The pick-up was still following.

Now do I signal to let him know what I want to do? Or surprise him? If he's not the sharpest knife in the drawer he may end up plowing into Seno's rear when I want to slow down for the turn. Or I could use my blinkers and my obituary could read, "Well, she signaled."

And the road I wanted to turn onto that would take me to the safety of the interstate...was somebody on that road in the southbound lane coming toward the intersection where I wanted to make the turn? Would they please get the hell out of the way so I could make a wide turn at a faster speed? I had about three more seconds for all this internal decision-making.

I didn't signal. I hit the brakes firmly but not hard for about three seconds then let up and steered. The intersecting road was clear and I swung into the lane right where I hoped there wouldn't be a car. Seno cornered like a champ and I suspect most of his wheels stayed on the ground. We made the turn and I glanced for a quarter of a second into the rear view mirror. The pick-up truck raced straight down Highway 70, not making the turn and I could have sworn I saw a trickle of smoke coming out of the engine. I didn't spend any time congratulating myself. I could see the hump of the interstate's overpass and we were over it and onto I-40 in a matter of seconds.

Sometimes traffic was a good thing. It meant people and the Highway Patrol and Stuckey's and gas stations and eventually a Days Inn with crisp white sheets in Lonoke, Arkansas.

Roadster Lesson #15: Motivation without morality will always require additional motivation and effort by others.

47

"Uncovering it, huh?" she asked in a thick southern accent.

"Yes."

"Purdy."

"Thank you."

"Are you a religious person?"

Sternly, "No."

Then she told me about how she just lost a necklace her son had given her while she walking her dogs on the lawn. So I needed this information?

"Better go look for it."

"Well, if I find it, it'll be God's will."

In the South God seemed to come up in conversation very causally, I thought.

In case there was any doubt in my mind where I was, the desk clerk said, "If we'd won the war, Hank Williams Jr. would be president." He was talking about the Civil War and for the first time I began to think maybe George Bush wasn't such a bad choice after all. Another indication I wasn't in Oregon any more...a little sign at the corner gas station that read: FLEA MARKET AND PAGEANT WEAR.

The next morning I learned that turtles pee when they're frightened. They get frightened when they're picked up. I was on Highway 89 and making the turn onto 165 when I found this turtle as big around as a dinner plate. He was out in the road, cringing and being passed by speeding cars. They were missing him by fractions of an inch.

I let him drain and then posed his big dark green self on the hood of my purple car. We had our photo session. Being careful to stay clear of his beak, I found a nice spot for him in the marshy ground. I left him pointed toward a small stream and away from the asphalt. The only food I had that I thought might interest a turtle was a banana. I didn't think an Atkins power bar was appropriate for wildlife. Hopefully he would live a long happy life in the mud and grass of Keo, Arkansas. It felt so good to help out a fellow traveler.

I drove up Highway 165 and saw a sign for the Toltec Baptist Church. That struck me as a tad odd. Weren't the Toltecs *pagans*?

But, of course, they borrowed the name from the Toltec Indian Mounds which were incorrectly identified by the woman who lived on the property 150 years ago. They looked Toltec to her and they did to me too, but they aren't.

Quite a facility and park interpreter Robin Gabe rolled the slide show at the Toltec Indian Archeological State Park and pointed me to the two paths through the mound circle and to the pond. I was the only visitor that early Saturday morning.

It took many generations to get the largest mound to its 50 foot conical height, piling a basketful of dirt at a time. A ceremonial temple, perhaps? There had been a moat around the entire encampment 1,300 years ago.

I was fascinated that a busy indigenous people would take valuable time to build such a structure. And how big would you have to build a mound to have it be that high a thousand years later?

According to the interpretive center, Indians tanned leather using deer brains and human urine. I wondered who the Indian was who came up with this idea and how did they discover this unusual mix of tanning solutions? Was it an accident? And how does the park service know this?

The mounds line up for solstice and equinox and if I were anywhere near this park on June 21, I would definitely be at the park for sunrise! (www.arkansasstateparks.com)

The Toltec Mounds were one of the largest and most impressive sites in the Mississippi River valley. There were at least 18 mounds here and the oxbow pond was unique to these mound builders. The people seem to have abandoned Toltec Mounds around 1050 A.D. and no one knows where they went or why, after 400 years, they chose to leave. Maybe they got transferred because of a merger. Or perhaps they were Sooners fans. I walked the grounds of flat, stubby grass and stood next to the pond, large trees growing out of the water. The day was quiet and not with its creepy bayou feel.

Back at the grey interpretive center I got Robin the park person to pose with a Mounds candy bar. A little visual pun. Then I was off to do battle with Memorial Day weekend traffic through Little Rock. When I'd accomplished that and come out the other side, I was fixin' to have lunch.

I had intended to keep my food plan light that day and I was searching for a tummy-compatible Subway sandwich shop. But once I saw the sign for Brown's and it read CATFISH and SEATING FOR 400 and BUSES WELCOME, I thought they would be able to handle me and my growing hunger. All appetites met their match at Brown's in Benton, Arkansas.

Next time I eat at Brown's, I'm waiting until I am "I'm-gonna-faint" hungry. While a piped in harpsichord played Patsy Kline's *Crazy*, people strolled the 100 foot long buffet. Brown's was the stuff of legends. Customers paid first and then started down the concourse of 150 different food offerings most of which had seen the inside of a deep fat fryer. As I sat and watched out the windows I noticed that most people waddled into Brown's. No matter. The catfish was truly wonderful and the chicken was moist. A paper card on the table read, "We continue to expand." So did the customers.

Onion rings, hush puppies, catfish, something in crab shells--I left Brown's with enough grease in me to lube a Cadillac. I enjoyed every single morsel and I'd do it all over again in a minute. If I lived in Benton, Arkansas at Exit 118, Seno would have to have a bigger engine to haul me around.

The largest gated community in the United States was my next destination. For most of the trip I had counted down the days when I'd be in the safe circle of my friend Marilu and off the road for the dreaded Memorial Day. I had stayed with her for one night once before and I knew what was in store.

Marilu had it "goin' on" as they say. She nailed human behavior and motivation faster than anybody I knew. She was also funny and opinionated, an unusual combination. She took certain things in stride and she was a Harry Truman-type give 'em hell when the situation warranted. A person would not want to be the opposing side of Marilu Grose of Hot Springs Village, Arkansas.

She also had a home that was visually soothing, organized and floral. She decorated with all my favorite pinks and burgundy. I knew I would be comfortable with her and with her house. I didn't know she was going to let Seno sleep in her garage! And she was a trooper about the car. The little roadster was such a difficult car to get in and out of that most of my friends wouldn't try to ride in it. Howard would rather take public transportation, I think. But Marilu couldn't wait to have her hair pulled out of shape flying through the hills of the 26,000 acre forest that was her hometown and laughing like a kid. Even when she fell out of the car and scared me to death landing on her hip, she thought about it overnight and had me put a folding step ladder in the bonnet. This allowed her to step out of the car as gracefully as a British royal.

Marilu seemed to know what I needed before I did. And she's had my number since we met at Oxford. We disliked the same weirdo from Louisiana and for the same reasons. We liked the crusty old lady in the wheelchair and we joked about Barry and his proper British efficiency. Well read and well traveled, Marilu could share information with heads of state or backwoods moon shiners. It was all pretty much the same to her.

Many of her friends of "the Village" were struggling with serious health problems or soon would be. She was no exception and she claimed that the timing of my visit was perfect because she was in between discomforts of hospital stays. The day I left she told me not to make the bed because it was going to be packed for her move to a new place. A temporary place until she had her new home built. Argh. How do some people do it? I would rather cross the country 12 times than deal with contractors and architects and attempt to build a house. What she was cheerily doing I would regard as Hell on Earth. And she was taking this new phase of her life like she took everything, with efficient good humor.

It was a great luxury for me to be inside a *house* and a great luxury for Seno to be inside of a garage. We hadn't had this blessing since Irv and Christina's in New York. I loved her house and I was amazed she was leaving it. A placid view of the lake waited every morning and squirrels performed acrobatics on her bird feeder. One afternoon a luna moth the size of a dessert plate sat on her deck. Flowers were blooming outside, fuchsia and purple things.

Hot Springs Village was a confusing maze of winding roads that looked like the pattern that ants make in one of those flat ant farms. Clearly the place was designed for the people who lived there and not visiting riff raff. I couldn't go anywhere without concentrating very hard on what I was doing and where I was going. But I was never lost and I got to the point where I could actually run errands for Marilu.

When she wasn't entertaining me with her stories, she let her friends do it. We went to a potluck that was a thank you dinner honoring one of her singing groups. People were warm and friendly and they would have been even if I hadn't been crossing the country in a roadster. All I had to be was "with Marilu."

I met a couple who may have to receive the Procrastination Award for Romance. What a story!

They no sooner introduced themselves as newlyweds then explained that they had put off getting married for 52 years. Anne and Ed met on a blind date when she was a junior in high school and he was an Air Force sergeant. After her graduation they were so set on getting married that they bought the rings. Her mama would have none of that, so the two had to go their separate ways. They both married other people, he for 46 years and she for 39 years! Both of their spouses died of cancer. They both married again. And again these marriages ended. So now we find Ed in Nashville facing becoming a widower *again* when he sits down at his computer and for the first time in half a century, decides to look up his old sweetheart, Anne. Now here's Anne in Fort Worth. Can you imagine what it must have been like to get an email from your long lost love?

When they got together, it was "like we'd never been apart." They were married February 23, 2002. He left his baggage in Tennessee and she left hers in Texas and they were starting fresh in the beautiful forested community of Hot Springs Village, Arkansas. Both of them had a certain devilment about them, sparkling eyes and great smiles. They looked like two kids that shouldn't be left alone with a cat, some string and a tin can. I asked them how it was going and she said, "I'm as crazy about him as I was 52 years ago."

So Michael Phelps, the high school guy my parents disapproved of, if you're out there...

Marilu and I had breakfast with two women who were like characters out of an off beat book. One was a Lake Wobegon

Scandinavian and the other was Sara, "the original steel magnolia," who had a husband named Square. I think this was the southern pronunciation for "Squire." He looked my roadster over very slowly and pronounced me certifiably insane. The Crystal Chimes, a female version of a barbershop quartet, were all dressed in red, white and blue and performed at a Memorial Day picnic. I thoroughly enjoyed their singing and humor. Vera Liermann, Evaline Keith, Rita Daniels and Marsha Bresanahn sang marches and even did a little encore just for me. I couldn't have clapped more if I'd had two more sets of hands! Things were getting to be out-of-control wholesome there for a couple of days.

Marilu was becoming the Perle Mesta of Roadster Cruising. We would get into Seno and she would wave at everybody, stop at the guard posts and visit with the guards, laugh and wave at people she didn't even know. It was a parade just having her in the car. She was a great audience for me and Seno.

One evening as I was pouring over maps, I discovered some interesting names in Marilu's state. If I needed Romance, Hope, Heart or Success, I could find it in Arkansas. I could visit Sweden, England, Moscow, Laredo, Oxford, Berlin, Lisbon, Atlanta, Nashville, Florence, Poughkeepsie, Newark, Athens, Austin and Concord and never cross the state line. "Did you know," I asked Marilu, "that there are two Morning Stars, two Evening Shades, two New Hopes and two Hookers?" No, she didn't. We asked about this at the post office the next day and the postal guy said that they go by zip codes and without a zip code they have look up street names. "We have a person whose job it is to sort out things like that," he explained. I had never in my life known that a state would allow two towns within its borders to have the same name. Hadn't Franklin, New Hampshire been named that because Webster was already taken? Is this duplicating of names a uniquely Arkansas quirk?

Marilu told me that she had "some car friends" and I figured that if they were really into it, they'd regard my purple buggy as the mutt that he was. I tried to tell her that but she arranged a meeting at their shop/warehouse anyway.

I met Jim Davis and his evil sounding Li'l Red Truck. Retired from Chrysler he and his enthusiastic wife Marleen were nice about my Brand X wheels and still let me in the shop. A group of guys all worked on an assortment of vehicles and motorcycles together and swapped stories. The shop was immaculate and as the legend goes, one of them didn't return a tool to its proper place and was called a "cabbage head" by someone else. Eventually they all became known as The Cabbage Heads and had baseball caps with cabbages sewn on them.

I got to see iron (vintage cars) so odd that I couldn't identify some of them. There were racing murals painted on the walls of the garage area as back drops for the vintage racers. In one corner was a Messerschmidt, a tiny three-wheeled car whose top opened like an airplane cockpit. It shared the corner with a 1957 Issetta whose single front door opened like a refrigerator. About as safe as climbing in a refrigerator too... A little knot of men were polishing and putting the finishing touches on a 1950 Jaguar Mark V in preparation for a concourse show in Kansas City. The wood inside that car was like jewelry. A piano would die of envy for wood like that. I was a kid in a candy store! The Cabbage Heads rocked!

Then John Hollansworth came ambling through and introduced me to the Green Dragon. This 1917 Peerless had been in the Great American Race four times. The entry fees alone to do this would buy a Mercedes. The Peerless was a large, high-wheeled speedster with large silver pipes running outside the body. I had been lucky enough to see the Great American Racers only once in Olympia, Washington so I was glad to get a picture of John with his Peerless.

I had four ultimate experiences in Arkansas. One, I managed to outrun the menacing white truck, two I ate at Brown's and now three John took me for a ride in the Green Dragon! It was at least as thrilling as racing for my life across Arkansas on Highway 70 and a lot more enjoyable. I cannot accurately describe the sound of the engine. It was the 1812 Overture performed at Tanglewood. Not easily impressed with engines because I don't understand them, even I could swoon over this amazing sound. If this engine played baseball, it would be Babe Ruth. If it were a pastry it would have been Mattie's Vermont cream puffs. Harley-Davidsons could sing but this thing was Enrico Caruso. Somebody play the soundtrack of this vehicle at my memorial service.

A lot of people cringed at the thought of owning an old car. How could you insure something like that? Very creatively, actually. John Hollansworth's next project was a very unusual racer, a 1934 Pierce Arrow. (Free sepia photograph of this wild Salt Flats record holding speedster, go to www.hagerty.com) "Memories are what makes a car important," John said. And if the car doesn't conjure up some memories, then you can always go out and *make some.*

I was falling all over myself and Marilu was laughing with glee. She and Marleen were both more than patient while I did everything but lick the cars. I'd make a complete pest of myself if I lived in Marilu's neighborhood. Jim Davis looked at me like, "Girl, you need to get out more often." I've not had a lot of luck containing my enthusiasm for old wheels. Check that, I've not had a lot of luck containing my enthusiasm *period*. The root meaning of the word *enthusiasm* was "the god within" and it might be a form of constipation if you didn't let it out!

So what's Memorial Day without a ride on the lake, Jim asked. I looked at Marilu like, "Can we, mom?" Everyone knows the look. "Can we, huh? huh?" I'm a great audience for anybody with a little fun in mind. I respond like a beagle puppy; I get excited and bump into furniture.

Hot Springs Village had six lakes and some of those were peppered with enormous homes bordering on castle status. Marilu says there are some modestly priced homes *somewhere* in the Village. We only had time to see the creme de la creme. That included Jim and Maureen's house. This was my fourth peak experience in Arkansas. The four of us hopped in the Davis' boat and the engine doing thwubba, thwubba in that low, throaty marine baritone and we were off across the lake, wine glasses in hand, for dinner at the Last Chance, my last night in Arkansas. I only hope I can repay some of these gracious people should they ever come to Portland, Oregon. Coming back that evening I got the water tour of homes. Jim even had an old restored gas pump on his dock. Their home was decorated by Maureen, a grandmother who missed the kids. I could relate. We had to get off of that subject in a hurry because I was now 48 days without a Gracie fix.

Jim and I were not going to ever get completely sick of cars that evening so they connected to Matthews' web site on the internet and we shopped, scrolling down the pictures and descriptions of the cars Dale had for sale. "Hey, you buy one," I offered, "and I'll drive it over here." (Any excuse to get back on the road. If I kept suggesting this idea perhaps someone would take me up on it.) At the bottom of www.memorylaneclassiccars.com was a picture of Seno and me in the driver's seat waving. When Marilu and I pulled away from the Davis' circular drive that evening and they stood a few feet apart waving to us I got the impression that they wanted to be doing my trip too.

We Oregonians like to think that we invented trees but I don't think I've ever seen thicker forests than within the confines of Hot Springs Village. Across Marilu's small lake, without my glasses on, the trees looked like broccoli florets they were so dense. And for those who hear Arkansas and think "double wide," think again. There was a dizzying array of roads and plenty of houses, unseen because of careful planning and extremely healthy trees. There were a half dozen golf courses, lots of churches, boat ramps, stores. Basically, everything was there but the mess. Nothing messy anywhere. *Anywhere.* Hot Springs Village would never be Trenton, New Jersey.

Journal Entry: May 29, 2002

It's 5:30 a.m. and I've been up for a least an hour attempting not to freak out as I listen to thunder and rain in quantity. The white rooms of Marilu's house light up in flashes when the lightning strikes. We're supposed to go to the Red Hat Society luncheon and then I am supposed to leave today...seven hours from now. I look at the maps and figure I'll never make it to Reno at this rate. I had better call Addie [travel agent] *and get a plane ticket for Billings to Reno just in case I don't make it. Feeling quite panicked and can't find my I.D. for plane travel. I have at least 3,000 miles before I'm home.*

Roadster Lesson #16: You will not get across Arkansas on a low fat diet.

48

The slamdunked hat I created for Marilu was a smashing red hat. I think it was probably, yes, it was *definitely* the best hat at the luncheon. Two chapters of the Red Hat Society (the Scarlet O'Hatters and the Spa City Belles) met at Diamante for very vivid pictures around my roadster and a great send off for me. Seno, of course, was in his purple and red and all the ladies were too. It stopped raining long enough for us to get from parking lot to restaurant without getting our feather boas wet. This was crucial because when a feathered lady gets wet, she's going to smell like a turkey farm. Not something we were going for.

What did Red Hat Society ladies do? Answer: anything they want. To wear the "regalia" (that's purple outfit and a red hat) the only requirement was to admit to being at least 50 years old and have even a particle of humor. There were no rules. There were no dues. There were no officers. There were no fund raisers. Hopefully what was left might resemble just a good time. RHS chapters had teas and luncheons but they also went on cruises, posed for the press, rode trains to places to shop, went to horse races, posed for the press, attended expositions and plays together and posed for the press. They shopped, swapped and got silly together. But wherever they went, they got attention. One chapter in Illinois went to a male strippers show and threw purple panties on the stage. It was entirely possible that the goal might be to say "stick it" to whatever expectations the world had for "women of a certain age."

Most women stopped wearing hats in the 1950's. Hats made a statement and many females were told that they shouldn't be making statements. Hairstyles changed and the last thing you wanted to do with your big hair was crush it under a hat. Change was long overdue. I have always loved hats; I have 400 hats; I wear hats; I make hats; I am a "hat person." Men that I didn't even know would come up to me and say, "It is so great to see a woman wearing a hat. Why don't more women wear hats?" Seeing a woman in a hat, any kind of a hat, was a bit of a surprise.

Now make it a red hat! A "Mother! How *could* you!" bright red hat. We are morally obligated to embarrass our children, ladies.

Now find a purple outfit. Dresses are nice but if you live in cowboy country, wear purple jeans. If you're in Florida, wear a muu muu. I'm fond of prom dresses myself. And you know those bride's maids dresses that women give to the Goodwill about 24 hours after the wedding? They go to a good cause. A lot of them end up at my house. And it's not a collection, it's a wardrobe. It's not illegal to wear a tutu to the grocery store. And by the way, anything you dislike doing (like going to the grocery store), just wear a prom dress and it will change the experience. I believe in the Therapy of Costumes. A lot of what's bothering you would just simply go away if you would wear something today that you'd never dream of wearing.

Don't you imagine that negotiations for world peace would go better if all the world leaders got together and wore old prom dresses? You know this would work. You just know they'd think more creatively. Would probably make the negotiations go much faster too because those crinolines get scratchy...

It is pretty obvious that in order to have a "good life" today, you need to "think outside the box." That requires stretching your comfort zone way, way out of whack. What better (and safer) way to stretch yourself than do the simple, perfectly legal, act of changing what you wear. You are not your clothes! Whatever you are wearing *right now*, quit. If you're wearing a prom dress, go get into a sweat suit. If you're in a suit, go find your old poodle skirt. You know this works. When you went as a floozy to that Halloween party, you didn't walk like an auto mechanic! Peter Sellers said, "Play the costume." Ask Dustin Hoffman about his revelations when he became *Tootsie*. Anytime you need to change your perspective, change your outfit. Women used to know this. They used to say, "I'm upset. I'm going to go buy a new hat." And then they felt better.

Anyway, now women gathered and wore purple and put on their red hats and something magical happened. They lightened up. They laughed more. But something else happened. They got noticed (something most women avoided and then complained because they were "invisible") and other women saw it and it was good. And then the press saw it and the colors knocked their socks off and when they recovered they took pictures and then miles of purple and red ink started appearing in newspapers and magazines.

So the two chapters of Hot Springs Village, Arkansas hosted a beautiful luncheon that Wednesday afternoon. They were friendly and gracious and smiling and encouraging and gorgeous. Each and every one of them. We sipped iced tea, munched our salads, posed for pictures with bright purple parasols and then I got in my roadster and drove away.

Curving Highway 7 rolled around in the Ouachita National Forest and then north into the Ozark National Forest. It was good road, definitely not straight but I could run between third and fourth gear most of the time. It was heavy overcast but the rain was holding off and I counted every minute as a gift. I could feel the pull as the elevation got higher and once we stopped on top of a small mountain just to take a breather and see the view. Most of this country was thick with trees, the leafy kind and they came right up to the highway. Or there were the few small white farm houses. "Towns" were gas station stops and independent grocery stores.

I had taken a little edge off my pressure by calling Addie and getting the plane ticket as back up. I absolutely had to be in Reno June 14 for a speaking engagement. The conference people didn't care if I arrived by stage coach as long as I was in the ballroom of The Nugget ready to perform at the appointed hour. If it turned out that I didn't need the ticket I could regard it as medication. It made me feel better to have it. It would be worth it just to steady my nerves. The trick was to guestimate where I would be when I would need the ticket! I was betting that I could make it to Billings, Montana.

I was contemplating miles and days and routes when the sky just opened up. This "gully washer" had such a volume of water that the roadster was literally washed off the road. Fortunately there was a small turn out, a tiny crescent-shaped patch of gravel. On complete impulse I dragged the car cover out from the leg area of the passenger side of the car, pulled the strap off of it, slippery when wet, unfurled the cover, put it over my head and then over the cockpit area of the car.

And there we sat.

Using the car cover was inspired but I should have done it quicker. Realizing that this impulsive solution was actually a very good one, I began to sort things in the front seat so that the cover would ride beside me instead of crammed down below. There wasn't much else to do while I was under there being pelted by rain. I rearranged everything in order to accommodate this quick draw idea.

It was sort of neat sitting there under my rain cover figuring out what to do next.

The rain subsided and I continued on, air drying out many things. I knew I was headed northbound but other than that, I didn't know where I would spend the night or what was up ahead. I would just travel until something seemed right.

Harrison Village Campground looked right. Swimming pool, laundry, TV room, all kinds of facilities that I wasn't going to use. But it looked like Seno would be parked in grass, under a tree. So we signed up for a space. My only criteria was that it be level and we got that. Again the only amenity I had was all that I needed: a wooden picnic table. And we were so close to the Arkansas-Missouri state line that I could have thrown a brick into the Show Me State.

Things went well. My stuff was organized and I was in good shape from the loving care of Marilu. Everything was clean. Me, the car and my clothes. That would not happen again on the trip.

I was expecting a duplicate of the pleasant night that I had spent camping in Vermont. Didn't happen. My feet and calves cramped like never before in my life or since. I was not prone to that sort of problem. It was excruciating and all the usual adjustments and movement didn't help. Both my feet curled up as if they were hands. I was in such terrific pain that I had to break down and get into my painkillers. It could not have been vitamin deficiency, I'd been taking all my supplements religiously. I don't know what happened but it was as if my extremities had been poisoned.

The next morning presented an unusual weather phenomenon. It was either a heavy fog or a very fine mist...so I called it *mog*. Visibility wasn't great but I wanted to make tracks and I love to be on the road by five a.m. Seno and I quietly picked our way out of the campground and to the highway. Everything was instantly coated with a fine, feathery wet breath. My glasses were sprinkled with tiny hazy water drops that wouldn't stick together and run off.

Every morning I had a checklist of things that I mentally had to do. I put a handful of tissues in my left pocket in case a bathroom ran out of paper. I had food and water handy that my hands could find without looking. I packed my maps and my journal just a certain way. I checked the odometer for mileage every morning to gauge the gas.

And every time I got in the car I had to overcome fear. Every day I had to adjust to passing trucks and the whipping they gave me when they passed. After an hour of driving I started to breathe again.

Mammoth billboards, costing thousands each, lined up like soldiers marching across the landscape outside of Branson, Missouri. I had never seen advertising quite like this before. The best one was "Great music squeezed fresh daily" with a photograph of a guy with an accordion. It was for the Lawrence Welk Show.

I was on a mission this morning, however. I needed to find the Beverly Hillbilly's car. The Klampetmobile. The old relic that had all the junk on it. A friend in Oregon thought he wanted to build one and my task was to find it and photograph it. It was located in an unlikely spot, a college museum.

The Ralph Foster Museum in Point Lookout, Missouri was three floors of an eclectic mix of donated items. Instead of racing in and racing out, I found myself wandering around getting interested in the History of the Ozarks and famous people who had lived in the area. I learned that Thomas Hart Benton "did his first mural at age six on wallpaper" and I thought that perhaps his mother didn't regard it that way when she first saw it. Had she requested a mural?

And I learned that polar bears have black skin and their livers are poisonous because they contain an excessive amount of vitamin A. Lincoln had a five dollar *Confederate* bill in his pocket when he was shot. And Booth tried two kidnapping schemes before he did his deed at Ford's theatre. Where was the Secret Service then? Oh, perhaps we didn't have one. The Ozarks was part of the Louisiana Purchase in 1803 and Thomas Jefferson got the land for three cents an acre. Way to go, Tommy!

I had the Beverly Hillbillies car to myself. There were so many advantages to getting up early! I hopped around the 1921 Oldsmobile touring car and photographed it from every angle. It was quite a large car and I could easily see the actors on it.

As I drove back through the green lawns of the College of the Ozarks I noticed a lot of what appeared to be students doing clean up work. Must be campus clean up day, I thought, which on most campuses was Party Day with Rakes. Well, here, every day was campus clean up day. The beautiful College of the Ozarks was home to 1,500 students who actually worked in lieu of tuition at "Hard Work U." These kids weren't here to party. The College was ranked in the Top 20 Liberal Arts College by *U.S. News & World Report* and it was number one in students graduating with the least amount of debt.

Loved the swan pond, a prominent feature in the middle of the campus. Everything was clean, tidy, perfect. Kids were pulling weeds, mowing, sweeping. In the gift shop were student made products including apple butter and ceramics. What a novel idea! Perhaps it will catch on. (www.cofo.edu)

In Branson there was the World's Largest Banjo, Andy Williams singing in his Christmas sweater, magic shows, blue grass, comedy, Americana. But one off-color comment, joke or song will get a performer bounced out of Branson. Or so I heard. There were stage performances going on all hours of the day and night. The only way to do Branson was park in Arkansas and take a bus in. Dennis Miller claims that Branson was "Las Vegas with missing teeth."

All I want was the money the shows here spend on full color brochures. The racks of screaming, slick graphics were everywhere. Half of the printing industry may be supported by Branson.

Next stop was Bonniebrook, Home of Rose O'Neill. Everyone knows her "product."

At one time 36 factories in Germany were producing her art in bisque form. She made over $2 million just in royalties.

During WWII there was a war embargo between England and Germany. The only record of that embargo *ever being lifted* was for a shipment of Rose's items. Even the war lords had to step aside so that the children of America and Britain could get their Christmas supply of...Kewpie Dolls.

The cute little dolls were originally illustrations and Thomas Hart Benton called Rose O'Neill "America's greatest illustrator." She was the highest paid female illustrator in the United States, she had homes in several pristine places around the world but she had a special place in her heart for the family home in the Ozarks which had the first indoor bathroom in the county. After two unhappy marriages and two divorces Rose had a dream which led to the creation of the Kewpie Doll in 1909. The impish little characters were named Kewpie as a quirky version of Cupid.

An interesting wrinkle to the story has a recent development. Because of WWII Rose eventually had to have the dolls made out of composite material. An American purchased a porcelain factory in Germany a few years ago and while sorting through his real estate purchase, he came upon the original molds for the Kewpie. So now they can produce them just as they were created back in the 30's. An original Kewpie would have a hefty price tag. And the best collection of them can be seen at the Ralph Foster Museum on the first floor or visit Rose's home and the Kewpie Museum just north of Branson.

In all the hundreds of wonderful Kewpie dolls available for purchase there I never did see one exactly like the one I had as a child. I walked around Rose O'Neill's house and I can see why she loved it. There was a brook running through the property that made a chime sound. Can't say that I really connected with her non-Kewpie sculpture displayed in the yard, although it evidently wow'd them in France. Illustrating a mythological story, this one large cement thing looked like a couple trying to get it on and trying to turn into broccoli at the same time.

Back on the highway and out of the vortex of Branson, the road was heating up, all the cooling clouds burned off and I settled into "make time." That only lasted until I saw the huge green billboard that read: LAMBERT'S, THE ONLY HOME OF THROWED ROLLS. Marilu had told me about this place where they pitch the dinner rolls from across the room.

Since 1942 Lambert's Cafe has been stuffing Americans with what they wanted. Food and lots of it. I think I saw some of the same diners here that I saw at Brown's in Arkansas. About 50 people were waiting outside to get in, listening for their names on a public address system. Seno landed a prime parking place and I waltzed right in--being just one person had *so* many advantages. Inside Lambert's looked like several gymnasiums decorated with flags, kites and license plates with a dozen squadrons of people ravenous and just off the road. It was packed with happy people and even happier wait staff because they really did *throw the rolls.* And they were those yeasty, hot, already-slippery-with-butter pillow rolls. I was lucky and caught both of mine. The chef salad was as big as a microwave oven and I took it with me and ate it for two more days. They came around with fried potatoes and fried okra, all you wanted. The iced tea was served in a container bigger than my helmet. I didn't ask for a doggie bag, I asked for a doggie suitcase.

Why do they have the tradition of throwing these rolls anyway? Well, it used to be that the owner would try to pass out the hot rolls in the usual way, by saying, "Would you care for a hot roll?" This didn't work too well on extremely busy days and, as legend has it, one customer said, "Just throw the #%X*! thing!" They've been throwing rolls at Lambert's for over 25 years.(www.throwedrolls.com)

I met Jason who was right on Seno when I was ready to leave. He pointed out his black Corvette roasting in the hot sun. I asked him what he thought people should know about his state and he said Missouri was the "Show Me" state and that was not just a slogan, he felt that people there wanted to see it to believe it. I certainly had to see Lambert's to believe it!

The Ozark hills provided me with scenes that I hadn't seen anywhere else. Like a long, long stretched roller coaster, the high hills took the roadster up, up for a great view and then raced down, down playing tag with trucks that can't go up fast (so you pass them) and then come barreling down (filling your rearview mirror with their grilles). There are at least seven of these thrilling hills before it starts to flatten out and becomes the Missouri I remember from my childhood years of living in Belton near the Kansas border.

I traveled all day through Missouri. The asphalt was taking on the temperature of a warming oven. At Humansville I stopped to get a photograph of their unusual town name on a large billboard. I needed to cool both me and Seno's engine under a tree in a city park. A live frog jumped out from under the car, I caught him in my purple towel and tried to photograph him with the business across the street as background, the Quick Jump convenience store with a frog for a logo. I just thought that the live frog with the store's logo was too good to pass up.

I told myself that Seno needed to cool but it was really just an excuse to go into the junque store on the corner. I found a photo holder about the size of a toothbrush, just the right size to slip in between Seno's battery and the fire wall. I couldn't buy anything unless I had a space for it. I struck up a conversation with the lady who ran the store and a fellow named Bill Clark. They told me about the French Indian fellow named James Human who founded the town on a land grant. He became Judge Human and everybody agreed we could use more human judges. I was asked the usual questions about my trip and I said, yes, I'd been gone 50 days now and had covered over 5,000 miles. I found a lovely purple silk rose thinking perhaps I could pin it under the dashboard so that it wouldn't get crushed. The lady who owned the store was sincerely interested in my driving around the country all alone. Alone? Alone. It was as if she had never heard or thought of such a thing. The idea of *going* also appealed to her. I used to live in Missouri, I told her, I can understand. Finally she just looked at me and said, "You are richer than Bill Gates to be able to do this."

Roadster Lesson #17: People will give you gifts. Accept them.

49

I stopped in Clinton, Missouri, the only town library that charged me money to use their computers for the internet. One dollar.

Because of the painful cramping I had endured the previous night, I didn't even consider camping out this Friday evening. I found a chain motel in Harrisonville and settled in next door to a freeway and a Wal-Mart. It wasn't exciting or glamorous but I wasn't feeling particularly excited or glamorous. I wanted a dull evening of stupid television, a hot bath and security for my traveling partner. I got everything I wanted.

The next morning as I was unrolling the cover and preparing for the day's drive, I looked in the crawl space cockpit and I said to myself,

"How can I get in there and drive this thing today?"

It was a conversation I had nearly every day for 50 days now. Every day that I drove the car I had to talk myself into getting started. And every day it took about an hour to get adjusted to the fear. I never really knew if some morning I just wouldn't be able to do it.

Then a fat guy hauling suitcases appeared in the parking lot. He stopped, looked at the roadster, waddled over to his van with Minnesota plates, crammed the suitcases in it and then walked back to get a better look. I just kept folding the cover and strapping like I did every morning. Finally he said, "You'd better be careful. If you roll that car, you could get hurt."

I acted shocked. Like this was complete news to me. "Really?" There would be absolutely nothing but air between my cranium and the earth if I rolled the car. His observation struck me as hilarious. And of course having him point it out to me was one of the funniest things I'd ever heard. It was like telling Cleopatra, "You'd better be careful with that asp..." I finished packing and took off.

I had visited 18 museums so far on this adventure and I was learning a few things about museum management. Sometimes people collect things and the compulsion gets out of hand and perhaps a spouse may step in and say, "Do something about this mess or else!" and the collection gets put in a building and the whole exercise may then be called a "museum."

Now the person who collected all this wonderful stuff may not really be interested in having people come and look at it. Their "museum" may even appear in some guide books but they do what they can to deter people from actually finding and viewing the collection. I found such a museum in Missouri...and since they wanted to remain anonymous, I intend to honor that. So if Independence, Missouri was your destination, you might just want to apply a thick coating of Nair on your curiosity and pass on the quirky museum there.

Instead, waste no time in getting to downtown Kansas City to the revitalized City Market area to the *Steamboat Arabia*. This exhibit was really two miracle stories, each exceptional.

In 1856 a large stern wheel paddle boat was bringing a supply of cargo, a mule and some passengers up the Missouri River. There was much needed hardware and supplies like boots, tools, farm implements, glassware and medicine that frontier people were counting on. This was a floating Wal-Mart complete with buttons, fabric, whiskey, perfume and china. There were also moms and kids and merchants and doctors and gamblers and all sorts of travelers headed west. The boat hit a jagged log and started to go down. Everyone jumped off and watched the vessel with 200 tons of cargo sink into the Missouri mud and disappear as if in quicksand. It kept sinking, mule still on board, until its big smoke stacks were out of sight. Down went jewelry, doorknobs, whale oil lamps and a doll. Eventually 45 feet of mud and dirt covered the grave of the *Steamboat Arabia*.

And that was where it all stayed for over 100 years. During that time the Missouri River shifted, established a new curve to itself and the surrounding farmland. Then these treasure hunters, armed with partially correct historical information, found the thing in a Kansas field. They managed to dig down and bring up the cargo which was daunting because for every shovelful of dirt, they got a bucket of mud and water. In an effort that can only be described as heroic, they brought up what was left of the steamboat and nearly all of its cargo, painstakingly cleaned it and preserved it. This was the first miracle.

But the second miracle was what they did with the treasure. This was now the largest collection of pre-civil war artifacts in the world! And how much would a Civil War buff pay for a pair of "new" 1856 boots in perfect condition? This could be the biggest historical garage sale in the history of America!

Florence Hawley, gracious and hardworking wife and mother, had never intended to become a museum curator and gift shop manager. She and her husband Bob, their kids and their kids and the other treasure hunters did a remarkable thing. They kept the entire collection together. Then they found a 30,000 square foot building in a funky part of Kansas City, gutted it, resurrected it and installed the collection. Instead of a nice quiet retirement, Flo had to deal with school children tours, Japanese tourists, purchase orders and staffing. What was even more remarkable to me than their efforts to get the cargo up on dry land, was the superb quality of the museum and every time I asked "Who did this display?" or "Who designed that?" the answer was always some member of the family.

The *Steamboat Arabia* could not have fallen into better hands. The arrangement of the exhibits, the graphics, the displays, everything here exceeds even the Smithsonian. It was worth veering off my trail several hundred miles to see this. Flo and her grandson Matt came out to my car and we had an exceptional visit explaining our amazing stories to each other.

One of the items found on board the ship was a bottle of perfume. It was still good! So they had the contents analyzed and then *reproduced!* I bought myself a special gift. A bottle of perfume called "1856." And I learned an interesting piece of trivia. Whale oil does not burn as well as kerosene. So if an old lamp had one wick, it was kerosene and if it had two wicks, it was older--a whale oil lamp. And there were so many pairs of boots on the *Arabia* that it would take another four years to clean them to preservation standards. And the stubborn mule that refused to budge? The animal's skeleton was right there on display near the ship's hull.

The two miracles in Kansas City should be considered a rare gem presented to America by these exceptional treasure hunters. (www.1856.com)

Leaving Kansas City I didn't get the highway I wanted but I figured anything headed north would be OK. So I lost a bit in my search for I-35, the only real route possible to Des Moines. The heat was becoming intense. I stopped to fill Seno and bought myself bottled ice water. As I drove I sprinkled cold water on my long-sleeved silk shirt. This was followed by almost instant evaporation. I made it 45 minutes and had to pull over to recuperate. I rested in the shade, laying on the grass near a tourist information booth housed in a caboose. My recovering time was taking too long. I learned that when I got overheated, I needed air-conditioning to revive quickly.

The interstate trucks and I flew by the "Welcome to Iowa" sign and John Wayne's birthplace and the Bridges of Madison County. With hours of road behind me I exited for dinner, more for the air-conditioning than food. The place was called the Country Quilt Cafe and had a field hand selection of food. A hand gun perky lady was more or less running the place and she asked most of the patrons about their crops. I had parked the roadster in the shade, on the east side of the building where it wasn't visible. I was glad this farm lady hadn't seen the car; I never would have gotten out of there.

I had bisected Iowa west to east just seven weeks before. They reported record heat then, the surprise 92 degrees. Now I was bisecting Iowa south to north and once again suffering in the oppressive heat. Inside my boiled brain I figured it must always be like this in Iowa and they just print headlines about record heat just to amuse tourists. They couldn't kid me, it was hot like this *all the time.*

The sun was going down but the temperature wasn't. Seno and I stayed in the right hand lane. When a semi would come up on the left, I'd speed up a little just to run for awhile in the shade of the truck for a little relief, then finally drop back, the sun hitting full force again.

So far I had driven through 27 states, ten state capitols, gone 6,258 miles, visited 107 bathrooms and 19 museums, identified nine different species of road kill, received over 500 thumbs up or waves, heard "good luck" over 100 times and had six "God bless you's." The worst bathroom on the trip was in a Front Royal, Virginia gas station and the best bathrooms were tourist rest stops in Ohio and Arkansas and the ultimate bathroom was the Hen House in Lee's Summit, Missouri. I had been traveling alone for over a month.

As I continued to lose brain cells to the heat I talked to myself about travel in general. Traveling is a "little death," I decided. You may have your drivers license or your passport but you don't really have an identity with other people until you open your mouth. When you're traveling you are what you are right at that moment. You cannot be your reputation, your heritage, your successes, your resume. All of the applause was gone but all of the little mistakes were gone too. You're just who you are.

I continued to enjoy the role of back up singer to Seno's spotlight performances. He just drew a crowd wherever we went. The workers on the loading docks in the Kansas City fruit market, Wal-Mart shoppers, rest stop families, museum parking lots. Everywhere. The car was a magnet for car buffs and for people who knew absolutely nothing about cars. I've traveled in other cars, even old cars, vintage fat-fendered cars, but nothing could beat the purple roadster for bringing instant smiles to the people who saw him.

As I slaved away in the heat, 65 miles per hour seemed more like 20 miles per hour. Getting to Des Moines was becoming an endurance test. But I wanted to see Ellen de Lathouder and she had generously offered her guest room to me. It was 8 p.m. when I finally arrived on the right street in the exact middle of Iowa. I had put in a 14 hour day.

Journal Entry: June 1

If I had a dog along, he'd be dead by now.

OK, so I had a mental picture of Iowa and Tudor-style old homes, rolling lawns and ironwork gates didn't fit the picture. Seeing Ellen's piece of paradise was like seeing Tiffany jewelry on Buck Owens.

I saw her house, inside and out, before I actually got to see her. Fan-like trees cooled the upscale, old neighborhood built in a miniature canyon. Luscious green grass rolled up and down lawns like carpet. The little street curved in this draw and on either side, the houses were displayed as if on shelves. Ellen's house, up a long driveway, was over 100 years old. She was out seeing a movie that wasn't her choice and invited me to make myself at home. What a great treat to have a few minutes to gather my thoughts and stop vibrating before I had to speak to another human being.

By now I had my routine simplified so that I had one bag and my maps and helmet to haul inside her home. And what a home! Eclectic, certainly. A narrow weathered table in the kitchen. A funky little loo tucked ingeniously under a stairway. Antiques, country chic, Indonesian god with an offering hole in his head, architectural house parts, odd candles, hardwood floors. There was something stunning about the mix. It worked. I just stood and stared trying to figure it out. How could it look so good, feel so good and appear to be so *undecorated*? French doors opened into a solarium. The kind of feature in a house that when you see it, the sale is made on that one thing. The large old fireplace opened in both the living room and the solarium. The whole place seemed comfortable, lived in and so at peace with itself.

Then Ellen arrived, poured wine and we discussed how people use space until midnight. She was as comfortable and orderly as her lovely home. What I couldn't fathom, and what delighted her, was the I-haven't-been-decorated look of her home. It had plenty of interesting personality but it didn't have that stiff, don't-touch-anything feel that I get looking at photographs of rooms in magazines. I mean, nobody leaves a hanky stuck in a book on a coffee table with a single rose petal on it. And the lemons on the kitchen counter. Does anybody leave lemons laying around like that?

Her home didn't try to impress and was impressive. Just like Ellen.

Ellen and I had met in the living room of Magdalen College more than a year ago. Part of the Oxford course we were taking involved a visit to the "living room" of Britain's megalith builders, Stonehenge.

We had a long conversation on the bus ride back to the college. Both of us were interested in arranged space, and how it was designed, and more importantly, how it affected the people who move around in it. From standing stones to pillows on furniture, we instinctively knew about feng shui before it became a Saturday seminar in suburbia.

I slept under a feather comforter that night and could have luxuriated til noon! But we had friends to meet at the Drake Diner, an upscale place with frosted windows that seemed a natural backdrop for a roadster. We had a great girl talk with Ellen's two chums and discussed the value of women in the lives of women. They were very supportive of my nutty trip and with a "go, girl!" from them, I was off again. Back out in the Iowa heat.

North of Des Moines I saw a strip of clouds in the distance. Seno and I ran for it! The day before I had welcomed the trucks bearing down on me because they brought shade. So the clouds were a welcomed sight. I was dousing my shirt with my water bottle so a little sprinkling from above was just fine with me.

A sprinkling was all those clouds had in them but they had cooled the day down to the low 90's. Despite my speed which cools the roadster experience substantially, in the heat it felt like baking under a heat lamp. Now, at least, there was a covering between us and the mean Iowa sun.

I had five more hours before I could stagger off I-35 into St. Paul, Minnesota and into the loving arms of my buddy Lynette. She appeared like a character in a King Arthur story, a large red parrot on her shoulder. She was gargoyles and fairies and fantasy and creativity and talent and generosity. She still had the long, long hair that she had 20 years ago when we met in Arizona. Michael, her spousal unit, was more enthusiastic than I remembered, probably because of Seno's presence parked on their block. Lynette's son and neighbors gathered.

I was anxious to show off the car and everybody was anxious to go for a ride. Then the roadster pulled a terrible stunt. Once shut off he wouldn't start again. We had a real comedy routine with Michael doing the "pop the clutch" trick while we pushed. We were joined by what appeared to be a fraternity group of guys from across the street. Lynette said to me, "Alyce, you couldn't just calmly come for tea or anything could you?"

Seno came to rest in their garage and then everybody just sat down. Sometimes it's just the only thing left to do. A major car event was going on in St. Paul that night and it looked like the roadster was not going to making a showing.

Lynette's funky old house was two blocks from the governor's mansion, a stunning brick building that looked like a Catholic girls school with an iron fence. Michael explained that the mansion was gifted and if it wasn't occupied, then the deed stipulated that it was to be torn down. Jesse Ventura, the love/hate child of Minnesota, abandoned the "house" and now chains and padlocks decorated the iron gates. Lovely. Surely all of America would rise up and protest against raising a wrecking ball to this great mansion. But then, we've had a lot on our minds...

Lynette had cautioned me to arrive on Saturday and not Sunday. Over 200,000 celebrants were due at a blow out block party called Grand Old Days that basically shuts down traffic all over St. Paul. So I had made it in time. Michael and Lynette and I joined the throng for cheese curls, lutefisk, rock 'n' roll, $4 ice cream cones, Arcadian accordionists, street vendors, Peruvian ragtime, dogs, velvet hats, impromptu dances between strangers, beer spilling on the sidewalk, Zydeco, balloons--it looked like Portland's Saturday Market. I felt right at home. I asked Michael what the difference was between Minneapolis and St. Paul.

"Minneapolis likes to think it's New York--the Mini-Apple. [say that out loud, you'll get it!] St. Paul doesn't care."

It was actually more entertaining to tour Lynette and Michael's home than to boogie down Grand Avenue sampling Scandinavian fare with the local 200,000. Lynette was an artist in the very advanced sense of the term. Children's book illustrator, sculpturer, muralist, designer, 3-D imagin-eer. At her brick fireplace two fairies about the size of four year old children lean toward each other with spread wings. One holds an Instamatic camera and looks at you as if to say, "Would you smile when I tell you, please?" Lynette sculpted these big fairies!

"I thought there was something wrong with me but listening to Alyce at least I know there's two of us," Lynette said.

There were deerstalker hats on the mantel, a salute to Michael's fascination with murder mysteries. We had a long, delicious conversation about Colin Dexter, the Inspector Morse writer that I had met in England. Michael wanted to know everything I could remember about Dexter. I told him most of it.

If Lynette wanted a curve instead of an angle in her space, she simply made it happen. It was one thing to have the idea, it was another to pull it off. She could do both. She sculpted things right into the wall--a dragon-like creature emerged from a corner of her kitchen. If there were no flowers, she painted them. I had to pay attention to what I was looking at because her trompe l'oeil were extremely convincing. The entire ceiling of the room where I slept was covered with Van Gogh's starry night, Lynette style. And in the bathroom, created out of cut yellow tile was a sunburst behind the toilet. "So light can shoot out of your bum," said Michael. I would love to empty my big old house and turn Lynette loose in it with a million dollars. It would be an environment beyond belief. This girl does not know how to be boring!

Meeting Hamish wasn't boring either. A little background...I was literally raised with collie dogs. I have black and white photographs of baby Alyce on a blanket in Ohio surrounded by collie puppies. I've had dog hair in my life for decades. I adore dogs almost as much as I adore their 4-wheeled counterparts (automobiles) and dogs seem to know that. Well, Hamish, the perky Scottish terrier (terror?) didn't get the memo. I got down on the floor to greet this cute black fur ball and in his nearsightedness and enthusiasm, he bit the edge of my jaw near my chin. He probably mistook me for an interloping dog and didn't appreciate the intrusion. I know that dog bites can hurt but fortunately this one didn't. After that he kept his teeth on my shoes, an acceptable compromise for us both. I had an inch long gouge under my jawbone but Hamish just added to the drama of my story, "And I was bitten by a dog!"

Tink, the big red parrot, enjoyed watching a Nero Wolf mystery with us one evening and every time Lynette would leave the room, he would patiently try to follow. I watched as he stood at the top of the stairs waiting for her and if she didn't return in 60 seconds, Tink would climb down the steps, grabbing each one with his beak first. He would make it all the way to the kitchen, just in time for Lynette to scoop him up and return to the TV room with popcorn or wine or whatever. During the next commercial break, this scene was repeated. He would watch her leave as if, "How could you leave me?" then wait a few seconds, hop off the couch, walk across the floor to the top of the steps, wait, then start his descent. The huge red bird was totally devoted to Lynette.

Garrison Keillor lived on Lynette's street. I had not listened to his PBS show in weeks and I missed it. I loved Guy Noir and Dusty and Lefty and powder milk biscuits. Unlike my VCR, I had no way of taping the radio shows so it was just entertainment lost. The closest I got to Lake Wobegon was to show Seno where the Big Guy lived.

Lynette's son Noel, bless his heart, examined the stubborn roadster and jiggled a few wires. Hopefully this solved the starting problem. I hoped so because I was leaving with all determination to make it to Reno in the car.

Just to make my visit complete, I fell down in the street injuring my left hand. Two fingers took the brunt of my weight as I ker-splatted on the sidewalk. The bleeding holes began to swell and turn purple before we made it home for ice.

I must have looked like the Perils of Pauline pulling out of St. Paul and returning to life on the road. I imagine Michael and Lynette breathed a sigh of relief that I was actually off their property and I could perform my antics of destruction elsewhere.

It was a bit of a thrill to see the word WEST on the Highway 169 sign and know that now I was officially headed toward home.

It was a long haul from Mankato, Minnesota to the South Dakota border. A cooling cloud cover was a relief from the Iowa sun even if the mist threatened to turn to rain. Minnesota, roughly translated, mean "sky-tinted water" and that was pretty much what it was all the way to Mitchell. I knew I was leaving the Mall of America behind but that place was nothing I could tackle in 20 minutes.

The roadster seemed to be running better than ever. Was the car as happy to be headed westbound as I was? I was glad to connect to I-90 because this highway was peppered with interesting things to see, some kitsch and some actually historical; I have enjoyed its many attractions on several road trips. Just past Sioux Falls, however, was a new one on me!

I noticed something odd in the distance and as I zoomed closer there was a billboard on my side of the road proclaiming WORLD'S LARGEST BULL HEAD. That got me to pull off at Exit 374 and I was on my way to South Dakota's version of "Wayne's World."

The massive Egyptian Long Horn Bull was 60 feet tall and weighed 25 tons, placed out on the prairie many miles from anywhere. As far as I could see were rolling green hills that would be tawny brown in a month. The bull head looked like a very surprised long horn--the horns went straight up in the air. Constructed out of railroad plate iron, the head came with bats and creepy, crawly creatures inside. Wayne enjoyed pointing these things out especially to the kids.

Wayne was a piece of work himself. The wide prairie landscape was his Field of Dreams and a few nightmares. He sculpted vultures, ladies, fish, rocking horses, dragons and birds. He gave me and a curious family a personalized tour of his Sculpture Park which included a glance inside his head and humor. Partly cartoonist and partly serious philosopher, Wayne Porter displayed his work like no other artist I had ever seen. His "canvas" was this vast South Dakota acreage and his "paint" of choice was metal.

The cod fish holding the umbrella was Wayne's comment about how some people need to create their own rainy days and make themselves unhappy. The god Pan played the saxophone in the park surrounded by dancing women with wiry hair and purses. The Jack jumped out of Pandora's box releasing evil from an old gas tank. A huge head showed how imagery came into Wayne's mind and the astonished look on the face indicated that even the creator of these amazing sculptures wasn't sure where all the inspiration came from. The Pink Horse was a large rocking horse afraid of what was behind it and depicted the dreams that "we are afraid to ride."

A school of large fat metal goldfish seemed to swim across the grassland toward Seno. Two of the fish could have eaten the car. Wayne liked to do big things in metal and paint with splashy color. Several of the fantails were as purple as the car!

Unlike many galleries, Wayne encouraged photo taking and would pose next to his creations and even interact with them or show how to take the most interesting picture.

Wayne explained the original use of some of the metal pieces. "Bucker teeth are used on farm implements to make haystacks." "Old disc blades." "Truck springs and railroad spikes." "Tire rims and mower sickle sections." His art exhibit wasn't free but I'd definitely say it was worth it. I climbed back into my cockpit pleased to have the kinks out of my body and I possibly had a few kinks removed from my head from enjoying the sculpture.

Just as I was coming into Mitchell, South Dakota to call it a day, the roadster's left rear fender broke loose.

Roadster Lesson #18: Don't buy coffee at a Dairy Queen.

51

"Nothing is harder on mortal man than wandering." --Homer

The words *travel* and *travail* have a common origin. People who stay home a lot were making more and more sense to me.

Journal Entry: June 4

I am nursing a swollen left hand, a dog bite and a broken car. My right hand must work overtime steering because the fat sausage fingers of my left hand can't grip very well. I had barely enough energy to wrap Seno in his car cover and I'm afraid I wasn't the most gregarious person the desk clerk has ever checked in. My hair looks like fine dried weeds. I look in the motel room mirror and I wonder, "How am I going to turn this into Alyce Cornyn-Selby?" I've got nine days to get me and the car 1,880 miles, across mountains and desert. Tonight's a low point. But unless I want to spend the rest of my life in Mitchell, South Dakota I'll get myself together soon.

The next morning I rolled out of bed and rolled out the duct tape. I tried gluing braces on the fender struts. That lasted two blocks. Rattling down the street I went into downtown Mitchell to see the familiar Corn Palace. I was to the point that I just didn't know what else to do.

New billboard ads along I-90 had read: FROM EAR TO ETERNITY and YOU'LL BE A-MAIZED.

For more than 100 years the citizens of Mitchell have stapled and glued corn kernels, grain, cobs and corn plants to the side of a building called the Corn Palace. Every year they take it all down, come up with a new theme and then do it all over again. Why do this? Over 400,000 visitors come to see it every year and letting them down would be unthinkable, I guess. Nine different kinds of corn was used on this year's display, no paint or artificial coloring was allowed. During the day there were free guided tours and at night they turned on its lights. The designer of Radio City Music Hall was the designer for the building in Mitchell that gets decorated with thousands of bushels of corn every year.

I parked the crippled roadster across the street at an attraction called the Enchanted Museum. I took his picture there just as a sarcastic point. Neither one of us was particularly enchanted that morning. My New York buddies were probably right. The car wasn't built to withstand this kind of brutal cross country trekking and obviously neither was I. Two rings were swollen solidly onto and into my left ring finger. One was a ring with a large flat red stone and the other was my plain gold band, what I called my "no pest strip."

A native (I could tell by his plaid pearl-snap shirt and jeans) was crossing the street to a municipal building and he said, "Great car!" I winced. "Know any welders?" I asked. "Sure," he said, "Two blocks that way is Bailey's."

I brightened immediately, slipped into the cockpit with a whole new lease on life and thought, "Mr. Bailey, can I please go home!" Twenty minutes later, and ten dollars lighter the fender was welded on and I was on my way to the interstate. Whew!

I don't mean to say anything negative about South Dakota roads but this fix lasted about two hundred miles. (At ten dollars per fix, that pencils out to five cents a mile.) This also was not a reflection of work done by various people on the car. Welding, as near as I could understand it, was like nail polish. The old welds needed to be ground off before the new stuff would stick. To do otherwise was like applying new nail polish over old. Icky. The other more important factor, however, was that no welding could make up for the bad idea of attaching those struts to the brake drums. Vibration would eventually wear the welds out even if the welder were God himself. I resigned myself to red duct tape striping the car body with it and wrapping it repeatedly to secure the fender.

I-90 was straight as a metal ruler across the plains. There were a few trees, no farm houses or cows or dogs to entertain me. The only interruption in the miles of prairie were billboards. And I read every one of them. Within an hour or two my heavy helmeted head was listing forward. I tried singing, rubbing my legs, stretching my back, shifting position, thinking awake thoughts and finally gave up. I was falling asleep at the wheel! I had slept, or was certain that I had slept at the motel in Mitchell. I pulled in at a rest stop, parked as far away from where travelers were congregating, put my large purple beach towel over my cockpit to block the sun and I went instantly to sleep.

I woke up in a half hour and figured, "Ah, there, now I'm set for the day." I drove back onto the interstate and continued west. I was moving right along, making good time, the car was holding together and then the sleepiness overtook me again. I knew I couldn't be getting carbon monoxide poisoning because I was doing 65 miles per hour in an open car! But it was as if I was heavily drugged. This time I barely made it off the highway. There was an exit and at the end of the ramp, an intersection with nothing around, just a narrow two lane road. I was dozing precariously and I maneuvered the car out of the way of the intersection and parked. I again got out the towel and again went instantly to sleep.

After 30 minutes I woke up, enjoyed a red delicious apple and slowly crept the car up the ramp and back on the interstate. The vibrating massage of the roadster, the light warmth of the sun, the sheer boredom of the expanse of land...I have no explanation for my inability to stay awake. My eyelids ached to close. I had never been a nap-taking person. I probably hadn't taken three naps since I was an infant. I could not fathom what was wrong with me. Could it have been that allergy pill I took that morning?

Could be, I thought. But this was too severe a reaction to blame it all on one pill. I couldn't keep the car on the road. I'd come to just in time to see Seno's right front tire riding the fog line. Drugs in the hospital didn't hit me this hard. Whatever it was, I wished I could get it in pill form for when I did want to sleep and couldn't! For the third time, my heavy arms barely got me off the road and this time to a look out point parking lot. By now I had my towel handy and had no compunction about sacking out in a public place.

Again I slept for 30 minutes and awoke just as before. It did not occur to me that 54 days of travel had perhaps taken its toll. Someone or something inside of me might have wanted more rest or may have wanted to quit this entire exercise. At this rate, I thought, it was going to take me three weeks to cross South Dakota! Telling myself to snap out of it wasn't helping.

Murdo was a favorite stop on I-90. Perhaps being around car stuff would charge my Alyce batteries. I had been through the Pioneer Auto Museum and Antique Town so many times I could have given the tour myself. My favorite vehicle here was an old White truck that someone had made into a traveling camper. Long before anyone thought up the term RV, this thing was equipped with a kitchen and beds. It seemed like a wonderful old relic to hit the road in. In all probability, it didn't run at all. There was an Elvis motorcycle here. Tom Mix had his name embossed in a set of tires on a car here--as the car rolled down the street, it wrote his name in the mud or dust. I shopped in the gift store, hoping the air-conditioning might stir a level of alertness. I got a big kick out of the display counters made out of the sides of a cream and pink '55 Chev. Drank something cold. Even retail therapy wasn't stimulating me.

Back in the car, I pulled on the stick and continued west on I-90. At least it wasn't raining. Nothing seemed to snap me out of my haze. Surely Wall would do it.

I loved Wall Drug. I loved their *Readers' Digest* story of how they got started by offering ice water to travelers headed west. I loved the fact that it was one place I could get a five cent cup of coffee. I loved the goofy things like the jackalope that I could climb on and have my picture taken. There were statue type dance hall girls, bar room hussies, slo-eyed cowboys and mountain men all sitting on park benches or cowboys leaning on posts, a prospector pulling a donkey. Fat vacationers in shorts and old ladies in print dresses interact bashfully with these "characters" while somebody snaps their photos.

Wall Drug was a kitsch museum all by itself. There was a western store with cowboy hats for the Japanese tourists and T-shirts for all the relatives back home. There wasn't just one Wall T-shirt, there were 37 different designs that said Wall Drug. What was a drug store became an entire town full of Black Hills gold jewelry, cedar boxes, post cards, rubber tomahawks, rabbit skins, tin sheriff badges and ten miles of shelves filled with stuff that even I wouldn't buy.

How many places besides Powell's Books and Wall Drug can you name that have to issue their customers maps?

Wall Drug was a jolly, trashy, touristy place that I wouldn't dream of missing and yet, on this day, it was as if I had lead weights on my feet. The coin operated mechanized band couldn't cheer me. The roaring animated dino couldn't rouse me. The honky-tonk music just seemed like so much noise. I sat quietly in the crowd and ate my buffalo burger and drank my cup of practically free coffee. This was not perhaps the best state for me to be in to make route decisions. For some unknown reason I thought that I should take a little side trip through the Badlands instead of staying on the mesmerizing interstate to get to Rapid City, my goal for the night. According to the map I could sample just a corner of the Badlands.

My injured hand throbbed. I gave myself a little sympathy...maybe three minutes worth.

When I backed away from the block long building I noticed that the block long sign read TED, BILL & RICK HUSTEAD'S WALL DRUG STORE. And hadn't I read that it was *Dorothy's* idea to offer that first glass of ice water and put signs out on the highway?

Around Wall is 591,000 acres of prairie and grassland. I headed south to Badlands National Park one of the worst decisions of the entire trip.

Two hours later I thought, "I should just light a match to the car, it would be more humane." The roadster and I were being beaten to death on a gravel dirt road miles longer than I ever imagined possible. The fender clanged like a bell. Half of the plastic Red Hat Society license plate frame was splintered and gone. What was left of the red duct tape was stretched or ripped. The paint on both rear fenders was pock marked with several hundred rock chips.

The car and I were both coated with a powdery dirt. Going into the sun, I had to wipe the little windshield just to see. There were no other vehicles out on this terrible excuse for a road. And there seemed to be no end to it. A serious error had been made and I was the only one making decisions for us that day.

After several lifetimes I finally reached black asphalt. I had a permanent ringing in my ears, my internal organs still vibrated and the car was shaken as if inside a child's rattle. I still had more than 30 miles before I would arrive in Rapid City and fight my way through their construction at Cambell and East Omaha streets. Would this awful day ever end?

Once I had checked into a motel and drank about a quart of water I went out to Seno to apologize and wipe him off to access the damage. It was like getting blood off of a patient to see where the critical places were. Applying the cool towels to his fenders was putting cold compresses on wounds and hoping he'd forgive my terrible choice.

Sometimes in life a person knows they've done something so stupid that they just want to turn themselves into the authorities and rest in jail for awhile. I had that feeling that night. Somebody else take the reins because I am obviously incompetent.

Roadster Lesson #19: On the Road of Life, you will do stupid things. Acceptance comes before forgiveness. You *will* do stupid things.

Things had to get better and they did. Except for the paint chips, the major damage was just to my ego. I pulled the ragged duct tape off and applied new. In a flash of creativity I bought a bottle of purple Rit dye at Wal-Mart and poured it full strength over the paint chips on the fenders. Surely that would make the white dots go away by dying the suckers purple. Great idea! Didn't work.

A trip through South Dakota would not be complete without seeing wildlife. But I hadn't expected varmints to nest under the cover of my car. When I did my daily ritual of rolling back the cover, tens of moths flew out. I had killed a dozen of them in the room but now they were getting personal. The pesky things had even infiltrated the bonnet! I had nothing on board that was wool so I was mystified why they would be attracted to my stuff. The moths made front page news in the *Rapid City Journal* with this June 5 story: "All the participants are here for the million moth march. Pestilent miller moths migrate through city. The invasion likely will last another ten days."

They were called miller moths because the scales on their wings fluffed off leaving white flour everywhere. The newspaper said there was nothing to do but wait it out. The disgusting things flew around like they were student pilots on acid, crashing into things like drapes, mirrors and my face. They ate flowering plants and were probably attracted to Seno because of his intense purple color.

Rapid City had a smorgasbord of things to see. Storybook Island with nursery rhyme settings, Sioux Pottery (see it made), the world largest's reptile collection, chuck wagon suppers, Ellsworth Air Force Base, a twelfth century Norwegian chapel, caverns and the Mistletoe Ranch Christmas Store. There was a AAA starred attraction, however, that I wanted to see. It was Bear Country U.S.A. and their ad showed six absolutely adorable bear cubs. "Where beauty is alive and natural." Then I read the fine print: "Drive through wildlife park."

No matter how stupid I was, even I knew better than to drive an open cockpit roadster through a car wash or a wildlife park with bears.

The entire southwest corner of South Dakota harbored more attractions than a visitor could take in on an ordinary vacation. Mount Rushmore, America's ultimate graffiti, may be the best known but it wasn't out there alone. Interests run the gamut from opera to religion to wildlife to wild west "history" and history. So I wasn't likely to find a Monet out here or a skyscraper. After at least five trips to this area, I still hadn't seen it all. And I wasn't going to be able to see it all on this trip either.

What I did see, however, was the Rapid Free Redicals and the Red Hat Honeys at a luncheon at Minerva's in Rapid City. These two Red Hat Society chapters got into their purple and red and we had a fine old time. I had met Peg Seljeskog at the Chicago convention and she was one of those great ladies who handed me her card and said, "Drop by." They showed me their photo album that included photographs taken at the convention and there I was actually looking like a female. That seemed so long ago. I could barely remember the long purple Victorian velvet dress and the elaborate red hat with satin trim and huge plumes. Would I ever be that person again?

Peg had hurried this impromptu luncheon; she was clearly a moving force wherever she went, however. The women were so happy and so friendly and so *funny!* It must be a tad different living near this high concentration of tourist activity. Peg told me that tourists have actually asked, "Where do you put it (Mount Rushmore) in the winter time?" After being asked this question enough times, she answered, "Rushmore Cave." Another Red Hatter said that several tourists thought that Mount Rushmore was made of cardboard and was taken down every night. On my dumbest day I haven't been this dumb. I began to feel better. The ladies blamed the crazy questions on what they called the "Disney-ification of America." We're a nation of people so used to convincing props that we think the real thing is fake. Interesting.

A handsome television reporter joined us and did some filming. We were also interviewed by Mary Garrigan of the *Rapid City Journal* and I guess I was at least as interesting as the moth invasion. Mary was the only reporter to actually "get it" that I was financing this whole project on my own and the significance of leaving my business for two and half months to do this trip. "Roadster-driving dreamer urges people to fulfill 'someday' wishes now," Mary wrote.

After many hugs and many more "good luck's" and sadly leaving that cute TV guy behind, I had my sense of humor back and was ready to hit the road again. I was making good use of the purple chiffon dress I had found in Vermont. It was warm out, the dress was breezy so I left it on for the drive through Rapid City and my southbound trek toward Hot Springs. I should have gotten a ticket from the fashion police for wearing a red hard shell motorcycle helmet with a purple afternoon tea dress but I had a sneaking suspicion South Dakota didn't hand out fashion tickets.

The sky was that intense blue that it gets in unpolluted country and there were roly-poly clouds just hangin' out. A lovely afternoon in fabulous green rolling country. The car seemed anxious to get up to highway speeds. I noticed that the clanging fender only sang at slower speeds. I suppose the air helped lift the fender after 35 miles per hour and the metal strut stopped slamming into the broken welds.

I tried to get past Motion Unlimited but it was like a carbohydrate addict trying to get past a pasta bar. I remembered seeing a motorcycle there that was tricked out as a hearse. I was glad I stopped because Peggy Napoli gave me a personal tour. She and her husband Bill had been restoring cars since 1969 and this museum was the result of a shared compulsion. The exhibit portion was constantly changing. And they also sold cars but my Internal Financial Director wouldn't even let me look at those! They had cars for sale from $500 parts cars to fully restored classics.

I got to see what my '40 Ford coupe would look like if it were painted purple. That was useful information. The aeroplane car was a one off thing that looked like one of those kids airplane pedal cars only bigger. I loved the motor home that was almost 90 years old. Peggy said it was still operational! (When do we leave?) There were over 85 motorcycles, 100 pedal cars, 2000 toys and a model wearing a red poodle skirt. Picture all these wheels and all this iron and there was just us two female gear heads wandering through the boys toys. (www.motionoldcars.com)

As long as the weather was holding I needed to make tracks so I left a lot of details behind at Motion Unlimited that I wasn't able to see. Sometimes travel leaves just enough time to sample rather than indulge. I had about 50 miles to cover and the drive was so pleasant than the miles flew by. The land gently rose and fell, the sunlight showed the distant mountains. Ah, this was what I had come for! A smooth blue highway for just me and a handful of pick-up trucks.

A gas gauge would have been a handy thing to have. Seno's gauge had never worked so I made it a policy to fill up every 100 miles or so. It was time so I pulled into a Texaco and, purple chiffon waving furiously in the prairie wind, filled the tank. In Oregon I didn't fill my own gas tank, it was not allowed. But in the rest of the U.S., I was on my own, sister, and I was definitely getting the hang of it. After this trip I wouldn't be intimidated by a gas pump again.

I flung my right leg over the roadster's side and holding the dress, hopped into the drivers seat. I took a big drag off my water bottle, peeled a banana and ate it, then looked around for a trash bin. One was located near the front door so I drove up to it, using Seno like I sometimes did, as a sort of moving chair. I lobed the banana peel into the can, a perfect 2-pointer. Sal watched this excellent maneuver and introduced himself.

Someone has to remodel kitchens in missile sites and it was Sal. I suppose he was tall, everybody looks tall to me when I'm in my little car. He did not ask "why" I was on this adventure across the country; he said that he'd be out on the road with his motorcycle if it weren't for those pesky kitchens. I didn't even know missile sites had kitchens. What do they cook in missile sites? Gut bombs? I snapped his picture and told him I'd have the web guy put his face on my web site, now did he have anything he wanted to say? Yes, he said, "Hi, Bruce!" to his daughter Christina. I didn't ask why he called his daughter Bruce, remembering the guy in Vermont who named his daughter Porsche. Someone needs to tell my daughter to thank me for not naming her Rolls-Royce.

I turned south on Highway 71 at Hot Springs and enjoyed one of the nicest afternoon drives of the entire trip. The temperature was perfect, I could drive without a jacket or without sprinkling water on myself to stay cool. It was sunny bright and the asphalt was like smooth frosting. The roadster and I were in travel heaven. And I was close enough to my destination that I wasn't paralyzed with fear about making it or not.

The Black Hills Wild Horse Sanctuary was the brain child of award-winning writer and major eccentric Dayton Hyde. I met Dayton when he was speaking at the Willamette Writers conference at the Hilton in downtown Portland. An unlikely place to meet a real cowboy. As I watched this tall, droll ranch hand tell writers to get out of their valleys, it was clear he wasn't your editorial office person. Looking more like Clint Eastwood, weathered and soft spoken but packing an anvil with his advice, Dayton was the real wild west, despite his success doing something as non-physical as writing. He was plains and prairies and mountains and wildlife and conservation and ranch land. He wrote about the last massacre in Oregon, about sand hill cranes, about horses and responsibility. This Mother Theresa in Chaps had dreams and projects that boggled the mind.

And irritated the hell out of the Bureau of Land Management.

People Magazine included Dayton Hyde in their "Most Amazing Americans" issue and television's *20/20* won an Emmy for their story about his efforts with the wild horses. I had known him for nearly 20 years, had visited his Oregon one-room cabin and stayed next to the 300-acre lake that he built with a Caterpillar D-9 and his son. That was back when he had to climb a pole to use the telephone and clip into the wire while dangling 20 feet in the air. I had produced a film called *Hyde Out* about his lake and his land and his caring. The ultimate applause was when he saw the piece and it brought tears.

This was my third visit to the Wild Horse Sanctuary, Institute of Range and American Mustang (IRAM).

Dayton had a burr under his saddle. He had seen wild horses corralled in a feed lot in Nevada and the sight never left him. He was passionate in the belief that these horses, standing in pens, should run free. That simple idea changed his life but affected many, many more people and certainly hundreds of horses. With over 16,000 acres of South Dakota, Dayton created a sanctuary where "over 300 wild horses run free across endless prairies, hooves striking thunder, manes and tails flying in the wind."

I crossed the Cheyenne River and slowed down to make the right hand turn onto the dirt road. I drove very slowly to keep from kicking up a huge cloud of red dust. A group of horses, probably 20 or 30, turned toward me when the fender started clanging like silverware hitting a Ball jar. They seemed to stiffen and suddenly the whole herd took flight like customers in a convenience store that have just heard gunfire. The stampeding horses fled over the hill in the direction of the Headquarters. "Oh, great," I thought, "they'll tell Dayton and I'll be in trouble." Twenty year friendship be hanged, Dayton didn't cotton to anyone disturbing the horses. I didn't have a choice but to continue slowly over a hill, past a pioneer cemetery and into the encampment of a few outbuildings that made up the office.

Dayton used to say, "My closest neighbor is 15 miles away and that's too close." This was wild sage and pine country, land that didn't read the *New York Times* or watch *Entertainment Tonight.* In fact, the only television viewing possible out here was movies played on a VCR. I had to eat a big breakfast, Dayton said during one visit, because if the truck broke down it might be days before we could get help. This was land that cautioned a person to watch their water and their gasoline levels, carry tools and a first aid kit.

Then here comes Alyce in this goofy tin slip of a car and wearing a purple chiffon dress. Shades of *Priscilla, Queen of the Desert.* It wasn't difficult to find Dayton. He was struggling to get out of a big hefty pick-up truck, flailing with a metal crutch. No, he didn't want help, he said as he grimaced so hard I thought he would break his teeth. I probably hadn't seen him for six years. I tried not to take it personally when he wouldn't even say, "howdy." Hip replacement surgery will do that to a person.

Last time I had visited Dayton I had helped him with some fencing. Any visit to Dayton was just following beside him as he did his work listening to him talk. Building a fence was terrifically taxing physical labor! Just slamming the post hole digger into the hard ground was bad enough. I could hardly lift the logs that went into the holes. So to say I was helping was a bit of an overstatement. To work this hard land Dayton had to be as strong as barbed wire and frequently he was as prickly.

Now imagine that you tuned into ABC's *20/20* program one evening and you see a story that really touches your heart. Five years go by and you can't forget that story. So you locate the hero of the story and call him and go see him. Your life is never the same because you uproot yourself from Alabama and join forces with him to save the wild horses. This was Susan Watt's story.

Probably the luckiest thing to happen to the solitaire Dayton Hyde in recent years was the arrival of Susan, a pretty woman with dark hair who can't be insulted by this aging cowboy activist. Not only was she infinitely patient with an infinitely impatient Dayton but she spent most of that night out in the barn tending to a newborn colt that wasn't going to make it without her help. Let's just canonize her now and get it over with.

All visits to see Dayton are punctuated with drama like this. There was always back breaking labor to be done, hoses tangled in farm equipment, an animal needing help, water worries or wood to be chopped. I never visited here that I wasn't ready to head back home happier with my own lot in life.

His home was originally a homesteader's place probably 150 years old or more and sturdy to have survived the wind and severe weather on this prairie. Dayton used the main part of it for an indoor bird aviary, a wood stove and a bed. A new and beautiful pine addition more than doubled the house. I slept in the 1850's upstairs bedroom that had Susan's touches all over it. A sweet bed and breakfast style of room with big farm bed and comforter.

"Where are the teepees?" I asked because I hadn't seen their familiar silhouettes. I recalled spending some time in one of these things; they were rented out to hardier campers.

"Rattlesnakes," he replied. Dayton liked to play games with the inside of my city brain. I looked at Susan. "The rattlesnakes loved the teepees," she confirmed. Later I wondered, "What did the Indians do...?"

In the morning Susan was back out at the barn after only a couple hours of sleep. She was grateful that I volunteered to fix breakfast. Good grief, it was the least I could do. A Lazy Boy type chair was elevated on a platform to make it easier for Dayton to land in it. With him directing from his chair I learned how to make bacon in the George Foreman grill, a flying saucer-looking thing I'd never seen before. Bacon was never going to be on the list of foods that I could allow myself to eat. I hadn't cooked a meal for nearly two months so I flopped around in the kitchen like a teenager.

The phone rang and I answered it when Dayton waved a finger at me. A fellow from Illinois wanted to make a reservation for his family to see the wild horses. I wrote the information and told him he'd have a great time and yes, his daughter was going to see more horses than she could imagine. Plan on "taking steep, primitive roads and fording the dark waters of the Cheyenne. The journey is rough but the destination is spectacular. The prairie sweeps for hundreds of miles and the rugged wilderness of Hell Canyon drops away behind the Black Hills." The spooky petroglyphs on the sanctuary's cliff were worth the trip from Illinois. And yes, I knew *exactly* how far away that was...

Then there was the Wild Mustang sponsorship program where a person could directly help with the feeding and caring of these horses by writing a check. Beats the heck out of trying to set posts in the ground or hauling hay.

I got a reference from Dayton for a welding shop. I was ready to toss my gear in my car when Dayton warned, "Careful of rattlesnakes in the engine!" I knew this time he wasn't kidding. A warm engine with no bottom on the car was an invitation for reptile hitchhikers. What was I supposed to do about this problem? It certainly was something I hadn't thought of in all my "what if's" as I was preparing for this trip! I decided that the blasted things could just cook in there and fall off, I wasn't going to open the engine compartment and suggest they find other transport.

The roadster and I slowly passed over the lumps in the field getting to the dirt road. As we crept past the barn Susan came out and waved. The little horse was still alive. A group of ambling horses, mamas and babies were crossing the same field and headed toward the barn. They walked all around my car sniffing it and leaning into the cockpit. I sat very still not wanting to startle them and if I couldn't touch their warm muzzles I could at least see them. They exhaled while looking over the front tires. At one point at least ten horses surrounded the car checking for anything familiar. Dayton wasn't with me so they decided I was only marginally interesting. I very carefully moved away in first gear and bounced over to the gate and onto the dirt road. As I climbed the hill I listened for rattlesnakes in my engine expecting to hear something like a blender going off but nothing unusual happened.

This whole experience was a far, far cry from having lunch in downtown Manhattan with Irving. Or was it? We had seen the surrealist exhibit at the Metropolitan Museum of Art and what could be more surreal than driving a Bugatti through a wild horse sanctuary?

53

Hot Springs, South Dakota was as good for Seno as Hot Springs, Arkansas had been for me. I found the G of G&H Welding. Gale, the welder weight champion of the day. A man not easily impressed, when I told him what I was doing ("well, I'm driving this car across America and...") he just motioned me to put it on the hoist. He welded a plate to the top of the broken strut and I was once again ready to roll. Everybody had a story. And his? Gale fights fires for a *hobby*.

Seno got tanked in town and had his oil changed. The engine was tight as a turnip. Not only did it not have any rattlesnakes in it, it had no leaks either. I mailed photos to David, bought apples and a sack of baby carrots and we were good to go before noon.

The drive through the Black Hills National Forest was one of the most golden of experiences. It was beyond the roads of my fantasies.

Seno waltzed me around the curves and up over the hills with grace once he was in one piece. I watched a lone antelope leap from a distant point, cross a valley and then bound right across the road, a performance for my eyes only. Prairie dogs, just a few feet from the edge of Highway 385, popped up and watched us go by. There were no fences. The prairie had become foothills and now became mountains. More evergreen trees gathered. So did buffalo, big shaggy things right there with nothing between us but air. I saw deer up walking around, not the road kill deer that lined I-35 in Minnesota.

Where was everybody? It was after Memorial Day. Were people closeted at home waiting for a knock on the door from their local terrorist? Were Americans really avoiding America? I could understand not wanting to fly because the airline industry had ruined flying as a pleasant activity years ago. No one would voluntarily ask for the worthless security searches that were now bordering on medical. ("One airport security guard examined me so closely, we still write.") But what about Fred and Ethel in their RV? Where was dad and mom and the kids in the van? This was a national forest and only a dozen miles away from Crazy Horse and Mount Rushmore.

Traffic is a funny thing...we complain about it but we miss it when it isn't there.

When I started this trip I never really thought I would make it. That is, I never thought I would do the entire route. Surely, with 8,000 things that could go wrong, something would. I told myself that at any time I could quit, give up, ship the car, and come home. But now things were going relatively well and I was "doing it." It occurred to me that I needed a closing point, a finish line. I couldn't just wander in and pick up where I'd left off, whatever the heck that was. I needed to be complete with it, however it ended. It started in Pacific City, it should end in Pacific City. Such a sweet, wet place. So different than the dry hills of Wyoming. And there should be a marker of some kind. How would I mark or commemorate this journey? Why not give something? So many had given to me on this trip--given their time, their homes, shared their friends, their talents, their stories. I was in karmic debt. I needed to give back somehow. What did Pacific City need? Oh, simple! I knew exactly what they needed! They needed what I couldn't find there! A "WELCOME TO PACIFIC CITY" sign! I began designing a large wooden sign in my mind with sandblasted letters and bright paint.

I had wanted and expected "windshield time" on this trip, that altered consciousness reverie that a person gets into when rocked in the bosom of Mother Road. I hadn't gotten it with Seno, he was too all consuming to let a mind drift far. But I found that with the gentle road from Hot Springs, South Dakota to the outback of Wyoming, I finally had mental grazing time.

I had the magnificent road almost to myself. In twenty miles I may have seen two other cars. Folks had stopped to photograph the comical prairie dogs and the startling sight of a herd of buffalo. I continued climbing north until I reached Custer, then hung a left smiling to myself at the WEST sign. The map indicated that I was on the scenic route to Newcastle, Wyoming. That was an understatement.

I pulled over for a mid afternoon snooze and was joined by a doe who did the same. She stayed there as if enjoying the company of the car. This was not something I did every day. My adventure was becoming a divine adventure. How could an experience be both exciting and peaceful? How could I have predicted that I would be napping with deer? At this point I could have cared less if I was going to have a long life; I was having such an exquisite life!

Now I was officially in Wyoming, the same state that had intimidated the hell out of me with its expansive, never-ending horizons and big views. Now I was smiling and loving every precious minute of it. Highway 16 was surely the Highway of Mother Road herself. The afternoon temperature was rising but my bliss must have air-cooled me. I arrived in Gillette, not wanting the day to end but lacking daylight to continue. I couldn't help but notice a huge billboard that read: CRAZY WOMAN and I thought (think DeNiro here), "You talkin' to me?"

If I couldn't drive any more in this clean, clear country, at least I could camp in it. Seno and I gently rolled into a grassy campground behind a windbreak of blooming lilacs at the Crazy Woman Campground. Dozens of South Dakota moths flew out of the bonnet when I unpacked my gear on the picnic table. Seno had more bugs in him than a Windows upgrade.

The campground newsletter explained that it was not clear what caused the original crazy woman to go crazy. She set her wickiup on the banks of a creek and on moonlit nights, she could be seen leaping back and forth alone across the creek. The Crow Indians considered this "Crazy Woman" a symbol of good luck. The campground had chosen her name because they thought she might bring safe travel and good fortune to campers who stopped there. On Wyoming and Montana maps there were Crazy mountains, Crazy Creek and Crazy Horse. There was also evidence of a Crazy Person attempting to drive across this rugged country in a topless old roadster.

The two-story high lilac bushes waved their blossom stalks overhead. They looked like a stadium of sports fans doing "the wave." Their perfume swirled around the camp sites and reminded me of the lilacs back home in Oregon.

I hadn't really thought much about Oregon for quite awhile. There's nothing quite like the challenge of 40 miles of bad road and the delight of 40 miles of fabulous road to take your mind off of home. Despite the welding shops and my side trips it looked like I had a fighting chance of making it to Reno. I tried not to think of crossing the desert on I-80 in Nevada. "Take it at night," I had been advised. Yeah, like being a lone female in an open car driving at night was some kind of good idea. Like Scarlett O'Hara, I just told myself I'd deal with that tomorrow. It was quite enough to shower, bandage my hand, have dinner on my picnic table and then crawl into my sleeping bag and sleep in the arms of my roadster.

Roadster Lesson #20: Sometimes there's nothing you can do. In a perfect world, there'd be no junkyards.

54

Longest stretch of wide open, uninhabited road so far--67 miles from Gillette to Buffalo, Wyoming. It was a great travel morning and there were only a dozen vehicles on I-90 at that hour. The horizon was ringed with blue pointy mountaintops but the road here was wide and sweeping. This was where wolves got danced with.

Seno's little engine was right on pitch. I could never relate to men who could analyze the source of engine problems just by listening. "Hear that knock?" they'd say and try as I might, I never heard anything. After weeks of listening to the roadster's purr right behind my head, however, I could discern any difference in his mood.

The sound that I could hear that morning seemed to be coming from the speedometer. When I glanced at the one gauge that worked, the needle bounced between the numbers 35 and 65. This gyrating was accompanied by a screeching sound. The noise would stop and so would the spastic needle but only for a few minutes. The speedometer kept this up for an hour and then finally quit completely. The car ran fine without a speedometer. I wasn't concerned. But it was another thing that didn't work on the car. I left the interstate for breakfast in Buffalo, Wyoming.

I felt morally obligated to order a biscuit with my eggs and continue my research efforts in the search for the ultimate breakfast biscuit. Of course, when I find it, future research will be suspended. So I've never awarded The Best to anyone yet.

Happy tummy and happy Alyce were back in the cockpit but we weren't going anywhere. Seno had chosen to do his ignition thing again. I knew that if and when he chose to start that I would have to drive non-stop to Billings, Montana. My friend Jan Barry was waiting for me to arrive. I also knew that 127 miles was a long time to go with three cups of coffee filtering through my kidneys. This would not be easy, but it would be necessary. I took an extra trip into the bathroom and prepared for a nerve-racking drive.

Back in the car I strapped in mentally and physically. I wiggled and jiggled wires and finally got Seno to fire up. There was nothing wrong with his battery or his engine, it was with the ignition and I knew that this last firing was going to be his *last firing*. In other words I wasn't going to be able to shut the engine off because he wasn't going to start again.

"All that's left is to do," I told myself and off we went. With the Bighorn Mountains to my left and Montana's Crow Indian Reservation in front of us and nothing but wild wind for music, it was a bit more somber driving. I passed turn offs for Sheridan, Wyola and Lodge Grass. Jan would most likely be working. I had kept her up to date on my progress around the country so she knew I was floating around out there in the universe somewhere. I didn't really want to begin our visit with a rescue.

This piece of the highway, if all went well, would take me a little over two hours. I hoped Seno didn't mind running that long without a break. I hoped Alyce didn't mind running that long with a break. I didn't dare drink any more water. "Hare Krishna, Hare Krishna, Krishna, Krishna..."

The sky clouded and a few drops of rain fell on the car. "Don't do this to me," I prayed. The clouds boiled up but we got no more rain out of them.

The Wolf Mountains and the Little Bighorn Battlefield came up on my right. We kept flying northward to Hardin where I-90 curved to the left and headed straight for Billings. I had visited Jan before but I did not know my way around this mid-sized Montana town and I certainly didn't have the foggiest idea where to take a car with an ignition problem. I pondered this for 40 miles.

Who knows who fixes what? Well, an auto parts store would know the answer to that question. Even though Seno was 27 miles past his gas fill time, I'd have to risk running around Billings until I found a parts store or something that looked vaguely automotive. Fortunately people in Montana don't do anything much that doesn't involve a pick-up truck so I easily found a parts store, parked Seno next to the door (still running) and I kept my eye on him as I stood in the doorway and conversed with the clerk. He pointed out a repair place almost within view. I drove over to it and explained my situation to the stunned auto mechanic. He gave me that "flying saucer with Robin Williams in it" look but came to long enough to tell me how to get to his buddy Jerry at the Exxon station near 27th street. Next thing I knew I was navigating around Billings like a native. Jerry said it was OK to shut off the engine. I took that as a positive sign. Only somebody who thinks they can fix a car would suggest parking it. To me, a car that didn't run was a lawn ornament.

It was time for me to get out of the way and let the repair gods take over. I got on my cell phone and called Jan. She was running around Billings too, doing errands and before I knew it I was standing in front of her smiling face and we were shrieking happy greetings at each other. Like two long lost sisters-in-crime, we could pick right up where we left off from her visit to my house. Jan's personalized license plate was her nickname: SPRKL8D (Sparkle Lady). And she was. We immediately had to eat something, buy something and get tattooed. It was a female bonding thing.

Jerry had the roadster's ignition fixed and showed me a piece of metal no bigger than my thumbnail that was the problem. I handed over my credit card with the stretch marks on it and Jan and I were off for home, me trailing her in my little purple car.

That night we rode around Billings on her tricycle, a custom red thing with a Corvair rear end and a motorcycle front end. I climbed on board this jeweled toy in the seat behind her. I was amazed at how stable it was and how comfortable my perch was. Jan drove all over downtown Billings and we viewed as many of the Art Horses as we could find. The air was so cool and fresh. I got so excited that I pulled the tie out of my hair and just let the wind blow through it.

The Art Horses were full-sized standing horses and colts decorated by various Montana artists. The goal of these fiberglass fillies was a fund raising project for the preservation of the historic Northern Pacific Railway Depot in Billings. The real benefactors were people like me who got to see this range of creativity. One horse was painted with a purple scene of a Montana countryside. I needed to bring Seno back and pose with that one. The most clever was the red Bale Earnhorse, Jr. horse, a la race car, decorated with sponsor stickers and sporting a gearshift, a racing seat and an interesting exhaust system. There were 37 horses in all, ranging from the Apple-loosa to Night Mares to Charlie Horse to Horseradish.

Jan and I talked until midnight about finances, men and lipstick. It was so very, very good to see her even if our visit was going to be so short. Montana was Seno's 30th state and this was the last friend I'd see on my journey, the last push pin. In order for me to make it to Reno, I'd have to leave on Sunday.

When we did finally manage to stop talking and get to sleep I was surrounded by three dogs that acted like I was a rock star when I entered a room. Addy and Inde were happy goldens and Dickens was a mix. A mix of nobody-is-more-adorable and feed-me and fluff like a keeshond. Henry and Harvey were brother cats, velvet white with splotches of bright yellow, not chestnut, real yellow, like lemon.

The next day we did more girl stuff. We had a lot of catching up to do, both of us excited and happy to encourage the other. We had terribly important information to share about supplements, make up, power bars, Reiki and art supplies. When Jan showed me her red leathers that she bought at the Sturgis motorcycle rally, I had to photograph her in them on her trike. We gave her neighbors an eye full. She had a bathing suit on under those cutaway chaps but still... She must have been the sexiest thing in Montana that day. We raced the film to the one hour film processors and had a gift print made for her beau who was out of town at a fishing derby. So Montana! That evening we went to a party and, of course, the roadster had to come along.

Several friends at the party were commercial airline pilots. They seemed to have implants in their heads tuned to the weather channel. "Snowing in Yellowstone," one said. What? Another confirmed it. My route was Billings to Yellowstone to Craters of the Moon (Idaho) to Reno. At least it had been. In order to do this I had just enough time to reasonably make it if I left the next morning. But with snow?

Yellowstone snow wasn't going to be like Oregon snow, I thought. Yellowstone snow would be deeper, colder, wilder, tougher. Not snow I could drive in like that stuff I left behind in Baker, Oregon my first day driving. It was June! It wasn't supposed to be *snowing!* A week ago I was crossing Iowa in nearly 100 degree heat!

"Oh, yeah," they all said, "we've gotten snow on the Fourth of July!"

Journal Entry: June 8

Now the huge hanging question is what next? Ignore the weather prediction and go anyway? Stay just one more day and make a mad dash for it? Stay and use the plane ticket and leave my car behind while I go to Reno? What?

Sunday morning I worked on the internet for hours trying to figure a way out of Billings. I kept finding different weather web sites, hoping for a different report. If-you-don't-like-the-result-change-the-data approach. The web cam at the Old Faithful Lodge confirmed a snowstorm in progress at Yellowstone National Park. That was out of the question. So how about other routes? South to Cody? High wind warnings were threatening to close these highways to trucks. Mountain passes and long distances made this impractical if not impossible. West to Bozeman and then south? Butte, even further west, was showing snow on its web cams too. There was snow above 4,000 feet everywhere. I was flooding Jan's desk with mileage charts and weather reports from different sources. When she woke up for breakfast, she made the decision easy.

"Just stay here and fly to Reno," she yawned.

So I did.

We shopped, did Reiki, hiked with friends, cleaned up the back yard, began doing Wishcraft exercises together, went to a bar-b-q and a bowling tournament. I met a guy who wrote jokes for George Gobel and he said that Lonesome George never learned how to drive a car.

I watched Judge Rick Anderson throw the book at a couple of guys in a courtroom in Billings where Jan worked as a court reporter. The judge and I had a conversation about old cars. He, too, craves a '40 Ford coupe. And I told him what I told everybody else. "You buy one from Matthews and I'll drive it over here and deliver it."

55

On Thursday morning a very sleepy Jan did above-and-beyond-the-call-of-duty service by taking me to the Billings airport for a 6:15 a.m. flight to Salt Lake City and eventually Reno. For the first time in 63 days I would be leaving my roadster, separated by the 1,106 miles that we were supposed to do together.

I was asked to take off my shoes at the airport and there was a thick layer of dog hair, like a shoe liner stuck to my feet. I was too heartsick to care much about the security screenings. It was the Trip Interrupted. I hadn't finished the trip. Leaving Seno. It just seemed awkward. This was the first time I had flown in many months and I had hoped that I would never again have to deal with the dreaded airlines industry. My reluctance was not fear but disgust. It was as if I thought I had been released from a habit, only to find myself lighting up again. I was back. The living rooms of airports.

But it could always be worse. Veteran road tripper Charles Kuralt was booking a flight out of Juneau where, at the counter, he said, passengers were weighed and then assigned to a pilot. I'm sorry, that wouldn't work for me. Can you imagine? I'd be stuck in Juneau until the spring thaw or until I lost 15 pounds, whichever came first. Just give me the skinniest pilot and we'll work from there, OK?

I was just a good, quiet, cooperative passenger that day, going through the worthless hoops and questions and wand-waving and other illusions of security. I couldn't even console myself with an overpriced airport muffin. "Oh, Alyce, snap out of it," I finally said to myself, "Seno is in a nice dry garage and you won't have to worry about him for days. Go have some fun." Little did I know that I would collect memories in Reno that a) would be the most unusual segment of the whole adventure and b) I'd never in this world forget. My true identity was going to be mistaken and I was going to love every minute of it!

Once I laid eyes on the huge parking structure at the Gold Nugget in Sparks, Nevada I was relieved that my roadster was in Billings. My room was two city blocks away from where Seno would have been parked. I would have needed a prescription for a very heavy drug to have accepted that arrangement. So without the car I could enjoy the chinga chinga of slot machines that started when I arrived in Reno and didn't stop until I left.

It was Reno so I easily found stage make up to conceal the dog bite on my chin and to cover the black and blue marks on my still swollen left hand.

The American Escrow Association was almost as much fun as roadster travel. They laughed at my jokes, took notes when I said something remotely important, gave me standing ovations, invited me to their banquet, awarded me a screen saver made out of Seno's photograph and then put on their version of The Gong Show. It was wonderful to see someone else get silly on stage. They bought all my books, asked for my autograph and then gave me a beaded stars and stripes frame of my route and my roadster. How could I say *thank you* enough to people like this?

I just got up on stage and did the very best job I knew how to do. Susan Reiman, the conference chair, hadn't seem disappointed that the famous purple roadster didn't make it to Reno, but then, where would we have put him? No, he really was better off cooling his tires in Montana. And she was so busy she didn't have a moment to spare on the details of making her conference a success. She was obviously well-liked and good at what she did, but I was amazed that she had energy and compassion left over to be nice to hundreds of people.

When I led the "Teamwork & Team Sabotage" session on Saturday this group was so sharp that four of the teams scored the maximum amount of points possible on the exercises. This was higher than usual by a long shot. Speaking to groups as bright as this one was like dancing with a partner who knows how to hang on.

In the lobby of the Gold Nugget was a gold rooster and it has quite a tail...a cocktail. But it has quite a tale too. This objet d'art was originally commissioned to be a symbolic logo for a restaurant, but made of 18 karat gold? The U.S. Treasury Department didn't think the rooster was art and said the casino was in violation of having more then 50 ounces of gold in its possession. The rooster was confiscated and sent to jail. It took a jury trial to free the bird. Our tax money at work here. This nine and half inch tall bantam bird would technically be art even if it were made out of bubble gum. It was beautiful and this crazy story was new to me.

On my tour of the National Automobile Museum in Reno I came across the Thomas Flyer, a large grey open car that won the 1907 Around the World Race. A mechanic who was pressed into service at the last minute ended up being the one who stuck with the car and won this race. The information on the wall said, "There has not been another attempt at a round-the-world auto race since 1908. As the current world record holder, this is the most historic automobile in existence." I had two things to say about that. One, please note that the Thomas Flyer was a *topless* car. And two, when do we leave?

The rest of my Reno stay was *Victor, Victoria* meets *Buck Rogers.* Portland diva and performer extraordinaire Poison Waters was doing a command performance at the Fire and Ice Coronation Ball at the Reno Hilton. It was a happy coincidence that I was in the Biggest Little City in America on the same night. So I got togged out in formal wear brought to me by my friend Howard (who drove down from Portland to help me) and we waltzed into the ballroom like I almost knew what I was doing. I wore a black and white satin floor length ball gown with a cape made of miles of white chiffon ruffles. My hair had a rhinestone clasp in it that held a large, curving black plume. When in Rome...or Reno...

It was fantastic to see so many familiar Oregon faces and that made me feel like home couldn't be too far away. Lotta Liquor was doing the drop dead gorgeous blond-in-white number very effectively and the always-out-there Maria was already up on stage sharing the MC duties. (I was a better corporate speaker by watching and learning from the style and performance ease of Maria and Poison.) I recognized other members of the Royal Rose Court, like Retro Rose Emperor ShelleY and the Lovely Suzanne and regal Meesha Peru. All of these people operate in a world that used to be fantasy but has now become somehow very real if not a tad quirky. Someone asked, "You're going to walk, aren't you?" Walk? As opposed to flit? or fly, what? Poison said, "Oh, of course, she is." Next thing you know I was back stage with some folks I kind of knew and some folks I really didn't know and some guy who looked like Eddie Murphy telling me, "Just walk out there like you're Miss Universe." Getting into the spirit of the "well, girlfriend" thing, I turned to him and said, "You mean I'm not?"

Because protocol was extremely important here and I was the greenhorn, I was the lesser of all royalty and I had to go first, with

Poison, the Grand Exalted Beauty of the Universe-Or-At-Least-Oregon would go last.

Just then the announcer called my name and there I was spotlighted on stage at the Reno Hilton for all of the royal courts from Seattle to San Diego to see. "Walking" meant that I was to walk out on stage, acknowledge all of humanity and then stroll gracefully the full length of the runway, roughly the length of a football field and be presented to the Reno royalty, the Emperor and Empress of the Silver Dollar Court. My amount of strolling gracefully *in my entire lifetime* probably doesn't add up to the length of a football field. The reigning Empress was adorned in a flaming headpiece and matching wings with sequined bikini and thigh high white platform boots. The Emperor wore a white tuxedo with no shirt. The program read, "A Fire and Ice Masquerade Extravaganza." I certainly couldn't argue with that.

The curtsy was optional. If I didn't screw that up I would be rewarded with a commemorative pin. Then I was to stand, posing ever so lady-like while the rest of the Oregonians did the same. My advantage was, there was no time to think about *whether* I was going to do this, I just went along like flotsam and was up there before my inner Gang of Bandits could hold a meeting in my head and talk me out of it. My disadvantage was, I hadn't been in girl shoes for three months. I walked like an auto mechanic. I hadn't really felt like a female since my one night in Chattanooga when I took myself to dinner. I stayed in my spot, blinded by the spotlight, until Her Royal Highness in Abundant Charisma Poison Waters arrived center stage to great applause. How she got all the looks cards, plus the extrovert cards, plus the funny cards, I'll never know.

Once down off the stage I looked at the "pin" in my hand. It was a metal cloisonne-type thing almost as big as business card. I looked at Howard, my car buff friend, and said, "Dash plaque." He nodded.

Later out in the hallway, Poison couldn't get 50 feet without fans begging for photographs with her and asking for her autograph. She graciously obliged every request. It was a good thing I had plenty of practice playing Second Banana to Seno so I wouldn't get a complex being around Poison. (www.poisonwaters.com)

On my glitziest day I couldn't hold a candle to these professional glitter queens. The most beautiful crowns and tiaras I'd seen this side of the Atlantic were on their heads! Where *did* they shop? I must know. After hours of seeing courts presented from Tumwater to Tijuana, my blood sugar was in the basement around midnight. I still had to struggle on those spike heels through the Hilton lobby to the front valet parking strip. This felt as long as that drive from Buffalo to Billings.

Howard was my witness. Someone pointed at me and said, "There's one of *them.*" I'd just received the ultimate compliment. I'd been mistaken for a drag queen.

My head was going to be so big I wouldn't be able to get it back into my helmet.

56

Journal Entry: June 18

Up at 5 a.m. and out to the Reno Airport. Flew to Elko, then Salt Lake City, then Jan picked me up in Billings. Hurt her back. Lunch downtown. Unusual roast beef and walnut salad. Home to work her computer and design a photo business card for her with her tricycle. Thank heavens Jan is as easy going as she is. Easy on others. Not on herself. Arranged and rearranged stuff in the roadster. I call this nervous activity "packing." Now I have to leave again and I look at the car and go...WHAT? In this?! But unless you want to have your mail delivered to Billings, Montana, get in the car, Alyce.

Very reluctantly I left Jan, standing in her pj's in her front yard waving good-bye. A dozen raindrops peppered the car but no matter. I had to leave. And I had my rain togs on and everything ready for the press to Yellowstone.

Once again connected to Seno, I felt our relationship was now like a married couple that had been together for too long. We were joined in this endurance test and had no way to complete the journey without each other. The roadster needed me to get him home and I needed him to get me home.

Together we drove into the Beartooth and Crazy Mountains. Did the 116 miles to Livingston, Montana which had been in a flood watch situation the week before and one of the reasons I couldn't leave Billings. (I had taken the Beartooth Scenic Highway just a few years before and I didn't really want to pit the roadster against the 11,000 foot Beartooth Pass.) Made the left turn and Highway 89 took us into a Scotland-like valley of breathtaking beauty. Every mile presented a scene to be photographed or painted or cherished in some way. The town of Gardiner was buzzing with grandpas and campers and kids and rafts and motorcycles at nine in the morning. I could have spent the day answering questions in the gas station.

I slowly took the curves through this interesting town that was the last commercial area before entering the north gate of Yellowstone, the World's First National Park. Three million people visited the park every year and half of them were in Gardiner that morning. I had traveled to the Cadillac of National Parks but I had never been to the North Gate.

Suddenly Gardiner just ended and there was an open field sloping up from the town ringed with mountains. At the beginning of the slope was a very large stone entrance arch with nothing around it. Looking like a Stonehenge trilithon on this plain, it made a striking impression. Most people pulled over to photograph it, park their vehicles in the roadway or stand grandma up with the arch behind her. I tried to get a shot of the little car and the huge arch but I was shooting into what little sun there was.

An amazing thing happened. Seno and I started up the roadway and the arch just seemed to overtake us. "For the benefit and enjoyment of all" was carved in its top and the magical word: YELLOWSTONE. Suddenly it struck me how very far I had come, how many thousands of miles I had driven to get to this one spot, how completely impossible it was and how I never in this world expected it to happen. We really were now in Yellowstone. *Completely without my consent*, a cowboy yee-haw! leapt out of my throat. I suspect that both arms went up as well. It was an Olympic medal moment.

Because Yellowstone was so famous and so old (established 1872) it had been the focus of every kind of interest group. This had resulted in a variety of ways to "see" Yellowstone. Through the eyes of astronomers? There were special programs called "Stars Over Yellowstone" listed in the park newspaper. Through the eyes of wildlife lovers? This park had been called the most successful wildlife sanctuary in the world. See it geothermally? More geysers were here than anywhere in the world and most of them available for close up and personal viewing. See it architecturally? If the Old Faithful Lodge can't take your breath away, you weren't breathing in the first place. See Yellowstone as a sports enthusiast? Horseback exploring, hiking, cold creek fishing, canoeing, if you could do it outdoors, you could do it here. See it as a photographer? Yellowstone provided a *lifetime* of film possibilities; the options were almost painful. Yellowstone must be the reason Kodak boxes are yellow. More film gets consumed here than anywhere else in America.

What they didn't tell me was in the fine print of the AAA Tour Book, back home on my desk in Oregon. "According to National Park Service figures, about 80 per cent of the park roads are in a structurally deficient state." See Yellowstone in many ways, but don't see it from a car that you're even remotely fond of.

The drive up the steep switch back to Mammouth Hot Springs was easy enough. At the top of the grade two ambling elk, walking around like runway models, ignored the astonished visitors. I took a simple side trip down into the geysers' loop, parked and walked to get a better view of the terrace-like formations. When I turned back to the roadster there was a mom posing two kids next to the car. I said, "We can do better than that," and lifted Anika and Tasha into Seno's seat. People were pulling away from the boiling, stinking geysers and surrounding the car. It was the only time I thought that stopping the car was going to cause traffic jams. There were just so many people and they were all on vacation, time on their hands and this little purple car was just so interesting. I needed to keep moving. Otherwise the car was going to be trapped like a rock star in a backstage hallway.

The overcast day was turning serious. I checked my fuel, my water bottle and my bag of hard boiled eggs. That one semi-sunny moment in Mammouth was the end of the pleasant weather and the pleasant road conditions.

First came four miles of pockmarked road construction. There wasn't six square inches that was smooth. The road was chewed with a million holes as if machined into the dirt. No amount of careful driving or sashaying could have lessened the impact. The left fender weld blew.

Four miles seemed like 400 when spent in first gear, sitting and just taking the beating. But we made it through to smooth asphalt. By now my duct tape scenario was becoming routine. I knew just how to wrap the fender for the stress it would have to take. We got in line with the other travelers on the road southbound. Then the rain started. I figured, OK, I've got my gear on, I'll do all right. The sky turned as dark as night and rained in earnest. Everyone slowed.

Once again I had the problem of air flowing over the helmet. Without speed, it just didn't work. The face shield had to be cracked open to avoid fogging and the water drops wouldn't run off the curved surface at slow speeds.

The rain started an angry pelting. Water was standing in the roadway. Vans and passenger cars were pulling off to the side. It was noon but blacker than many moonlit midnights and in the downpour all I could see was headlights. I pulled over into a paved viewing area and fumbled with my tiny business umbrella. I didn't know what else to do. The alternative was to find a bucket and bail. The rain came down like it was being dropped out of a firefighting helicopter.

I wiggled out of the hard shell motorcycle helmet still holding the umbrella. I wiped the shield as best I could and just hung out under the bumbershoot relieved that I had it for protection. The downpour continued so I served myself lunch. When it still didn't quit, I took a nap.

Thirty minutes later when I awoke the other vehicles had left the pull out and the rain had stopped. The sky said, "I can still get you, my pretty and your little car too!" so relief was not exactly in sight. Traffic had thinned slightly and I took a deep breath and thought that although this was pretty awful, we'd survived it and could continue on to Old Faithful.

A clog of cars and vans had stopped for a herd of buffalo. I had the caution yellow WARNING sheet right next to me in the car. It read, "Buffalo can weigh 2,000 pounds and can sprint at 30 miles per hour, three times faster than you can run. They are wild, unpredictable, dangerous and many visitors have been gored by them." They didn't seem all *that* far away from my car. Connecticut, that's how far away from my car I wanted them to be. But traffic was stopped. "Excuse me, people," I thought, "I'm in an open car here, let's move along, shall we?" I felt like I was sitting in a purple egg shell with a target painted on the side of it.

Seno and I were not through it by a long shot. The dreaded orange road signs again appeared. The rain had filled the millions of holes, some of them as big as old-fashioned dish pans. As we started into five miles of the most hideous excuse for a road I had ever seen, the rain came back. The roadster and I were getting it from above and below. Our top speed never got above three miles per hour.

The "road" was a strip of mud, dimpled methodically with holes and sprinkled liberally with gravel. Suddenly liquid mud shot up on either side of my cockpit as if we were driving over geysers. *Why!?* Fenders were put on cars to keep this from happening! Unless both rear fenders had fallen off... I took my eyes off our forward movement and leaned my helmeted head over to my left and got a face full of spraying mud. I was driving through a fountain of grit. The taped left fender was still there but from my vantage point I could not see the right fender. Wet mud must have shot three or four feet up in the air on either side of me.

When we climbed out of this rut of a road an hour later and onto pavement both Seno and his driver were painted with a thin coat of wet mud. I made it to the first pull out, a viewpoint for a waterfall and yanked wet, gritty gloves from my frozen hands.

Why didn't the road crew work on just one lane at a time, shutting done one and letting cars go through on a smooth surface? Even waiting for several cars to go, a la one-lane bridges, would have been as fast for travelers as pulling their vehicles through this awful mud. But my film teacher Homer Groening said, "Don't ask 'why' questions and don't answer 'why' questions."

The scenic viewpoint lot was full of cars and vans, people photographing the falls and Seno. I did my best to answer questions while trying to access our damage. The right rear fender had finally given up too. It hung like a punched tooth. I had to wipe it and the right side of the car clean in order to get the duct tape to stick. I poured my drinking water on a polishing cloth and went to work. Now the only thing holding the rear fenders on was 60 yards of bright red duct tape.

In order to get myself mentally through those nightmare five miles, I had promised myself a cup of coffee, a latte, a great big one as soon as I could find a source. I pictured that cup in front of the hood ornament and that image encouraged me to keep the car rolling when what I wanted to do was just stop and scream. Or cry. Or throw a fit. Or give the car away and take a limo home.

A handsome blond boy was fixated on the roadster. Yellowstone was all around him and yet he had the look of love that only a five year boy can have for a car. But he was a gentleman and wasn't about to intrude on my work. I met Chris, the kid's dad and felt I should apologize for the looks of the car. I couldn't see the car for the mud. They couldn't see the mud for the car.

I picked Daniel up, put him in the driver's seat and gave him my helmet. He pretended to drive the car. I needed to keep wiping, turning the cloth over and over and folding it inside out, hoping I'd have enough surface to clean the fender. I was prepared to use my purple chiffon dress if I had to. The roadster wasn't moving anywhere until I had two miles of duct tape securing those fenders. Then Daniel's mom said, "Would you like a cup of coffee?"

That should pretty much end the argument "Is there a Supreme Being?" Somewhere, somehow out of the back end of that van, she produced the most luscious hot cup of milk and coffee I think I have ever tasted.

Roadster Lesson #21: Many wrongs can be righted with one cup of coffee.

57

I could have exited Yellowstone National Park at Madison but I continued south to Lower Geyser Basin. I felt as if I had paid, Big Time, for a Yellowstone experience and I wanted something good out of it. I needed to see something beautiful and tranquil. The Firehole River provided sapphire blessings to my mud-caked spirit. Fishermen waded out from its cold banks and leisurely casted lines into the little white caps. It was a Cabela's calendar scene. I followed the river to Fountain Paint Pots. Yellowstone was so weird, so freaky. The roads seemed to run too close to the bubbling geysers. How did they know for sure where to put the roads? The Yellowstone caution signs also reported that a person could get fatal meningitis from the hot water, and advised against letting it splash on skin or touching your face after being exposed to the geysers' steam. Wafts of white stinking clouds rose in puffs over the landscape. To a primitive mind this must have appeared to be hell on earth.

I turned into the driveway marked for Old Faithful's Lodge and when I arrived at the gas station a van pulled in behind me. Three excited females, all wearing purple, said they had followed me into the North Gate at Gardiner. They needed my address to send pictures of me and Seno going under the arch! (Someone had captured our Olympic moment on film!) I met Nancy Boldt of Fort Madison, Iowa and her travel mates Sally and Elizabeth Flesch. The three of them were making their Yellowstone annual pilgrimage-sans-husbands. They seemed to be having the time of their lives and I posed them next to Seno. We promised to stay in touch and very sincerely wished each other all good travel for the homeward bound return.

I bought a bag of huckleberry yogurt-coated pretzels, parked my road weary butt on a lodge bench and just relaxed for awhile in the afternoon sun overlooking Old Faithful. It was a sun that only lasted about 15 minutes but I was there for it. This had been the roughest driving challenge of the trip and I needed to take just a moment, acknowledge that, readjust my shaken head and let Seno take a breather. He was a complete mess. He looked like he had been delivering mail in a war zone.

I had no intention of trying to find a welder in Yellowstone. The place was a zoo with steam. After 68 days on the road I was like the old guy who shows up at the Vatican in Rome and says, "Good grief, not another cathedral." If Yellowstone hadn't tried to eat me and my car alive, I might have been more interested in exploring. It was, without any doubt, the outdoor gem in the crown of the USA. The next car I bring to Yellowstone will have no paint at all, be equipped with tractor tires, have reinforced sides, have a defroster to end all defrosters, cup holders, a built in coffee pot, a floor heater and a top.

I backtracked to Madison and took a westerly left. There was more rain for my trip out of the park but it rolled off my windshield and my helmet politely like it was designed to do. As much as I loved commercial and touristy areas I couldn't stop in West Yellowstone. I kept moving toward Highway 20 and into Idaho toward home.

The sky hung in grey bags of rain, the edges of my horizon fenced in by jagged mountain peaks on both sides. The Targhee National Forest looked like a scene I had loved from the window of a train in Switzerland. Despite my wounded car, my doubts about holding the roadster together for these last 1,000 miles, I surprised myself by admiring the majestic views. Now there was little traffic. A calmness seemed to roll into the pristine valley, the asphalt was blissfully smooth and all was quiet except the constant purr of Seno's engine. Flat pastures with abundant grass fed herds of black Angus. If a person dreamed of being a dairy farmer this was the scene to picture.

That familiar I-am-the-Mother-Road-and-you-are-my-Daughter feeling was starting to return. I was still in the game. Still moving. Battered, sure, but OK.

Then along the highway, flopped over and bloated, was a large dead black cow. It looked like a Macy's parade balloon. All four legs were stiff and pointed toward the roadway. Its tongue hung out of its mouth. Someone had taken a can of white Krylon and spray painted GOT MILK? across the thing. American humor, I thought.

Humor, no matter how black or how tasteless or how seemingly inappropriate or misplaced, has got to be one of our most outstanding American traits. When we've lost everything else, we'll find a joke. While other cultures lapse into stiff upper lips or quiet meditation, an American will be inventing a whoopee cushion. In foxholes or surgery or space shuttles, the worst thing you can be is a sour puss. We Americans disagree with each vigorously on matters of politics and religion but deep down inside we all know that laughter is the soul's Preparation H. We are, all of us, perfectly willing to make fools of other Americans to prove that point. And if that doesn't work, we'll make fools of ourselves.

I knew I hadn't completely lost my perspective when I read the cow and couldn't help myself. I had to laugh. Perhaps on any other day I wouldn't have.

I made it all the way to St. Anthony, Idaho and gladly laid down my Master Card for Room 119 at the Day's Inn. A warm bath, cool white sheets, fat down pillows and pretty soon I thought it was quite funny that I had been so thrilled to arrive at Yellowstone National Park and was even more thrilled to leave it.

58

Exiting the motel the next morning, I now had the sound of clanging fenders in stereo. The crisscrossing layers of duct tape held them so that if their last welds broke, they wouldn't fly off and hit something, like another car. At 60 miles per hour that wouldn't be a good thing. Seno was beginning to look like he'd been put together with a grenade but everything seemed fairly secure so I gassed up and we were on our way south and west toward Idaho Falls.

There was a town and then poof! there was no town. Without a gentle thinning of residential or industrial leading to wild lands, the wild lands just abruptly met Idaho Falls. I faced our longest stretch of uninterrupted highway, nearly 70 miles of sage brush, buttes, distant mountains and one long strip of road. No Dairy Queens, no

Wal-Marts, no gas stations of any kind, not even a farmhouse or a double wide. There wasn't a mail box or a fence post. Most of it was through land that belonged to the U.S. Department of Energy. It wasn't raining so the road looked good to me.

For over an hour Seno and I flew over the speckled road and anything in the distance took a long time coming and going. It was also a long time in between seeing other vehicles. I didn't know that *there was this much of nothing* in the lower 48. Even Nevada punctuated the highway with a casino or a roadhouse. As long as everything was going so well I enjoyed holding the wheel and making the gentle adjustments that easily kept us on the road. I was rested from the horror that had been Yellowstone and happy to have the rising eastern sun at my back.

It was such an expanse that when I did roll into the town of Arco I pulled in at the first station, Seno's favorite, a Texaco station. Arco had the dubious distinction of being the "first city to be lit by atomic power." I wondered if that was on purpose and if the citizens there glowed at night. There wasn't even a postcard of the huge stretch of desolate country that I'd just passed over so I slipped back into the roadster, pulled on the stick and bumped over the gas station's driveway and back onto their Main Street. I looked to the right for an all clear and noticed some motorcyclists pulling into the station. I waved and they waved back.

I was taking the bleak and arid Highway 20 because I wanted to see Craters of the Moon National Monument. This unusual and forlorn area was a prominent feature in the terrific but nearly forgotten movie *Pontiac Moon.* In the film Ted Danson and his son drive a vintage Pontiac convertible to the Craters in an effort to get there in time for the first moon landing. I hadn't heard of such a place and once I found it on my Idaho map, I was nearly as intent on seeing it as the characters in the movie. A left turn out of Arco and I was on my way. The fields of sage I had just driven through continued on this side of Arco as well.

I was happy. And why not? It was dry but not hot. I had a full tank of gas and a good road with not an orange cone in sight. The countryside wasn't a green pretty one but it had an austere beauty about it. I was headed west toward something interesting to see and just that much closer to home. I was feeling healthy and had my lunch beside me. David, my webmaster, was working on having a sign made for my special surprise presentation to the citizens of Pacific City, Oregon. Soon I'd get my hands on my granddaughter and get to hear her joyful squeals once more when I called her "Warthog." And I could look at my daughter's huge blue eyes and thank her for taking care of my house and my bills.

Highway 20 was out beyond litter. It was out beyond road kill.

The road was totally straight in front of me and there wasn't a vehicle in sight in either direction. No cars had passed me and no cars were headed toward me. The remoteness of this empty land didn't unnerve me because I was going *through* it.

Then I barely became aware of something.

Driving an open car a person got used to a wide range of smells. Road odors of hot tar, diesel fumes and rubber frequently roll in and out of the cockpit. The honeysuckle in Tennessee, the soy sauce cooking on Hawthorne. But this odor became stronger and I inhaled deeply in my hard shell helmet. Burning rubber.

Then it occurred to me. *I'm the only one out here.*

The smell was not going away. "I think we need to stop," I told myself.

"Nah. The Craters of the Moon are down this road somewhere."

"That smell. It's pretty strong. What could possibly be burning?"

"Nothing's burning."

"Something's burning. Need to pull over."

"Where? There's no place to pull over!"

I slowed the car, scanning the edge of the road for the barest platform of dirt. I saw a little patch of gravel about the size of a wheelbarrow and pulled over. As I lifted myself out of the cockpit the smell of rubber was very strong. I glanced at the wheels on the left side of the car, nothing unusual. Then I walked around the boat tail and saw black goobies, like shredded cheese on the top of the duct taped fender. I bent down to get a closer look at the tire.

Expletive deleted.

The metal holding the fender had sunk its teeth into the tire and as the tire spun down the road, the metal put a wide and deep groove into the rubber tread. The rear tire had two grooves in it as if it had been on a lathe and chiseled. The fender had machined the tire down to its core. I touched the surface of the tire. It was very hot. Gooey rubber came off on my finger. I could see and feel the canvas-like surface under the rubber coating that had been the tire's tread.

My first thought was to yank the fender off the car. Two welds held it on and only one was broken. I was intent on breaking the other. I grabbed the end of the fender and pulled up for all I was worth. The weld held tight. I quickly opened the bonnet and got out my set of tools, hoping to slam the weld with enough force to break it. I had hammer and screwdrivers on Seno's hood when a group of motorcyclists stopped. Of course I hadn't noticed them approaching. They seemed to be the same group that exchanged waves with me at the gas station.

"Need help?"

"Yeah, I do!"

For the next hour five of us tended to my tire and fender. Mom Nelda and Joe Collins from Anderson, Missouri had been riding together on a motorcycle trike and her son Bradley from Gore, Oklahoma was on one bike, his wife Tina on another bike. Joe and I lifted the fender up high enough that the strut could rest inside the cockpit of the car. Now it couldn't do any more damage. A good look at the tire and we were all shaking our heads. I had been running at 65 miles per hour on hot canvas. I had less than a mile before the tire would have exploded and sent me air borne. At my rate of speed, that was less than one minute until blow out.

Fainting at that moment would have been totally appropriate.

This group of travelers was headed to the Oregon coast. They had jobs and vacation days and time was of the essence for them. They were doing a wide loop around the western half of the United States that would take them through California, Arizona, New Mexico and back to the Midwest. The last thing they needed was a road interruption.

"Want us to change the tire?" Bradley asked.

"Are you sure?" I didn't want to hold them up.

"We didn't know why we came down this highway," said Joe.

"No, we didn't," said Tina.

"We were sent by God to save you," they said.

We found enough pieces to put together a jack and up Seno went. Pulling the wounded tire off and getting the spare tire was simple enough. But then, another annoying problem. The powder coating on the spare wheel was thick and hard and filled the splines. The wheel wouldn't go on until this paint had been chipped out. Bradley took my hammer and screw driver and pounded it all out. Tina whipped out some handi-wipes for me to clean the melted rubber off my hands. And Nelda demonstrated her very cool goggles for me. When the spare was firmly on and hammered into place, we took bungee cords and tied them tightly around the fenders to help the duct tape.

They had never intended to take Highway 20 and weren't sure what had made them select it. They became TEAM IDAHO, my angels.

As I pulled away from the Rescue Spot the fenders were quiet, not a hint of a rattle and I watched the two motorcycles and Joe's trike disappear up the hill into the far distance. They had appeared seemingly out of thin air and now they were gone.

Roadster Lesson #22: There are angels.

59

After that experience, Craters of the Moon would have to be giving away free samples of moon rocks to impress me. I wandered through the park's book shop and into the exhibit that explained how a huge hot spot under the surface of the earth started in Oregon and gradually moved through Idaho and was now Yellowstone. I comprehended that new information but somehow it seemed less significant than what has just happened to me out on Highway 20. The desolate road. The tire with less than the thickness of lunch meat left on it. The motorcyclists. It was too perfect. I hadn't even gotten to the point of asking the universe for help or thinking what to do next.

I thought about how I didn't want to stop but did anyway. I was one minute away from an explosion that would have been a spectacular crash in the middle of no where.

It was one of those rare times that you shake your head and say, "What just happened here?" And this time it wasn't a geology question.

I looked out over the scene at the Visitor's Center and there were acres of black, churned lava. I noticed the park's exhibit map but I just couldn't get my brain to attend to the necessary work to follow trails. It was as if a deeper part of me really wanted to think about what had transpired so miraculously. I just got back into Seno and headed toward Shoshone where I asked an auto mechanic to whack the thing that held the right rear tire on. A brass hammer was needed to do it right and I didn't have one. He obliged with three good healthy strokes and I continued on.

I met two people from Cape Elizabeth, Maine at a Texaco Star Mart. I was wearing my purple T-shirt from Jackie's in Ogunquit, Maine and we were jabbering away like bridge partners after that. Russ Connors said he ran the Boston Marathon 13 times and ran the Dublin Marathon in two hours and 57 minutes. This guy hadn't been my age for a few years. His traveling partner Rebecca Hawkes had hiked all 48 peaks in New Hampshire above 4,000 feet. I didn't even know there *were* 48 peaks in New Hampshire and I was just there! These two were inspirational material for this roadster potato. But I was still in am-I-alive? mode.

This trip had been about breathtaking scenic views, amazing architectural accomplishments but on a completely different level, it had presented new information to me about people. Everyone from P. T. Barnum to ex-DEA cop Ross to Nelda Collins. Before starting the trip I could say that I loved America, I loved the land, the vastness, the intrigue of her mountains, the sapphire of the ocean's edge and cold rivers, the rolling prairie, the Lincoln Highway, the national park system. And I could still say that. But, my goodness, what could I possibly say to myself now about her people? From Janet who opened her home to me, a stranger, to Marilu who seemed to know what I needed before I did to Jan who hauled my suitcases at five in the morning to Poison Waters who glued my earrings to my head so I wouldn't lose them while walking the runway at the Reno Hilton. There was Irv who helped me find my rain pants and Peter who provided distraction from the drive I didn't want to take. There was the staggeringly creative Lynette and the gracious curator Flo.

And the literally hundreds of people who honked and waved when I wasn't sure I could make it another ten miles, how could I ever pay it all back? I couldn't. I just had to go do something nice for some other American. That was how it worked. This country was wall-to-wall stories of inspiration and courage. And I had the privilege of listening to just a few of them. The whole of their phenomenal support could be summed up in one simple gesture that I saw a thousand times, out truck windows, on street corners, from passing cars, from construction workers, from road crews, from cops: thumbs up! America, thumbs up!

There was Karl whose relatives had ridden the Underground Railroad and there was MariAn who had to run for her life in Manhattan on 9-11. There was the tenacious character with the cabooses in Pennsylvania. There was the New Hampshire dad who dreamed of turning his corn field into a campground. There was Dayton Hyde who wanted to save the wild horses and Susan who wanted to save Dayton.

I was brimming over with stories and now I had one, a big one.

That afternoon the back roads led me to I-84. This was significant. I was back on the first highway of the trip. Now I was going in the opposite direction. I was headed home. Sixty nine days ago I had been eastbound on this four lane interstate. If I could look over into the past and see the purple roadster headed eastbound, what would I have said to the driver?

Would I warn her about Illinois? Would I tell her, *no matter what happens*, just keep coming, it will all be worth it? Would I explain about how Americans really operate? Would I say, don't worry about the engine? Would I say, look, I know you haven't camped in 26 years but this would be different? Would I tell her about the throwed rolls and Mattie's cream puffs? Would I tell her that the snowstorm in Yellowstone might be an omen?

And would she listen to any of this? Or would she be like we all are, on our own journeys, needing to find things out for ourselves?

I think I would tell her, "It's *not* a lousy idea. And you will be able to handle it. Be prepared to have people help you. Keep going. And you'll be headed back *too soon.*"

I had been so humbled by the tire incident that I had no illusions that getting home was a sure thing. Like a good game of backgammon, anything could still happen. There was absolutely no reason to let my guard down just because I had less than 1,000 miles left to go. In fact, I knew that I could lose it all two miles from my house. I had lost friends in Viet Nam that had less than a week to go before their tour of duty was up. It's not over until it's over.

So I clung to the steering wheel, put a square of duct tape on my face shield to block the sun and continued west. I didn't know that Boise was big enough to have a rush hour but at five o'clock everybody who isn't in a hospital bed, everybody who is of legal age, gets in a car and sits on I-84. There was no construction, there were no accidents, but the road was clogged like a drain.

I exited at Nampa, pulled into an automobile dealership and called the youth hostel listed in the guide book. I talked with Elsa who told me two happy things: she had room for me and I was on the right road, keep coming.

Keep coming. The story of my Life. Just keep coming.

Journal Entry: June 19

All human beings have had close calls that they didn't even know about...a surgery that came within an eighth of inch of being botched, water and electricity that almost met but didn't, a germ that was unsuccessful because we wore gloves that day, a plane we missed that we never knew didn't make it and scores of accidents we weren't involved in because we left home 30 seconds too soon or too late. But when a close call happens and you know it, when you can put your finger right on the physical spot and touch the thinness of it, this is sobering. When you know, as surely as you know your own name, that you had only seconds between you and your end and the only thing that saved you was a fleeting odor of rubber that you had to talk yourself into paying attention to... I don't know. I'm going to have to think about this for awhile.

Roadster Lesson #23: Thou shalt not ignore thy nose.

60

Hostel Boise reminded me of the bunk house at my aunt's Kansas ranch. One story, very comfortable, large communal-style kitchen and separate from Elsa's main house. I was technically in the country with flower gardens but there weren't miles of confusing roads to sort through to find it. And Elsa was the jewel here. With the enthusiasm and smile of a six year old, we were instant play-mates. She had just heard about the Red Hat Society and was getting her outfit together so we played dress up and I took her portrait while she sat next to her piano. She shared lemon chiffon ice cream with me and we talked about our daughters.

I knew that I wouldn't be in the area again without stopping to see her.

The next morning I woke up and remembered I was still stunned to be alive. My last out-of-state moment was a fresh June Idaho morning with not-a-cloud sky. When I tossed my gear into the roadster I was wondering if I would make it home in one day or two. Looking hard at the duct tape and bungee cords, I still wondered if I would ever make it home.

Then, there on the grille, was a flash of irridescent blue and I saw the perfectly presented dragonfly, placed there as if it were a piece of jewelry. Elsa and I both looked at the beautiful thing. It was a gift, given to Seno by Mother Road.

"I'm going to make it," I said.

That Thursday morning I crossed the Idaho border into Oregon. There was no way I was going to repeat my outbound route. There were basically three possible paths from Ontario, Oregon to Portland and I was only familiar with one, I-84. This needed to be corrected. So I took the middle route, the one that would follow the Willow River and go through Unity, and over to Mitchell. Aside from seeing a part of Oregon I'd never seen before, I had one more museum to hit before turning in my tourist badge, the Kam Wah Chung & Company Museum in John Day.

I started into my westbound drive easily enough but noticed a certain impatience, an urgency in the accelerator. This was the back-to-the-barn pull that we all feel when we think the fun was about over and we really needed to rocket home. It robs us of the last precious drops of nectar that may be the sweetest. I fought the urge to bomb across the landscape. I hadn't taken the trip that way, I wasn't going to treat Oregon that way.

Seno climbed Brogan Hill Summit, elevation 3,981, and continued without stopping up to Eldorado Pass, at 4,623 feet. We took a short breather there to look out over the valleys. This was all new to me and I had it all to myself. Again, I wondered, "Where *is* everybody?" and "I can't wait to get back here!" It was unhurried and untouched and beautiful country. Mountains, crops, orchards, quiet farms, creeks, grazing horses.

In 1879 there were three times as many Chinese as whites living in and around John Day, Oregon. The Kam Wah Chung building, a trading post, was the center of activity here on the east-west military road. Doc Hay and his partner Lung On sold supplies to miners and townspeople but more importantly the Doc provided non-traditional medical care. He was a famous herbalist and a master of Pulse Diagnosis, a traditional Chinese method of detecting illness that is still used successfully today. More than 1,000 different herbs were stored in this building. Lung On was a successful businessman, gambler and ladies' man. This building, not a replica but the original building, became a religious and social center for the Chinese community. In these cramped quarters they could experience the sights, smells and rituals of their homeland that they must have missed very much. For those who were Chinese and wanted to escape reality completely, there was the opium den in the back with bunk beds. The walls are so blackened with a sooty look that I suspect you could get high by smoking the wood itself. The partners were not above selling whiskey during prohibition either.

The truly unique part of this story was that the building was boarded up in the late 1940's and stayed that way, completely untouched until 1969. The cold, dry climate kept everything well preserved. During nearly 30 years city officials *did not know* that the place had been deeded to the city as a museum. Researchers have praised the collection as the most accurate portrayal of what immigrant life was like in the American West.

The strange control freak who was the museum guide showed some of the ingredients Doc Hay used in his remedies: rattlesnake, tiger's bone, turtle shell, bear paws, dried lizards and the creepiest things that would give most people nightmares. Hay treated whites as well, those who could withstand his unusual environment. There were no windows and each room had a shrine. More than $23,000 in uncashed checks were found under the doctor's mattress. Did he know they *could* be cashed? Or was he content enough with life that he didn't want the money? Or was he just a big, fat procrastinator?

Despite the shrines and dried offerings, no one was able to identify what religion Doc Hay or Lung On practiced. The store's general merchandise included tobacco, canned marshmallows, peanut butter kisses and lard all in their original packages. The place had a dingy, creepy look. Doc Hay's socks were still on his bed. This museum was an oddity back in 1887 and it hadn't changed when I saw it.

Some of the road between John Day and Mitchell had been freshly paved. It was jet black asphalt, smooth as skin and the stripes glowing white. It twisted around through canyons like a light-hearted aria. I thought that I had never seen such a perfect road, so black, so photogenic! It was a pleasure to hear only Seno's engine and not one rattle, not one bump of a tire. Automobile manufacturers and advertising agencies look for stretches of highway like this. It was beautiful.

Outside of Mitchell we went over the Ochoco Pass and stopped for a breather. As luck again would have it, I met some interesting folks. They were celebrating their 55th wedding anniversary by taking a tour of Oregon; they lived in Willamina, over a couple of mountain ranges. Lucille and Robert insisted that I come visit, "bring the car!" so that I could let their blind son see it. This last part didn't make a great deal of sense to me but I learned on this trip not to question the offerings of the American people. All I really needed to know was that Lucille made my favorite kind of pie and she said she made the best rhubarb pie that I was ever going to taste. I told her it was a date. Just let me get the book written and I'd be right over.

At Prineville I had to be careful to find Highway 26. It was going to be the one to take me home. If I stayed on this road and watched the signs it would eventually bring me within three blocks of my house. But I was still over 170 miles from Portland. At least from here, things began to look a familiar and I could pronounce the names of things, like Kah-Nee-Ta. Nearing Warm Springs the road did a nauseating turn, it hugged the cliff and then threw Seno out like a yo-yo. Air seemed to pull the car sideways but there was no wind. This awful curve was no easier coming from the opposite direction. I had taken it 100 times and I never liked the feeling of that pull. The traffic from Bend to Portland was picking up through the Warm Springs Indian Reservation. As Bend prospered, this highway was more and more taxed. Frequently the passenger cars got frustrated with the campers. Now truckers were added to the mix.

Approaching the Cascade Range I pulled over to call my daughter and find out the location of my favorite four year old, granddaughter

Gracie. She led such an active life she could be at soccer practice or martial arts class or acrobatics or be in a kayak with her mom or pedaling behind Kel's bicycle. The kid had experienced a greater variety of activities than I had at age 30. There was no answer on Kel's phone, just the voice mail. I called my own voice mail and heard the message. My pupils must have dilated when I heard it. They would be at the Park Blocks Farmer's Market that evening and Gracie was *leaving in the morning for San Francisco!*

I threw the phone in my food bag and gravel shot out from under Seno's tires as we hit Highway 26 with a vengeance. The back-to-the-barn lead foot was nothing compared to a grandmother on a mission! After nine weeks, I was no longer able to hold that part of myself back. With complete focus I unwound that four cylinder engine and we passed everything remotely safe to pass. Beautiful white Mount Hood with its four lane super highway was a road I knew very well. We were up and over the summit, flying past Government Camp and holding the corners at just over a speed I was comfortable with. A sign you don't want to see when you're a grandmother coming home to grand kids: FINES DOUBLE IN TRAFFIC CORRIDOR. I had traveled over 8,500 miles without so much as a parking ticket. I didn't want an added expense to my already over-budgeted trip but more than anything I didn't want to take the time it would take for a cop to write a ticket! Coming through Zigzag and Brightwood I found what I needed, a speeding red SUV. I flew on their wing in the right hand lane, sure that they'd be stopped if either of us were. At a couple of points we were doing 70 miles per hour. I stayed in formation past Sandy and then took the painstaking stop-and-go route westbound on Burnside.

"You start out with a bag full of luck and an empty bag of experience. The trick is to fill the bag of experience before emptying the bag of luck."

Seno was still mud-caked from Yellowstone, his fenders duct-taped and strapped with bungee cords. I downshifted over and over and blew through three or four yellow lights. Look out, grandmother coming through! I didn't bother to change from my highway helmet to my town helmet, that would have taken too much time. Over the little rise near Mt. Tabor I hit the light just right and flew up and over that intersection and onto the straight descent into the city. The late afternoon sun lit the polished street and made it white. As I got closer and closer to the Willamette River, I said out loud: "I want a good parking place."

The light at MLK was green and now it was clear sailing across the Burnside Bridge into the heart of downtown. All this was done during Portland rush hour! Past the soup kitchens and the Greek restaurant, I knew exactly how to play these stoplights. I knew I'd never get the one on Fourth Avenue and I didn't. I crossed Broadway, got into the right hand lane and whipped through the Park Blocks. I found the parking space I had asked for and leaped out of the roadster like cartoon toast out of a toaster. I pulled the hard shell off my head, jammed a quarter in the parking meter and lit out for the Farmer's Market.

It had been so long. Kids grow so fast. Would I still recognize her? Will she still remember me? I walked the perimeter like a crazed animal. What if they decided to do something else instead? I called my voice mail. No other messages. Where was that kid? The crowded outdoor market swelled with more strolling people. I decided it made more sense to just sit down and watch the moving people that continue to mill. "Get a grip," I said.

"Oh, *you* get a grip! I want that grand kid and you're not going to talk me into leaving again for a long, *long* time!"

I knew who that was. It was Grandmother Alyce, one of the most intense characters in my head. I don't know how I was ever able to sedate her enough to do this trip in the first place.

Ah! there she was. My sweetheart. My little Gracie. She was about to sample some food thing. I knelt down next to her and said, "Hi, ya, how ya doin', Warthog?"

EPILOGUE

On June 28, 2002 Alyce and the roadster, presented the WELCOME TO PACIFIC CITY sign to the Chamber of Commerce (at the Pelican Pub, Cape Kiwanda) to commemorate the successful completion of the "Pacific City to Atlantic City to Pacific City" Drive of a Lifetime. It rained.

Seno and Alyce were featured in dozens of newspapers across the country. His fenders were eventually resculpted and reattached as specified by Team New York.

On July 20, 2002 Seno led the Red Hat Society entry in the Fort Dalles Days parade (The Dalles, Oregon) and helped the Purple Rhapsody Chapter win first place.

Terry Dickman of Sioux Falls, South Dakota won the "Guess Where This Photo Was Taken?" contest that appeared on the trip's web site: www.GoingTopless.info

Irene Dennis, the Maine friend Alyce didn't get to see, gave birth to a baby girl, Emma.

Aseem Hoesein was never charged with the theft of money from the Princeton, Illinois motel.

Susan Rogers, who was inspired by Alyce's trip, was accepted and plans to attend the university of her choice.

John Adair was pronounced cancer free and attended his class at Cambridge University in England as scheduled.

Team Idaho, the four motorcycle rescuers, made it safely home.

Lucille Johnstone really does make the best rhubarb pie in the known universe.

Alyce continues her career as a speaker and was able to remove the rings from her swollen hand six weeks after she returned to Oregon. Whenever possible she brings the roadster with her to presentations and personal appearances.

After examining the damaged tire, A-N-T Tire Company of Portland determined that the life of the tire was approximately 45 seconds.

ABOUT THE AUTHOR

Alyce Cornyn-Selby, international speaker and recognized authority on the subject of sabotage (overcoming self-defeating behaviors), speaks to fighter pilots, nurses, bank presidents, FBI agents, credit unions, corporations and associations from Honolulu to London.

She isn't a speech; she's an event.

Manager of the most award-winning communications team of its kind in the country, Alyce is uniquely qualified to illustrate *winning* in the world of work.

Award winning scriptwriter and film producer, Alyce brings visual drama and comedy to her programs. Alyce overcame a seven year fear of driving, a paralyzing fear of public speaking and obesity. She lost 100 pounds using a system called the Inner Theatre Method.

Named THE HIGH PRIESTESS OF PROCRASTINATION, Alyce is also the author of *Procrastinator's Success Kit* and *What's Your Sabotage?*, a best selling book at every convention since being published.

ABC, CBS, NBC, *This Week, Psychology Today, USA Today* and *Readers' Digest* have all featured Alyce's innovative concepts.

Contact the author:
www.justalyce.com
503-232-0433

www.GoingTopless.info
Across America in a Topless Car

Order books: 1-800-937-7771

ORDER FORM

Other books by Alyce Cornyn-Selby

COPIES

___What's Your Sabotage?..........................$15.95 each______

The Last Word in Overcoming Self-Sabotage
End financial, weight, relationship or career sabotage.
Alyce lost 100 pounds using this dynamic method.
The FBI wanted her research. So did Boeing, Microsoft,
the National Guard, the *New York Times*, Bank of America
and thousands of professional conferences and conventions.

___Procrastinator's Success Kit..........................$12.95______

How to Get Yourself to Do Almost Anything
by the HIGH PRIESTESS OF PROCRASTINATION,
includes 8 different styles of procrastination, how to handle each one,
how to live with a procrastinating spouse or boss. Invaluable!

___HIT THE ROAD,
Across America in a Topless Car......................$16.95______

Solo journey coast-to-coast in a vintage topless roadster.

___Why Winners Win..$8.95______

6 things winners have; 3 things they don't seem to have; motivating!

___Video: Self-Sabotage.....................................$29.00______

1 hour, the method explained for staff meetings or
for teenagers or you own private seminar; effective!

___I want them all: all 5 products ~~$83.80~~ $70........___$70._

Save $13.80!! Package Deal! *Save $13.80!!!*

Total for books $______

Shipping $2 for each book ______

Grand Total______

SEND YOUR **NAME AND ADDRESS** TO:
(CHECK PAYABLE)
Beynch Press
1928 S. E. Ladd Avenue
Portland OR 97214

Credit card orders: 1-800-937-7771 **(Higher shipping rates apply!)**